C. S. Lewis   MN.

Sketch of C. S. Lewis by Mary Shelley Neylan. See Chapter 14,
"A Goddaughter's Memories," by Sarah Tisdall.
Reprinted by permission of the Edwin W. Brown Collection
at Taylor University and Sarah Tisdall, daughter of the artist.

C. S. LEWIS

REMEMBERED

COLLECTED REFELCTIONS OF
STUDENTS, FRIENDS & COLLEAGUES

C. S. LEWIS
REMEMBERED

HARRY LEE POE & REBECCA WHITTEN POE
General Editors

ZONDERVAN®

GRAND RAPIDS, MICHIGAN 49530 USA

ZONDERVAN.COM/
AUTHOR**TRACKER**

ZONDERVAN®

C. S. Lewis Remembered
Copyright © 2006 by Harry Lee Poe

Requests for information should be addressed to:

Zondervan, *Grand Rapids, Michigan 49530*

Library of Congress Cataloging-in-Publication Data

    C. S. Lewis remembered : collected reflections of students, friends and
colleagues / Harry Lee Poe and Rebecca Whitten Poe, general editors.
       p. cm.
    Includes index.
    ISBN-10: 0-310-26509-6
    ISBN-13: 978-0-310-26509-2
    1. Lewis, C. S. (Clive Staples), 1898–1963. 2. Lewis, C. S. (Clive Staples),
1898–1963—Friends and associates. 3. Oxford (England)—Intellectual
life—20th century. 4. Teacher-student relationships—England—Oxford.
5. College teachers—England—Oxford—Biography. 6. Authors,
English—20th century—Biography. 7. University of Oxford—
Faculty—Biography. I. Poe, Harry Lee, 1950-. II. Poe, Rebecca Whitten.
   PR6023.E926Z599 2006
   823'.912—dc22

                                            2006003806

This edition printed on acid free paper.

Extracts by C. S. Lewis copyright © C. S. Lewis Pte. Ltd. Reprinted by permission.
For permission to reprint "The Establishment Must Die and Rot ... ," we would like
to acknowledge Curtis Brown on behalf of Brian Aldiss; copyright © Brian Aldiss
1964. George Watson's article "The Art of Disagreement: C. S. Lewis (1898–1963)" is
reprinted by permission from the *Hudson Review* 48, no. 2 (Summer 1995). Copyright
© 1995 George Watson.

Interior design by Michelle Espinoza

Printed in the United States of America

06 07 08 09 10 11 12 • 18 17 16 15 14 13 12 11 10 9 8 7 6 5 4 3 2 1

To John Stanley Mattson,
whose vision and commitment
have led to the preservation of
The Kilns
and the establishment of
the C. S. Lewis Foundation

CONTENTS

PREFACE

This is not a book of scholarship — though most of the contributors have had distinguished careers as scholars. Nor is it a collection of essays by "Lewis experts" — even though one of the contributors, Walter Hooper, has done more than anyone to make Lewis's papers, articles, and letters available to the world. Rather, this is a book of personal memories and reflections by people who knew C. S. Lewis — mostly as a teacher.

I first thought a book of this sort should be written when I heard Francis Warner and Barbara Reynolds, at the C. S. Lewis Summer Institute in 1998, recounting their experiences with Lewis in Cambridge when they were young. Then in 2002, as I listened to Emrys Jones, who had held the prestigious Goldsmiths' Professorship of English Literature at Oxford, evaluate Lewis as a teacher and scholar, I knew someone needed to collect reflections of Lewis as a teacher.

Most people know C. S. Lewis only through his writings, as well they should. His books have had an impact on the lives of millions. I know of many who owe their conversions to faith in Christ to Lewis's writings. But Lewis was not a professional writer. He was a teacher. And as I listened to Jones, I wondered how much influence Lewis had really had in that capacity. What had happened to his students? Was he continuing to have an influence through those students? What sort of teachers did Lewis produce?

This book represents my efforts to find the answer to these questions. It is not an exhaustive answer, but it is a highly suggestive one.

At first I thought others should collect these essays. The beginnings of this collection came in 1988 when Stan Mattson invited Owen Barfield, George Sayer, and Walter Hooper to speak at the first C. S. Lewis Summer Institute sponsored by the C. S. Lewis Foundation. Conducted in residence at St. Hilda's College, Oxford, the first summer institute took as its theme "The Christian in the Contemporary

University." In founding the C. S. Lewis Foundation, Stan Mattson was concerned to encourage a renaissance of Christian scholarship and artistic expression throughout the mainstream of contemporary higher education. The foundation was not formed as a C. S. Lewis veneration society. Rather, it took its inspiration from the life and legacy of C. S. Lewis in the matter of how to live and work as a vital Christian in higher education. Lewis provides the model for Christians who want to make a significant contribution in the academy.

In that first C. S. Lewis Summer Institute, Kim Gilnett and Walter Hooper interviewed Owen Barfield, who had known Lewis from the time of Lewis's return to Oxford after World War I. The transcript of that interview is the opening chapter of this book. Though Barfield had played an important role in Lewis's shift from atheism to belief that God must exist, Barfield was not himself an orthodox Christian. As Lewis became a leading voice of the Christian faith in the English-speaking world, Barfield became a leading proponent of anthroposophy. When Lewis came to faith in Christ, he and Barfield remained close friends — despite the theological divide that separated them. After Lewis's death Barfield served as the advisor to Lewis's literary estate. In his conversation with Gilnett and Hooper, Barfield introduces the man who was his friend. Several fine biographies provide the accurate details of Lewis's life, details that Barfield makes no pretense to recall with accuracy, but Barfield offers the impressions of a long friendship with Lewis.

Following Barfield, Walter Hooper presents a different perspective on Lewis. If Barfield was among Lewis's first friends in Oxford, Hooper was certainly one of his last. Walter Hooper did not study with Lewis, and yet Lewis had a profound impact on the young graduate student from America. Lewis took the time to meet him and encourage him. In turn, Hooper took the time to help Lewis with the secretarial duties that Warren, Lewis's brother, normally performed. In another of those bits of irony, Hooper has spent his life completing those secretarial duties as he deserves the credit for collecting the short essays and letters of Lewis to make them available in edited volumes. Barfield and Hooper provide the frame for the essays that follow.

A common refrain marks the response of those who agreed to contribute to this collection. They almost all used the same words when invited to participate: "Oh, but I was not a friend of Lewis. I only knew him as my tutor." This book does not claim to be, nor intend to be, an intimate portrait of C. S. Lewis. Those who knew him best have written important essays and books about their relationships. Those who are not familiar with these should read those volumes:

- Jocelyn Gibb's edited collection, *Light on C. S. Lewis*
- George Sayer's biography, *Jack: C. S. Lewis and His Times*
- James Como's collection of essays by many of Lewis's friends, *C. S. Lewis at the Breakfast Table*, reissued in 2005 as *Remembering C. S. Lewis*
- John Lawlor's *C. S. Lewis: Memories and Reflections*
- Douglas Gresham, *Lenten Lands: My Childhood with Joy Davidman and C. S. Lewis* (a fine volume by Lewis's stepson)

This volume, rather, explores the lasting work of C. S. Lewis as a teacher and an influence on young people. (Of related interest is a recent book by Joel Heck entitled *Irrigating Deserts: C. S. Lewis on Education*.)

My cousin George Poe, who chaired the French Department at the University of the South for many years, quickened my interest in Lewis as a teacher when he sent me a brief article from *Sewanee* magazine in spring 1999, written by the retiring dean W. Brown Patterson. The article entitled "C. S. Lewis: Personal Reflections," was an account of Patterson's experience as a Rhodes Scholar studying with Lewis. In time I had the opportunity to meet Dr. Patterson, who agreed to expand his article for this volume.

The irony of this investigation into the influence of Lewis came home to me later when I received a note from my high school history teacher. Ken Childs taught high school for several years after college before going on to law school and a distinguished career as an attorney. He had a profound influence on a generation of high school students. He challenged us intellectually, devoted time as an advisor to our student political club, and helped us learn to think. Because he also challenged us to think about how our faith relates to the rest of our lives, he had more to do with my early intellectual development than any other person. In his note, he invited me to join him at Sewanee to hear a speech by Lady Soames, Churchill's daughter, and to have lunch with his own college history teacher, W. Brown Patterson. How startling to realize that I stood in the tradition of the Lewis legacy! We never know what influence we may have on our students, but Lewis provides a model of teaching at its best.

Some of the contributors, like Patterson, chose to study with Lewis because of his Christianity, but not everyone in this collection shared Lewis's faith. George Watson admired Lewis as a scholar but never shared Lewis's interest in religion. Paul Piehler studied with Lewis in defiance of Lewis's God—only to become a convert himself after leaving Oxford. Some shared Lewis's "mere Christianity" but differed with him over his Protestantism, such as Peter Milward, who for many years has served as a Catholic missionary in Japan.

Not everyone who contributed to this volume actually studied with Lewis in a formal setting. Obviously, Barfield did not. The rest came in contact with Lewis when they were young adults or younger. Barbara Reynolds never studied with Lewis but attended his inaugural lecture at Cambridge on behalf of her mentor, Dorothy L. Sayers. Bishop Simon Barrington-Ward came to know Lewis when he was the young, new chaplain at Magdalene College, Cambridge, where Lewis faithfully attended college chapel. Philosopher Basil Mitchell knew Lewis as the president of the Socratic Club and succeeded to the office when Lewis moved to Cambridge. Laurence Harwood was a godson of Lewis. Throughout his life until Lewis's death, Harwood received notes of encouragement from Lewis at critical points in his young life. Sarah Tisdall was a goddaughter of Lewis and also received his attention. These accounts remind us that the true teacher has an influence beyond the formalities of instruction.

Though most of the contributions were written for this collection, some were originally presented in plenary sessions of the C. S. Lewis Summer Institute, and some appeared in whole or in part in journals. The details may be found in each contribution's opening footnote.

As an appendix, this volume contains a reprint of an article that appeared in the inaugural issue of *SF Horizons* in spring 1964. I am most grateful to Brian Aldiss for permission to reprint it. The article is unusual for several reasons. It appeared after Lewis died. *SF Horizons* is a nonreligious, nonscholarly magazine for science fiction enthusiasts. Most important for our purposes, the article is the transcript of a taped conversation on science fiction between C. S. Lewis, Kingsley Amis, and the editor Brian Aldiss. While many descriptions of Lewis's art of conversation within the Inklings and within a formal tutorial have been published, I believe that this article represents the only transcript we have of how Lewis actually engaged in serious and critical conversation.

The hardest part about editing this collection was bringing it to a close. Scores of others could be included in this collection. Christopher Armitage sent along a brief word when it was too late for a full essay, and we have included it to represent the many who are not included.

In the midst of this project, I invited a young colleague to join me. I had undertaken too many other projects of my own with deadlines looming and editors growing impatient when I suffered a back injury. My daughter Rebecca Poe came to the rescue. She stands at the beginning of a career in English literature, so it seemed appropriate that she should help edit this manuscript and learn from the masters who contributed to it. She has been a great help in some of the most laborious and painstaking aspects of locating and verifying quotations.

I also acknowledge my debt to those who helped in various ways to bring this collection to a successful completion. Marjorie Richard transcribed the tapes of oral addresses by Barbara Reynolds, Owen Barfield, Walter Hooper, Laurence Harwood, and Francis Warner. Paul Sorrell, of the Emma Waters Summar Library at Union University, obtained numerous volumes through interlibrary loan that allowed me to find the quotations that so many of the contributors included in their essays. Sharon Helton, the conference manager of the C. S. Lewis Summer Institute, struck up a conversation with a gentleman in the coffee shop across from St. John's College, Cambridge. The gentleman turned out to be George Watson, who was most gracious to us during our visit with him. Jill Fort, Faculty Forum coordinator for the C. S. Lewis Foundation, assisted me in too many ways to remember. I am indebted to Stan Mattson, president of the C. S. Lewis Foundation, for granting permission to publish all of the addresses that came from the C. S. Lewis Summer Institutes. Bob Hudson, senior editor-at-large at Zondervan, believed in this project from the beginning and worked diligently to see that it came to pass. I am most grateful for his support.

I deeply appreciate the support of David S. Dockery, president of Union University, who has offered his encouragement and support for this and so many other projects.

I appreciate the understanding and the indulgence of my wife, Mary Anne, and my daughter Mary Ellen while Rebecca and I spent too much time away from them in the last month of the editing process.

Harry Lee Poe
Charles Colson Professor of Faith and Culture
Union University
June 2006

Working at The Kilns

The noise and fury of twenty hands
rebuilding the house around me
never intruded on my thoughts
as I set to do the work before me.

Ripping up the rotten floor
and cutting new parquet
to match the old in Joy's room;
Cutting out the boards by hand
and nailing them together
to match the bookcase in the picture
of Mrs. Moore's room;
Tearing brick and mortar apart
with a miniature jack hammer
to open up the fireplace
in Jack's bedroom;
Scraping the ladder on the quarry tile floor
and drilling into the ceiling
to hang a towel rack above the Aga
in Mrs. Miller's kitchen.

My pen moved steadily across the paper
while I sat at the dining room table
until I finished my chapter,
looked up, and thought,
"Jack wrote here."

Harry Lee Poe

FOREWORD BY SIMON BARRINGTON-WARD

Not long ago, on one of the first of those really warm mornings of spring, I was strolling back across the Fellows' Garden of Magdalene, Cambridge, returning from early morning prayer in chapel. As I approached the "Monks' Walk," a path, which at that time had become a primrose path indeed, on a raised bank by the far wall of the garden, I suddenly had that sense of more than déjà vu, of almost a positive glimpse of a "sly shade" from the past. It was as if, at any moment, rounding the corner, I might encounter a well-loved presence, never far away from the college. And there came into my mind the words of "Jack" Lewis, the name by which C. S. Lewis told us to call him, in a last letter, written to the master of the college after his enforced retirement due to illness in 1963. The letter was written to acknowledge his having been made an honorary Fellow: "I am constantly with you in imagination. If, in some twilit hour, anyone sees a bald and bulky spectre in the Combination Room or the garden, don't get Simon to exorcise it, for it is a harmless wraith and means nothing but good."

In quieter days, when there was far less traffic near, I had often seen him pacing that path in his lifetime. At that moment I felt the pang of an overwhelming yearning for those halcyon days (in the late fifties) when I was a young, raw chaplain here and, with others in a small group of younger Fellows, experienced the mingled awe and surprise at having been joined, in our little, mellow, hobbit-shaped establishment, by this great figure. He, however, adopting none of the airs of the great man, acted with a kind of boyish zest, as if he too as a newcomer was happy to be junior alongside us. The fellowship was small, and the number living in college and dining most nights was even smaller. In the Combination Room where we sat after dinner, in a semicircle round the fire in winter and round the large window overlooking the court in summer, the Senior Fellow, Francis Turner, a small, dominant figure who could be quite formidable, influenced the tone of the evening by his moods.

Well had the evening tremblers learned to trace
The night's disasters on his evening face!

To be fair the gloom that Francis could on occasion communicate was relatively rare. He was in fact a deeply endearing recluse who was extraordinarily good to the many undergraduates who were devoted to him and who gave so much to the college. But it was he who would invariably choose the topic of our evening talk from his central chair, and Jack Lewis fitted in perfectly with this, taking his place in the group as one of us, sometimes pouring out the port as the Junior Fellow and submitting good-humoredly to Francis's central role. "Every common room needs a bully," he confided to one of my fellow juniors, "but an amiable bully, such as Francis, who will do us good and keep us all in order."

For us younger ones, the way in which Jack, this distinguished newcomer, seemed to identify himself with us was always a delightful surprise. One day I was coming back with him from one of the walks into the country, which, just occasionally, he would take in the morning. As we approached the college, lunchtime was close and he began to quicken the pace. When I asked him why he was hurrying since there was no fixed starting time, he replied, "Francis doesn't like us being late." "You don't mean to say *you're* a bit afraid of Francis too?" I blurted out in surprise. "Of course I am," he said, "Francis is one of the grown-ups." He then expounded his theory that certain people always have a kind of grown-up status to which the rest of us closer to the table, as it were, never quite attain.

One evening, much later, when Francis was away, Jack suddenly conjured up a wonderful little dreamlike fantasy. He told us how after the funeral of a certain late lamented college figure of revered memory, the younger Fellows had returned to the high table that night in a strangely boisterous, almost liberated mood, by which he, Jack, was not a little shocked. By the time we reached the Combination Room, things were getting a bit out of hand. People began calling for whisky instead of this dreary old port, and then, to Jack's horror, a voice could be heard crying out to the college butler, "Milne! We've had enough of all this boring conversation!"—a complaint *most* unlikely to arise in any company in which Jack was present!—"Bring in the television!" (in those days, a novelty in a nearby guest room). The aged butler tottered in bearing the machine and plugged its cable into a socket. Then, to the entire semicircle's great surprise, the screen came instantly alight and alive with the compelling spectacle of what, at first, appeared to be swirling mists, which were gradually clearing, as before a mountain peak, only to reveal, to the horrified faces of the company, the unmistakable physiognomy of the man they thought had been buried that day. Jack then did a little unmistakable imitation of Francis. "Mph! Mph! So you thought you would have a little novelty, did you? Mph! Well, you've got one, haven't you? More than you bargained for, perhaps? Oh no, Simon. Don't you go trying to turn me off. You see I have controls here. And *I* can switch *you* off!" This was in fact not more than a humorous extravaganza on the theme of the extent to which we all really needed Francis! Both he and Jack deeply appreciated each other.

Although Jack was unfailingly genial, full of spontaneous inspiration and immensely kindly, it could at times, in the beginning especially, be quite an awe-inspiring pleasure to be the person sitting next to him. It might seem at first partly an ordeal, partly a formative education. His immense scope and range of reference, drawing upon the widest possible reading of so much European literature, and his astonishing power of recall could make one feel that by comparison, like the unliterary friend he described in *An Experiment in Criticism*, one "inhabited a tiny world!" But he was so innocent of any attempt to impress. He simply assumed that we also were familiar with Aeschylus or Racine or had recently reread Boethius's *Consolation of Philosophy*! Such an assumption gradually inspired one to desire to expand one's own range of reading more rapidly. He would always take your little ideas seriously and help to make them into something, with the result that young people often felt they had been in amazing form after sitting next to him of an evening.

Again, another part of the ordeal arose when you attempted to disagree with him. When Nevill Coghill compared him to Dr. Johnson, he remarked that "both were formidable in their learning and in the range of their conversation, both had the same delight in argument and, in spite of their regard for truth, would argue for victory. Lewis had Johnson's handiness with the butt end of a pistol if an argument misfired!"[1] Some of us experienced this and felt a bit crushed or stifled at times! But we soon came to understand that this was just his "barrack room lawyer's" style (inherited perhaps from his father) and carried with it no ill will! The help and the inspiration he gave us so far surpassed the occasional, rather too heavy, even brutal sparring that we all seemed to become his lifelong debtors!

To the younger Fellows especially, and to the undergraduates, he could be relied on to provide unfailing help. Dr. Ronald Hyam, a younger Magdalene contemporary, tells how he came into the Combination Room one night worried about a lecture he had to give the next day for which he felt ill-prepared. In a desperate throw he asked Jack, not expecting anything much since this was scarcely Jack's field, "What can you tell me about eighteenth-century race relations?" After a long silence, Jack responded, "Of course you've read Captain Cook's *Journals*?" "Of course I hadn't!" says Ronald. He describes how Jack "proceeded with gusto to regale him with every possible bit of evidence which could be distilled from this voluminous source. His recall was flawless."[2]

John Stevens, a Junior Fellow teaching English, described his own feelings of awe and self-mistrust in the presence of the author of *The Allegory of Love* and the then just completed *Oxford History of English Literature in the Sixteenth Century*. John was struggling to learn Anglo-Saxon (not compulsory in Cambridge English) and Jack found out about this. For two years Jack was then to give up two hours once a week after Hall every evening in his rooms "reading," as John said Jack insisted on describing it, Anglo-Saxon with him, an extraordinary act of generosity with that most precious commodity, his time. John described his patience, his encouragement, his cross-references to a great range of illuminating parallels, and the time spent together with John afterwards when the conversation — and the wine — flowed.[3]

Undergraduates also describe their memories of Lewis voluntarily offering Anglo-Saxon supervision classes, his friendly welcome, the beer he offered, and his stories of former well-known students.

He also regularly met with an English Club to enable those studying English to meet him. They would also experience, on occasion, his rather dogmatic and devastating arguments with those who sought to disagree with him, battering them with his vastly superior knowledge! But they also so greatly valued his encouragement, and he would give generous praise to those whose papers he approved. So again on the whole he inspired them and helped them on, and they would never forget meeting with him. I remember attending some of his lectures, thronged with undergraduates, and receiving something more than imaginative and literary stimulus. A deeper awareness of a moral and spiritual framework, undergirding all things, held all his teaching and his critical writing together. For many of us this underlying root bore fruit, not only in his marvelous fiction and his religious writings, but also in his evoking in us the sense of the reality of a divine source and ground to our whole life. As I came away I knew that this experience had been shared by numbers of his young hearers, a whole generation of them.

But the central thrust of that awareness, which impressed itself most deeply upon several of us who came under his influence during his maturing years of the Cambridge chair and Magdalene Fellowship, struck home to me most forcibly on some of the walks I took with him near Cambridge. One day I made a mild complaint about the dullness of the Cambridge countryside contrasted with other places I had known and loved. He turned on me quite gravely. "You should never condemn any genuine countryside in that way," he said almost severely to me. "In every landscape you should try to feel for its real nature and quality and let it grasp hold of you. The day is coming when, beyond this life, we shall recognize that quality in the eternal fulfillment in which it will have its true place." I am reminded now of the last chapter of a book of his that I had not yet then read, although I think it had just been published, *The Last Battle*, where the children, who have passed through death into a new world, suddenly discover there all the landscapes they had ever known in their original country and in Narnia.

On another walk, at the sight of a flight of swans landing with a great flurry of water on the radiant river on a sunlit afternoon, I quoted Walter de la Mare, "Look thy last on all things lovely, every hour." Again came one of those unexpected rebukes from which I learned so much from Jack. "No. No. It should certainly *not* be, 'Look thy last …,' but 'Look thy *first* on all things lovely.' Every sight and sound that is good, every touch of beauty or rightness, is pointing ahead to its ultimate fulfillment in the world to come." Soon after that I read for the first time *The Weight of Glory.* "We are summoned to pass in through Nature, beyond her, into that splendour which she fitfully reflects." This was the supreme aspect of the gospel of which Jack somehow, in so many ways, made us more and more conscious, as I believe he became more and more conscious of it himself, that sense of anticipation, of what he called "eschatological Platonism," the knowledge that the ideal and the real are not laid up statically in some metaphysical realm but are emerging through this life and lie ahead of us, and so are to be met within, and through, and, ultimately, beyond this life. His ranging out over literature medieval and modern, his profound imagination, his constant gift of apt quotation, his wonderful writing and storytelling, his deep kindness helped to open this future reality out to us.

That is why what began with a nostalgic half sighting of Jack as we knew him in the Fellows' Garden and in the Combination Room at Magdalene must take us far further. I don't want just to look back *at* him, though it is good to do that. But I want, with all the readers of this book, to look forward *with* him, in faith and hope and above all love, to all that lies ahead of us. So the glimpse of that benevolent shade in the garden points not back but forward, as did the springtide in which it was given. This must be a *fore*-word indeed, a reminder of Jack Lewis's greatest gift to the young (of all ages!), to enable them, as he enabled many of us in Cambridge in the late fifties and since, to reach out beyond, to grasp with all the saints what is the breadth and length and height and depth, and to look to that day when, with them, we are to be "filled with *all* the fullness of God"!

Part 1

THE MAN

Before his death, C. S. Lewis named Owen Barfield as his literary executor. Barfield was one of Lewis's first new friends in Oxford when he returned from the First World War. Barfield played an enormous role in the change of mind Lewis had about taking spiritual reality seriously. Lewis wrote about their discussions and disagreements, but also about what he learned through these discussions with Barfield. To be a great teacher, it is first necessary to love learning. Long before the term "lifelong learning" had come into vogue, Lewis practiced the life of learning. Early on, his friendship with Tolkien centered around learning Old Norse! Lewis even preferred to think of himself as a "learned man" rather than a "scholar."

It is appropriate, then, that this volume begins with Owen Barfield. Barfield was interviewed at the first C. S. Lewis Summer Institute in 1988 by Kim Gilnett and Walter Hooper. The theme for the Conference was "The Christian and the Contemporary University." The first chapter reflects the conversational style of an earlier day and gives a glimpse of Lewis the man from one who knew him well.

One of the last people on earth to make the acquaintance of C. S. Lewis was Walter Hooper, a young American graduate student. Hooper met Lewis that last summer before his death and helped him with his correspondence and related secretarial duties while Warren Lewis was away in Ireland. Hooper has probably had more to do than any other single individual with the continued interest in Lewis simply by virtue of the enormous editorial work he has undertaken to make available the short essays and sermons that Lewis produced over his lifetime. Though Hooper did not study formally with Lewis, he represents the vast reach of Lewis the teacher to the millions who have read his work.

Chapter 1

C. S. LEWIS AS CHRISTIAN AND SCHOLAR

Owen Barfield

OWEN BARFIELD: I think the first thing I ought to do is to thank the administration for providing this magnificently comfortable armchair. It is so comfortable that if I fall asleep, you will know who to blame.

I'm not very clear, I have to confess, whether it's old age or some other reason, exactly what I'm expected to do. But I have been told that there were likely to be a great many questions, and it occurs to me that as the time is not unlimited and there are quite a number of people here, perhaps it would be best, and I'm subject to correction here, perhaps it would be best if we confined ourselves to begin with questions which I will do my best to answer.

KIM GILNETT: You met Lewis in 1919. Why don't you tell us a little bit about the occasion of when you met Lewis?

BARFIELD: Oh. Yes. It's not a tremendously dramatic one. I met Lewis through a friend. I was an undergraduate at Wadham College, and the man who became a friend was also an undergraduate there, Leo Baker, who was already acquainted with Lewis.[1] I don't know in what connection, before either of them came to university. Leo Baker and I were both interested in reading and in writing poetry, and I think Lewis and Baker and another friend called Paisley were already planning to produce a collected volume of their poems. Anyhow, Baker

Interview of Owen Barfield by Kim Gilnett and Walter Hooper at the C. S. Lewis Summer Institute, Oxford, 1988.

introduced me to Lewis by the simple process of asking us both to tea. That was when I first met Lewis in the autumn of 1919. I have a very vivid recollection, which may have been distorted because it doesn't altogether accord with my recollection of Lewis in later life. I recollect a rather lean young man, arriving on a bicycle at Wadham, looking a bit hungry. I think he was in those days. He wasn't then at all well off. Now exactly what we talked about, because it was about sixty years ago, I couldn't possibly tell you. It was certainly quite a number of subjects. What was already impressing me was Lewis's acuteness, so to speak. He always had his eye on the ball. Whatever we were talking about, he would have something pointed and relevant about it to say. He never spoke in a hurry or slurred his words at all. There was a kind of eagerness behind his thinking that often does come out, and I'm afraid in my own case comes out, in rather hurried and inaudible diction. He had this eager mind, so to speak, shining through his eyes. Shining is such an excessive adjective, but it was there. And somehow I suppose we felt we had something in common, and after that we met occasionally on our own. Sometimes with Baker, sometimes on our own. Not frightfully often during that term; not tremendously often while we were still undergraduates. When we did meet most was after I had finished the doctorate and was living someplace very near, and he had then become a don at Magdalen. I would go in to see him or he would come up and see me, and we began a rather long and complicated argument of an epistemological nature about which a book has subsequently been published, called *The Great War between C. S. Lewis and Owen Barfield* [sic].[2]

GILNETT: Tell us a little more about that argument in which you had an impact on his thinking, particularly before Lewis became a Christian.

BARFIELD: I don't know that this is a very appropriate venue to go into the philosophical details of the struggle, but I supposed it worked out, to put it as untechnically and briefly as possible, he was philosophically a materialist. He didn't believe that any access to the spiritual or supernatural world was possible for the human mind, and that any human mind that supposed that it had such access was living in a world of fantasy. I took a different view. I thought that what had come to be called "imagination" at the time of the Romantic movement, and had been developed a good deal since, was a line of communication between the human mind and a mind in the universe that was immaterial. That's the nearest I can get in a few words putting what the issue was between us, but it wasn't as brief or as simple as that, because it led to a long correspondence. We used to correspond at intervals and also to meet and argue verbally, and then he wrote a long sort of treatise, you would call it, in Latin, intellectually reminiscent of Thomas Aquinas's *Summa Contra Gentiles*, because it was *Summa Contra Anthropophia*, and I wrote a longish answer to it, and he wrote again, and that together with the correspondence was what was dealt with, I think skillfully and at a fair length, in the book I have mentioned. I don't think I can carry it any further; otherwise we shall be here until approximately this time tomorrow.

WALTER HOOPER: I wonder, Owen, could you mention when you first met the household?

BARFIELD: Oh—the "household" is a curious word to use. All my other friends were undergraduates, either living in college rooms or else in diggings in the town of Oxford on their own or with friends. Lewis was already established in a house in Headington. The house was called Hillsborough at some little way from The Kilns. The owner of the house was a Mrs. Moore, who had a daughter, Maureen, but we didn't see much of her because she was at school, mostly. He never said much about his domestic arrangements or about Mrs. Moore. It's a little bit of a mystery who exactly Mrs. Moore was. After a time, in addition to having tea with him in Oxford, he asked me, and sometimes my friend Harwood, out to tea there and then, to begin with, we never met Mrs. Moore.[3] But there was one incident that I know Walter Hooper will find particularly amusing. When Lewis and I were talking late at night in the living room of The Kilns—this is at The Kilns now—no, it wasn't, this was at Hillsborough. At a certain stage in the conversation he would say, "Excuse me. I must go do Mrs. Moore's jowls." I had no idea what that was. It was only some years later that I discovered "jowls" was either the ordinary Irish name or Lewis's name for Mrs. Moore's hot water bottle. So he used to have to go up and put one or more hot water bottles in her bed. That was probably his function. I gradually learned, I can't remember at what stage, how it came about that he was living with Mrs. Moore, but he had a great friend who was in the army with him in the first war, and they had agreed that if either one of them were killed, the other one would look after the parents of the surviving one. And in that way he came to live with Mrs. Moore, help her along, more or less as a surrogate son, really. I think I might add in that connection, I know quite a lot and I have read quite a lot of what has been written about Mrs. Moore since Lewis's death, a great deal of it very unfavorable, giving a very unfavorable impression of her. Now that may be not inaccurate as to the later years of her life, and I hardly ever saw her. She may have grown into perhaps a peevish old lady. At the time when I knew him then as an undergraduate and also for quite a number of years afterward, after I was married and my wife and I both used to go and visit them in The Kilns, my wife and I both had the impression that Mrs. Moore was really extremely good to these two brothers. By that time Warnie, his brother, was also living there, and she was extremely good to them, looking after them very well. I think I remember my wife saying on one occasion, "How she spoils those two!" I mention that to add a little balance to what you may have read about Mrs. Moore. She was not by any means only an ogre. Or ogress, I suppose I should say.

GILNETT: Was Warnie—Warnie had a difficult time with Mrs. Moore.

BARFIELD: I believe—I heard that. I wasn't going there so often. I was living in London; I didn't often hear, but I have heard, and I couldn't express an opinion about how reliable that view or rumor is, whether they didn't get on well or not.

GILNETT: Tell us a little more about Warnie. Obviously those brothers were together as much time as they could be. They were very close.

BARFIELD: Do you want more about Mrs. Moore, in connection with their both being together?

GILNETT: No. Actually, more about Warnie. Excuse me. Tell us a little more about Warren Lewis, the Major.

BARFIELD: It's a very broad question: "a little more about" him. He was in the regular army—I think the Army Service Corp, wasn't it? And I didn't see anything of him at all for the first few years of my acquaintanceship with Lewis, and then he retired and came and lived in Oxford. He had a room in Magdalen. He was there every day. He always came into Lewis's room and spent the day there, and he spent all his time with a typewriter, typing out this enormous history of the family, the Lewis family, incorporating all sorts of letters and documents. He also used to attend the meetings of the little group they called "the Inklings," which met every week in Lewis's room. I only went once in a dozen times when I wasn't living in Oxford. He and Lewis used to go for little walks, little walking tours together. His range of interest was certainly different from his brother's in many ways, although they were so close together. Warnie Lewis hated philosophy. He couldn't stand anything to do with it, and how he managed in spite of that to enjoy attending the Inklings, I don't know, but he did. But he was, in many ways, a thoroughly well-educated man. He wrote several books. His particular interest was life at the time of Louis XIV in France. He wrote four or five books which were really quite successful on that topic, but I didn't see him all that often.[4] He used to—at that time, my friend Harwood and I very often visited those two together, and Lewis's brother Warnie got in the habit of calling us "the Barwood."

GILNETT: I remember reading a letter that was written to you in 1929 from Lewis that indicated—this was right during the time he was considering the Christian faith—in which he said something to the effect—and I have to paraphrase—that the spirit is taking the offensive, and that if you didn't get up to see him soon, he may be checked into a monastery.

BARFIELD: I brought that letter. It's very short. I think I've got the right one. I won't read the whole letter, but:

> Terrible things are happening to me. The "Spirit" or real "I" is showing an alarming tendency to become much more personal, and is taking the offensive and behaving just like God. You'd better come on Monday at the latest, or you might find me in a monastery.[5]

I don't think I went. I wrote to him, but I don't remember that I went on. That, of course, was the beginning of his conversion. That's also when he writes in *Surprised by Joy* how reluctant he was to be converted. There was never a more reluctant convert or unhappy Christian, probably, than he was that evening.

GILNETT: It was to affect his academic life later on, the becoming a Christian, and he did a number of things: broadcast talks, and speaking to the RAF. There was an article that came out, and I can't remember who wrote the article, but it indicated that Lewis did those things because his conscience required him to do that. Is that your impression, that he felt like he was called to go out and speak, to write, to do the broadcast talks, something he didn't like to do?

BARFIELD: Yes, I never discussed it with him or asked him, but I would think that was so, that as a writer he wouldn't have chosen to write the sort of things he wrote—the broadcast talks that became *Mere Christianity*—but his Christianity was essentially one of action. It comes out a good deal in his private correspondence with people who wrote to him because of his Christian apologetic books. He would always rather warn them against thinking that religion meant having fine, warm feelings. You ought to do what you were called upon to do, what you felt it was your duty to do. You know the text, "The one that says, 'Lord, Lord,' will not inherit the kingdom of heaven, but he that doeth the will of my Father." I think that was essentially the leading thread, if that's the right word, in Lewis's Christian faith, or Christian experience. And I would think that he did all that writing of the apologetic nature not primarily because he enjoyed it. Though I think when he began to write he would always enjoy it, because he enjoyed putting things well, and he put them so well. But I think you are probably right, if you suggested it, that he wouldn't have chosen that simply for information. It would have an element of doing his duty in it.

HOOPER: I wonder, Owen, if you would tell them about the setting up of the Agape Files.

BARFIELD: Oh, that's getting into the legal technicalities. Of course, when he and I were undergraduates, and for many years after, we were both writing and even publishing books. It didn't mean anything in financial terms. Then he turned out *Screwtape Letters*, which sold like hotcakes, and after that he continued writing books at what appeared to me to be kind of breakneck speed. I could hardly believe—and to my even greater surprise, they sold. So he began to get quite large sums of money coming in. Well, he was earning quite a decent salary as an English literature teacher at Magdalen. He really didn't need all the money, so he used to give it away. And what he did was, he'd write to a publisher and say, "Send the next lot of royalties to the Home for the Benefit of Cats," or something of that kind. And after that had been going on for a year or two, I suppose in connection with his ordinary income tax, he would consult an accountant. The accountant pointed out to him that all these things he'd given away, although he'd given it away and he'd never seen the money, since he had acquired the right to the money and had parted with it, it was counted for tax purposes as his income. At that time there was an income tax on the lower level of income and also a surtax at a very high rate on larger sums. And it was worked out that he had probably now incurred a liability to income tax and surtax, which would absorb not only any royalty he had earned but also his ordinary salary. Certainly if he went on doing that, it would very quickly do so. So—the English tax laws and the American laws are a bit different. I can't go into all that, but I know in American law you can give your money away to charity and get it all deducted for income tax. You can't quite do that in England. If you wanted to make a donation to charity and not have to pay income tax on it, you had to enter into what's called a "Deed of Covenant," by which you agree to pay so much every year to charity concerns. And when you pay that, you deduct tax from it and in that way you save yourself the tax. The charity then goes back to the Revenue and recovers the tax you have deducted. It's all very complicated. Anyhow, we decided that he'd better do that. So he appointed me the trustee of his charitable trust and all royalties were paid to me and were distributed as he directed, for charity or for charitable purposes, not necessarily to an institutional charity, but a poor man who hadn't enough money to educate his children, and so forth. All sorts of personal cases came his way, either through friends or otherwise. I even suggested the name for this—"Agapargyry"—*agape* being the Greek name for charity and *argyrion* the name for money. And that's how we always referred to it: "Agapargyry" for a while or just "Agapod", or even "the Ag," as we used to call it sometimes. Now and then I'd get a line from him saying, "Send so much to so-and-so. I just heard from him that his wife's got cancer." That went on for many years. But of course, there again, I had to advise him to only dispose of two-thirds of his income in that way, because he still had to pay tax, of course, on his salary. And there was some question of surtax, as I say, but that's getting into technical detail we needn't go into, but that was the substance of it—just setting out of a charitable deed. (It also helped donations, for people to make donations. They could enter into a Deed of Covenant to pay me, the trustee, so much for, it used to be six years, and they could deduct tax. But …)

GILNETT: When his books became quite popular, he met some opposition here in Oxford, particularly on the scholarly level in different colleges, and this opposition to his Christian books was why he was not given promotion here in Oxford. Did you see any evidence of that? Did you have any occasion in the Inklings or in his daily life to hear Lewis comment about the opposition that he met here locally?

BARFIELD: Opposition from his colleagues?

GILNETT: Yes, opposition from his colleagues about his Christian stance in his popular books.

BARFIELD: No, not really. I mean I knew it was going on, but I couldn't give any specific instance of hearing it happening or even hearing of it. I knew what was going on. No, I don't think I could do that. I know, even before his conversion, he was very critical of the sort of atmosphere in the administration of the college: personal antagonism, and so forth, that would decide the issue. I have a letter he wrote in 1928 in which he uses all sorts of phrases like "cesspool" and so forth.[6] So I imagine that when it came to his Christianity, that they didn't share, because Magdalen was a decidedly secular college, very secular, pretty much common at that time, there must have been a great deal of hostility. But they kept it in terms of politeness, more or less, I think.

HOOPER: Owen, I know that you and I have often talked about the increasing popularity of Jack Lewis's books. I wonder what you would have to say about there being the conference in Oxford twenty-five years after his death. How do you explain the popularity?

BARFIELD: Well, they're good books. Do you need any more? Whether they're also popular among the kind of people who you're talking about, I doubt rather that they should be popular by a large number of people not only in Oxford, not only in England, very much more in America than in England, I should imagine. That they should be popular there is no surprise to me at all. It's a bit of a surprise how astronomically popular they are, I must say, but it's a very good thing, I think. Have you got anything particular in mind behind your question?

HOOPER: No. I agree with you. They're good books. But what interests me is that people often like bad books. It's delightful to see so many people who like the books that you and I agree with.

BARFIELD: Yeah. I say, yes, it is.

GILNETT: Are there any questions that you might like to address to Professor Barfield?

NIGEL GOODWIN: What a joy to have you here. Just a voice out front, and it's jolly hard, I know, to see from the stage, but hopefully you can hear.[7]

BARFIELD: I can't see any at all.

GOODWIN: I wonder if you could say anything about Joy Davidman Gresham's coming into the family and what you men felt, what the Inklings maybe felt, about her coming over. Some friends made the film fairly recently, called *Shadowlands*, shown on American and British television, but I wonder what you can recall of her coming on the scene.

BARFIELD: Well, I'm rather reluctant, you know, to go into personal reminiscences, not that I have any very intimate ones, but—one thing that occurred to me is how Lewis himself would have very much disliked the amount of interest being taken in what he would regard as his purely personal concerns. I expect that some of you know the book *The Personal Heresy*, when he rather emphasized that interest and admiration for a writer should be confined to his work and not go into the details of his personal life—what time he shaved in the morning, and so forth. But I suppose that one could give, without infringing any confidentiality, a general answer that Joy's arrival and their marriage obviously meant an unspeakable amount to Lewis himself, and in many respects, changed him, I think. It is also true that his friends of the whole, his Inkling friends and others, were not favorably impressed by Joy, and they didn't like her. On the other hand, it is the case that his brother, who if anything in the nature of jealousy were being entered at, whom you would expect to be the most jealous of all, got on very well with Joy indeed. They had a very happy relationship. I don't think I'm anxious to say much more than that on that subject.

AUDIENCE MEMBER: Mr. Barfield, I'd like to know what C. S. Lewis thought was his most important work and why, and in your estimation, if you concur with that, or what, in your estimation, was his most important work.

BARFIELD: What he regarded was his most important work?

AUDIENCE MEMBER: Yes, and what you felt his most important work was.

BARFIELD: I doubt whether he ever seriously addressed his mind to it. He was very reluctant to think about himself as far as the reputation or anything of that sort. As far as his fiction is concerned, I'm pretty sure he felt, and I certainly did, that his last book, *Till We Have Faces*, was the profoundest and the best that he produced. Whether he had any view of the relative importance of his writings as a scholar or his writings as a theologian or Christian apologist, I don't suppose he ever really gave any mind to it.

AUDIENCE MEMBER: Mr. Barfield, I wonder if you could tell us what impact Mr. Lewis's theology, his Christianity, had on your own personal spiritual pilgrimage.

BARFIELD: I'm afraid the answer is "not much," you know. Because although I was not brought up as a member of any church and was, I suppose, in my late teens, more or less certainly an agnostic, I had already become convinced of the essential truth of Christian revelation before we had our big argument. So that from my point of view, his conversion was something like coming around by him to what was already my point of view, although not quite in the terms and in the shape in which I should have expected or which appealed to me very strongly. But he does say in *Surprised by Joy*, talking about this "Great War" as it is called, he thinks I influenced him more than he influenced me. That is true, I think. There is another interesting point there when I was thinking the kind of thing I might say if I didn't spend all the time answering questions, which I'm much prepared to do, on this business of evolution: to my notion, my conviction of the essential truth of Christianity is very much connected to something I've always called evolution of consciousness. The human experience of the world and nature is not just a change of ideas but a change in the whole nature of perception, and so forth. Anyway, a very big emphasis on evolution. Now Lewis, as you know, hated the idea of evolution. He has, of course, a poem on evolution, but in his personal life, he did have an evolution and he did change very much, both from before conversion to a convinced Christian, and then as some people who have written essays on him since have pointed out, I think, it isn't just a life of two periods. In a way there were three. I'm speaking now of his mental life, psychography rather than biography. There was a time before his conversion, and a time afterwards, which went on for quite a number of years when he was writing his Christian apologetics, and the Narnia books and everything else. I think a third period at the end, not quite at the end, the last few years, when—what I said earlier about the essential nature of Christianity were not quite so true. That he came to value and to feel the importance in Christianity of the soul's acquiring some kind of union with the Spirit and not just like those who say, "Lord, Lord," but something like St. Paul's verse in the Romans. "No longer I live, but Christ liveth in me." I don't believe that was a reality to him in the early part of his conversion. I think he did at the end, but this comes out in *Letter to Malcolm*, in the sermon *The Weight of Glory*, and so forth. He did come around more to feel that there was importance in this as well. The point I'm making now is that he did actually evolve, but he didn't believe in evolution. I believe in evolution. I didn't evolve. I've been saying the same thing all my life.

AUDIENCE MEMBER: Do you know what C. S. Lewis's personal favorite work that he did was, and why?

BARFIELD: Insofar as he thought about it, not very intensively or interestedly, certainly in fiction he thought *Till We Have Faces*.

Chapter 2

WHAT ABOUT MRS. BOSHELL?

Walter Hooper

This talk, such as it is, might be called—and you must remember this title—"What about Mrs. Boshell?" I usually find if one can remember one word of a talk, you've got something which might be worthwhile. What about Mrs. Boshell? However, I will come to her in time.

Some years ago I had an interesting visit with a woman whom you have heard about as "the American lady." There is a volume of C. S. Lewis's letters which are addressed to an American lady. When I went to see her, it was about whether or not the Lewis estate should try to continue the payments which C. S. Lewis had been making to her, because she had told him how very poor she was. If you've read C. S. Lewis's letters you will gather that the lady was of very gloomy cast of mind. I think you would know that even if you had never met her.

So I was not very surprised when I walked into her flat in Washington, D.C. Her first words were, "Don't expect to enjoy yourself." That has come home to me in the last few weeks, and that is because of my connection, or one misconnection, with our beloved Stan Mattson, whom I love very much. He joins the list of those whom I like to think about in purgatory, or the outskirts of heaven. What sort of treatment I would devise if I were God for Stan Mattson! I would strike from his vocabulary forever the word "share," because—I might as well get it out of my system and say of him, perhaps, he should spend some time getting it out of his. When he first approached Owen Barfield and George Sayer and myself about this conference and what

Remarks made at the C. S. Lewis Summer Institute, Oxford, 1988.

we would do, I told him that I was frightfully busy at this time, editing a book of C. S. Lewis's letters, and he said, "Just picture yourself at a table with about nine people, and in the course of the dinner maybe you'd share if you feel like it, and others will share if they feel like it, and all will share, and so forth." Both Mr. Barfield and Mr. Sayer had been on the telephone to me after I had explained to them that all you do is "share," and now that they have seen the program, they too are devising treatment for Dr. Mattson that's more severe than what I have in mind. Anyway, for all of that sharing, you will now get such as you do hear from me. If you don't like what you hear, it's not my fault. So don't expect to enjoy yourselves.

Even so, a number of things have passed through my mind other than what I would actually talk to you about today. I still remember how I first saw C. S. Lewis, and I thought, "Nothing more remarkable than this will ever take place in my life." So, again, I am visited with something like that when I walk past this theater and see posters advertising a fortnight's conference on "C. S. Lewis: The C. S. Lewis Summer Institute." How remarkable that actually is; perhaps as remarkable to us as this meeting would be to C. S. Lewis.

Many of you have heard, I know, what Lewis has said about his friend Charles Williams actually giving a lecture on Milton's *Comus* in Oxford, not very far from here. It was in the divinity school of the Bodleian Library. If you've been there, it is a large fifteenth-century building that you go into to see the exhibitions. It was in there that Charles Williams gave that lecture in February of 1940. And Lewis says this about it to his brother:

> On Monday C[harles] W[illiams] lectured nominally on *Comus*, but really on Chastity. Simply as criticism it was superb — because here was a man who really started from the same point of view as Milton and really cared with every fibre of his being about "the sage and serious doctrine of virginity" which it would never occur to the ordinary modern critic to take seriously. But it was more important still as a sermon. It was a beautiful sight to see a whole room full of modern young men and women sitting in that absolute silence which can *not*

be faked, very puzzled, but spell-bound: perhaps with something of the same feeling which a lecture on *un*chastity might have evoked in their grandparents — The forbidden subject broached at last. He forced them to lap it up and I think many, by the end, liked the taste more than they expected to. It was "borne in upon me" that that beautiful carved room had probably not witnessed anything so important since some of the great medieval or Reformation lectures. I have at last, if only for once, seen a university doing what it was founded to do: teaching Wisdom. And what a wonderful power there is in the direct appeal which disregards the temporary climate of opinion — I wonder is it the case that the man who has the audacity to get up in any corrupt society and squarely preach justice or valour or the like *always* wins?[1]

We don't know. I don't know, anyway, whether they always win, but I think there is certainly something in that. The audacity which Lewis himself did not start with but which he learned is still *the* Christian way. It might be called simply the keeping together of faith and good works. I know it's been said, it's been disputed about, but in his own life, as I think over what to say to you, it seems to me that those two things can never finally be separated and, of course, shouldn't have been in the first place.

Most of you will know enough about his young life to realize that he did not come to Oxford as a Christian. In fact, of the few people I know who remember him from that time, many remember that he was, as one described it, "a blaspheming atheist" who was exceptionally gifted even then with wit and with the ability to actually say what he means. Sometimes a weapon which can be used for good and sometimes for very bad things is the ability to whip the other man simply by your tongue because you are so good at talking. I must admit I have always felt afraid of people who can talk well.

So it was that C. S. Lewis could master, and in one way keep, I think, Christianity at bay, because he could talk well and could talk like Dr. Johnson at times for victory. But talking is one of those things, like all things, which can be turned to good or evil — depending on how you put it. However, I suppose you also realize that it was gradual, by many, many different stages, that Lewis came to believe the gospel and to be converted. That is all told, much better than anyone else could put it, in Lewis's own autobiography, *Surprised by Joy*. We realize that mainly it is a philosophical conversion. There is some dispute amongst even his friends and his family about whether Lewis was ever converted. His brother maintained that he was not converted, that he was always a Christian and had been since baptism. Lewis, I notice, in all of his writing, continues to use the word "conversion," but when pushed from the other side to say when, precisely at what moment, he was converted, he would say, "No, no, it took a long time." So you must make up your mind, I think, about C. S. Lewis that here you are dealing with someone much more like St. Peter than St. Paul in that matter. There was no precise moment that he could put his finger on that did not actually bear upon this wonderful thing which continued to work in his life, all of his life, every moment of it, it seemed to me.

After his conversion he felt that the first thing he should do, as he says, is "fly the flag." He did that, first of all, by going to his own local church. He also at that time was looking after a friend's mother, Mrs. Moore, whom he had adopted after the war, when he came back to Oxford in 1919. All of these things came gradually into play when he comes before England as an apologist. That happened with *The Screwtape Letters*, and here is where Mrs. Boshell finally makes her appearance. When Lewis wrote *The Screwtape Letters*, the pieces were not actually for a book but for a periodical called the *Guardian*, which is now defunct. They appeared weekly, almost exactly as you have read them, in this newspaper. From the very first, Lewis, like his brother, took seriously the belief that one should look after widows and orphans in affliction, though, as he often said, "it does not say anything about having those widows come to see you." I don't know how on earth she ever came into the picture, but Mrs. Boshell's name appears in many letters of C. S. Lewis. The first time, I think, she appears is in a Lewis letter to the editor of the *Guardian*, pointing out that none of the money from *The Screwtape Letters* was to be sent to him at all. He did not even want it sent to his address. The money from the royalties should go to Mrs. Boshell, and there were no end of such widows.

Shortly after that, as *The Screwtape Letters* were being prepared for a book, Lewis began his great series of lectures on the BBC which later became the first part of *Mere Christianity.* I've been to Reading, where the BBC written archives center is, and there I saw Lewis's letters, and who should be mentioned in those letters? Where was the money to go for the BBC lectures? Mrs. Boshell. It appears with that same frequency with which we know a man who uses "share." Mrs. Boshell. She "shared" the money with a number of other widows.

Here again I think we find out how Lewis was finding his own way in what precisely he was to do. Lewis was not a man who readily accepted a speaking or writing invitation unless he felt he had something to say. His friends at that time rather got the impression that he never turned down an invitation, but he actually did. He turned them down when he felt, as he said in many cases, that the pot had run dry, that there was no more water in the well, simply nothing else to say.

One of his friends, Sister Penelope, a nun who was at Wantage, was also writing some lectures for the BBC at the same time as Lewis. She did not actually read them over the BBC, but someone else did. Lewis pointed out to her at the time—something which, I think, applies to all of his apologetical works—he said,

> Mine [his lectures over the BBC] are *preparatio evangelica* [preparation for the gospel] rather than *evangelium* [the gospel itself], and attempt to convince people that there is a moral law, that we disobey it, and that the existence of a Lawgiver is at least very probable and also (*unless* you add the Christian doctrine of the Atonement) imparts despair rather than comfort....
>
> Yes ... jobs one dare neither refuse nor perform. One must take comfort in remembering that God used an ass to convert the prophet: perhaps if we do our poor best we shall be allowed a stall near it in the celestial stable....[2]

In all that letter, the rest of it is actually a drawing with a huge stable and a gigantic jackass in the stable with a halo, and outside the stable on one side is a nun, and on the other side is an Oxford don in a mortarboard. But the largest thing, of course, is the ass—Balaam's ass—who is inside.

But Lewis found that the problem with his own country at that time was "how do you give them the good news which is connected with repentance if, in fact, they don't find anything to repent of?" That, of course, could occupy us a very long time, and I don't think that Lewis ever felt that he dealt in a completely satisfactory way with that. Even so, this was a part of his apologetic, and a part which he felt you cannot do without. In this case the gospel, the good news, remains the same, but how you impart this despair, I don't know. I think that changes. He thought it changes at times with people, but it is very difficult to get people to realize that they need something unless they think they need it. How can you bring good news if they think they've got quite enough as it is?

From the first, those lectures were given with a freshness and with a conciseness which has simply marked Lewis's style ever since. I don't think he had written anything before that which was really quite as pithy and racy, and yet which is quite as deep. Many, I think, have attempted to write like that, in the sense that they can write easily. It is simply very, very easy to understand and very easy to read. But Lewis's writings are extremely deceptive. Because one can understand them does not mean that they are shallow. Other writings might be very shallow, even though they might be difficult to understand. I remember Owen Barfield reading aloud to me one page by Mr. Altizer, the man who started the "God is Dead" movement. He read from Altizer's book called *God Is Dead*. Owen Barfield and I had rather the pleasure of that bit of poison since Mr. Barfield was in the United States right after Mr. Altizer had buried God. Owen Barfield discovered that he was going to be on the same platform debating with Altizer one day, but that morning he read this obituary by Altizer. It was the most turgid piece of prose I ever heard in my life. At the end of this I had to just say, "I can't understand a word you've said."

Lewis said you can always make the language more polysyllabic, but you don't necessarily make it clearer for that reason. And in Lewis's case, I think this has been a stumbling block for those who feel that good sense is always extremely difficult to come by, that unless you have a headache after reading a couple of pages of an author, you haven't got anywhere. One of the stumbling blocks I've noticed from the beginning has been over that fascinating question of just who precisely our Lord Jesus was and the disconnection of our Lord's own claims from *the* claim made by some that he was a merely moral man. Lewis takes that up and says, "You cannot say that, because a man who says he is God cannot therefore be a merely moral man; he would either be on a level with a man who says he is a poached egg or he would be the devil of Hell because he's lying, or he would be who he says he is. But we cannot come to him with any patronizing nonsense about him being a purely moral man, because he's not left that open to us."[3]

I remember this came up in one of the first books from the United States about C. S. Lewis as apologist, in which the author said, "I cannot accept this; it is far too simple." I brought that up with Austin Farrer, who at that time was the warden of Keble College, a very learned theologian here. He said, "No, no, that is where Lewis deceives his modern critics. It is because it is simply said one naturally assumes there is no sense in it." He said, "No, he thought it out very, very carefully. There is no other alternative, you know." And he said, "Notice that his critic says it cannot be that simple; there must be something else, but he does not supply us with that, if he knew."

So those lectures succeeded very well and brought, presumably, much happiness to Mrs. Boshell, who at one time appears to even be at The Kilns, all because Lewis got entangled with the BBC. He had asked that Mrs. Boshell be sent some of the royalties, in care of The Kilns, his own home. So they thought, "Well, we are writing a letter to him to say that we are sending it to Mrs. Boshell," and they just put it in the same envelope. He sent it back and said, "No, don't send it to me; send it to Mrs. Boshell." The fact that his address was the same was not satisfactory, and Mrs. Boshell got a separate letter. Mrs. Boshell seems to have done quite well out of *Mere Christianity*.

It was at this time that I think I am more and more impressed by how Lewis did it. I believe that many of us, especially those of us who are connected in some small way with universities, feel that it is enough if we are just perhaps learned people. I know that there is great fascination with simply publishing. Perhaps in the United States one must publish anyway. Perhaps the dangerous thing about that is not only that one will write things which are worthless but one will imagine that that is enough, that that is all we have to do. I find it particularly the case in this country with theologians who write learned books but who do not seem to have a completely Christian life. Partly because of that, they seem to feel that it is simply enough to write about the nature of God, though in many cases it sounds as if they don't believe that God has much nature. As Lewis says about most of the modern theologians who were operating at his time, "It doesn't sound as though God knows very much about himself, if you read the modern theologians." However, I find that for those Christians and for those priests who have combined theology with perhaps doing what they hope is a good job, good work in that sense, that you get a very different sort of plan than you get if you separate the two. I think you can very well simply do good works, if that is what God has given you to do. If you are a theologian, or if you are the head of almost anything and call yourself a Christian, I don't think your theology will be very sound if you simply do not do any good works.

In this case I'm always reminded of Lewis himself more than anyone. His life seemed to be almost totally that of a man who gave away so much. Mr. Barfield will be able to tell us much more about that than I can. But from the very first, with *The Screwtape Letters*, there is Mrs. Boshell, who is receiving the money, and there are a great many other widows. With *Mere Christianity*, Mrs. Boshell again received some money, and with the royalties to Lewis's other books Mrs. Boshell continued to benefit. What makes this interesting to me is that Lewis himself seemed to me to be a man who actually worried so much about money, as did his brother. I think his brother, Major Lewis, seemed to worry even more than he did. When you find this going on in someone who was as generous as they both were, it is to be remarked on.

I know that I was the one to whom Lewis dictated his letter resigning from his job in Cambridge. I thought, when I did that, that he needed a rest and we might actually celebrate with a drink, or at least a cup of tea. But he seemed to be rather sunk in thought, and I realized, of course, it's not very easy to leave a job without some mixed feelings about it. Eventually it came out, and he said, "Well, my dear Walter, you know, with me out of work and with winter coming on, we won't be able to have both a fire in the common room and one in the dining room, so we'll have to eat in the cove, we'll have to sleep in the cove, we'll have to do our work together in front of a small fire here in the common room." I said, "If you keep talking like that I will read you your bank account."

I actually could remember what was in his bank account at that point. He came out of that spell right away. Later, after he had died, I ran into the same problem with his brother. I went to see him one day; this was after he had paid his income tax. What he normally did was to keep in the bank a considerable sum. If he got over a particular sum he would invest it, and so keep a considerable sum, but not too large, in the bank. When I went to see him he was slumped down in his chair. It was the first time he didn't get up, and he said, "You're looking at a bankrupt." He said, "I wonder how it would be if Tolkien should be passing by and see the wagon when they come to collect me and take me to the poorhouse." We don't have poorhouses any longer; we didn't even then. Nor do wagons come and collect bodies, you know. Nor was Professor Tolkien likely to be walking by and see this wagon carrying Major Lewis away. Anyway, I discovered what had happened. He had paid his income tax, which took all of what he had in his checking account. He had paid his income tax with that. I said, "Yes, but you have other money too, because I've been helping you invest it." He said, "Yes, but I don't have that." I said, "I know, but it's invested; you can get it." "No, no, I don't have that; that's gone, that's gone."

So I found I couldn't get anywhere with him, so I had a little amount of money myself and I sent him that, and at the same time I wrote to Mr. Barfield and explained it to him. After that, we took half of his income and paid his income tax for him. This way he did not feel that he was paying any income tax at all! We rather worried about him spending too much, you know. So what do you do with the two Lewis brothers?

When I charged C. S. Lewis with being rather an alarmist, I thought how extraordinary it is. There you are, giving away two-thirds of your income, but when the time comes we're going to have one fire, a small fire, all winter long. It would never occur to him to actually take some of the money back and not give it away and use it on himself. He wouldn't do that.

As for the rest, his own life was an extraordinarily curious one. Those who visited The Kilns found it as I did, even when I went there, rather like St. Anne's on the Hill.[4] All this curious combination of people seemed to get on frightfully well with one another, though you couldn't quite see how precisely they ever came to be in the same house at all. His housekeeper seemed to really come to The Kilns because she enjoyed coming, and she really just enjoyed preparing her own meals and seeing what was going on. Lewis received so many gifts from other people, which he gave to her. She was extremely engaging as a conversationalist, and she liked to come and see who was there and what was going on. Paxford, the gardener, as I have said elsewhere, didn't get up until eleven, and he seemed to enjoy himself enormously. And precisely what he did, I never really could find out. His understanding of the gospel seemed to be totally confined to eschatology. He believed that the end of the world was coming at any moment, and for this reason, as the shopper in the family, the man who went out and got the food that we ate, he didn't think we should have too much on hand. He was particularly bad about buying sugar, as I know I've said before in another talk, but the sugar problem was a severe one in The Kilns. I remember when we were having such a distinguished man as Spencer Curtis Brown, the literary agent, coming for tea. I was preparing things for that tea, but the problem was, most people in this country take sugar, and I counted the spoonfuls of sugar from one vase into another, and I found there was only enough for C. S. Lewis. So I asked Paxford, who usually got a half pound at a time, if we couldn't have some before that afternoon. He said, "He may not take sugar." And I said, "Yes, he may not, but most people do. He may take it." "He may not, though." And I said, "I'm not very worried about him not taking it; I'm worried if he does take it. Couldn't we have some more?" And then again, in came the end of the world.

How would I feel about him? How would Mr. Jack feel about Paxford if there we saw the whole world ending, and all that sugar just being burnt up? I may mention, now that that charming man is before us, that Lewis did say that of all the characters that he'd created, the one most fully based on any human being was, of course, Paxford, who is Puddleglum, the Marsh-wiggle. Lewis told me that his life was made very interesting by Paxford, particularly when Joy was there. Paxford, he said, showed himself in as fully a Marsh-wiggle on the morning that C. S. Lewis and his wife were to go to Greece. Lewis told me, "There I was, with a wife who was dying, and we were flying in an airplane, which was very new to both of us, going to a foreign country where we didn't know, really, what was going to happen." A taxi came to collect Jack and Joy and take them to the airport, and Paxford came out, as usual, to say good-bye to them, and he put his head in the window. He was always listening to the wireless, and he said, "Well, Mr. Jack, there was this bulletin just going on on the wireless about a plane just went down. Everyone killed, burnt beyond recognition. Did you hear that, Mr. Jack? Burnt beyond recognition." As Lewis said, "On that note, we flew to Greece."

One detail among so many of simply how extremely generous he was: in having such a household, including myself, all of whom looked like we were refugees from somewhere else who just happened to be hanging around at the time and he says, "Come in," but an incredibly nice man. I have recently seen even a further example of this in editing the letters. This is not the complete letters; that's still a long way ahead, I think. But if you'll forgive my being so personal, over this year I've been revising Major Lewis's edition to the letters for a new publication, trying to make that book more like what he had planned for it to be before the publishers changed it, and this means adding a great many more letters to that book, so that it's about twice, two and a half times as long as it has been.[5]

In that collection of letters, one sees Lewis very easily and charmingly writing letters, particularly to his brother and to his father up until the time his father has died and his brother is, of course, living at home with him. This coincides almost precisely with the time that Lewis became famous and began to receive so many letters himself.

Something which before had always been a trial but nevertheless had its own peculiar pleasures, at least writing to friends, now was something demanded of him. Over and over again you see letters written on Christmas Day, or New Year's Day, or Christmas Eve. You think, "Will that man never get to the end of it?" How one's heart is wrung when you find, for instance, in a letter he says, "It is now 9.50 a.m. and I've already been writing letters as hard as I can drive the pen across the paper for an hour and a half; and when on earth I shall get a chance to begin my own day's work, I don't know."[6]

I found this when I was with him: that the letters, which he considered one other thing which one must endure about success of a sort, must be answered, if possible that very day. Yet those letters are some of the best. I think they were some of the best things for Lewis in the sense that they were a very pastoral thing to do. They also, I think, are one of the richest mines of his writing. How often he has learned to simply take what others would take ten pages in trying to write and condense to a brief paragraph, and yet in which everything is there. You cannot find an argument put more beautifully and precisely. For many people, this will be the only way they will learn theology: to simply read it in that condensed form. So Lewis, himself, I think, learned, partly through adversity, how you simply use the gifts you have — not the ones you don't have, but the ones you do have — to glorify God. This, I think, came best because he himself had already believed that this success, as he chose it, as he wanted it, had had to be killed.

In one of his letters written in 1930 to Arthur Greeves, he said something that has made an extremely important impression on me. Arthur Greeves had not succeeded in getting a novel published, something which he counted on for years and years and years. One of his friends told him no, it really won't do, and I think Lewis knew it wouldn't do. In the letter, he's trying to comfort a friend himself in 1930, about the time of his conversion. Slightly before that, he himself had one great ambition, which was to be a poet, and it hadn't worked out at all well.

He says this:

From the age of sixteen onwards I had one single ambition, from which I never wavered, in the prosecution of which I spent every ounce I could, on wh. I really & deliberately staked my whole contentment: And I recognised myself as having unmistakably failed in it.... Think of how difficult that would be if one *succeeded* as a writer: how bitter this necessary purgation at the age of sixty, when literary success had made your whole life and you had *then* got to begin to go through the stage of seeing it all as dust and ashes. Perhaps God has been specially kind to us in forcing us to get over it at the beginning.... As you know so well, we have got to *die*. Cry, kick, swear, we may: only like Lillith to come in the end and die far more painfully and later. Does it sound like priggery if I say "I implore you"? Heaven knows I do it as a friend not as a preacher: do it only because you stand very high among the half-dozen people whom I love. I implore you, then, seriously, to regard your present trouble as an opportunity for carrying the dying process a stage further. If necessary, go back to the Puritan language you were brought up in and think of your literary ambitions as an "idol" you have to give up as a sacrifice demanded.[7]

He then says in his next letter,

In my own case it is a very remarkable thing that in the last few religious lyrics which I have written during the last year, in which I had no idea of publication & at first very little idea even of showing them to friends, I have found myself impelled to take infinitely more pains, less ready to be contented with the fairly good and more determined to reach the best attainable, than ever I was in the days when I never wrote without the ardent hope of successful publication.[8]

And so he goes on, having decided that he would never succeed, having all his ambitions killed, to the remarkable man that he later became, though he never, I think, got over, to my mind and to his mind, what a remarkable thing he was called to do. In 1941 he had a

letter from Sister Penelope inviting him to come and address some of
the junior sisters in the convent at Wantage, which is about eighteen
miles from Oxford. He wrote,

> Yes, I will come and address your Junior Sisters next Easter
> unless "wife and oxen" have by that time taken the form of
> incarceration in a German concentration camp, an English
> Labour Company, or (to pitch on a brighter idea) some sort of
> Borstal Institution of the lower foot-hills of the mountains of
> Purgatory. But (if one may say so *salva reverentia*) what very
> odd tasks God sets us: if anyone had told me ten years ago
> that I should be lecturing in a convent—!⁹

Well, so he was lecturing in a convent, and even when I met him
in 1963, he kept saying, "How remarkable! Imagine me, preaching."
To us it seemed such a natural thing for him to do. But like all of us,
he still could look at himself and think, "What a curious thing. Having been an atheist for so long, what an odd thing for me to do. Who
would have believed that God could be that strong?" As to what he
set himself to do, I think one of the best examples comes in his letter,
his reply, his rejoinder to Dr. Pittinger at that time of New York, who
had complained about a number of his theological books. He says at
the end of his rejoinder,

> When I began, Christianity came before the great mass
> of my unbelieving fellow-countrymen either in the highly
> emotional form offered by revivalists or in the unintel-
> ligible language of highly cultured clergymen. Most men
> were reached by neither. My task was therefore simply that
> of a *translator*—one turning Christian doctrine, or what he
> believed to be such, into the vernacular, into language that
> unscholarly people would attend to and could understand.
> For this purpose a style more guarded, more *nuancé*, fine-
> lier shaded, more rich and fruitful ambiguities—in fact, a
> style more like Dr Pittinger's own—would have been worse
> than useless. It would not only have failed to enlighten the
> common reader's understanding, it would have aroused his

suspicion. He would have thought, poor soul, that I was facing both ways, sitting on the fence, offering at one moment what I withdrew the next, and generally trying to trick him. I may have made theological errors. My manner may have been defective. Others may do better hereafter. I am ready, if I am young enough, to learn. Dr Pittinger would be more of a helpful critic if he advised the cure as well as asserting many diseases. How does he himself do such work? What methods, what success, does he employ when he is trying to convert the great mass of storekeepers, lawyers, realtors, morticians, policemen, and artisans who surround him in his own city?

One thing at least is sure. If the real theologians had tackled that laborious work of translation about a hundred years ago, when they began to lose touch with the people (for whom Christ died), there would have been no place for me.[10]

Perhaps there would not have been, but how fortunate that it is. We find in his writings, I think, not only great learning but simply a very remarkable man. I know how fortunate I was to have known him, but I think those who didn't can nevertheless enjoy a great deal of him, and most of what he says that is best is in his books. And he sounds like his books. But even then, I still think that it's a good thing to hear about him. I welcome this Oxford 88.[11]

Finally, one point; even at the end, I don't think that success, such as it was, ever spoiled him. I use this as an example. I know this isn't exactly giving alms to Mrs. Boshell, who eventually died, but the way he treated a particular man in Cambridge, whom I've met too — Lewis sent me over there to Cambridge to deal with his books and belongings and to move his things back to Oxford and sell some things. During the few days that Douglas Gresham and I were in Cambridge, I met a member of his college who was not actually a teacher, and the man was so incredibly boring that I found it hard to know whether I'd been standing in front of him five minutes or five years. I couldn't even remember my former life. I seemed not to have any. Lewis asked me what I thought of X, we'll call him, and I said,

"X is really the greatest bore I have ever met. He is unique. He differs from other bores in that he interests me by the intensity of his boringness." To which Lewis replied, "Yes, but let us not forget that our Lord might well have said, 'If you have done it unto one of the least of these, my bores, you have done it unto me.'"

Ladies and gentlemen, I am sorry that I have "bored" you with this "sharing." Thank you very much.

Part 2

THE TEACHER

Many of C. S. Lewis's students have held important teaching posts around the world, influencing yet another generation. Many have made significant contributions to the field of English literature and other academic subjects. While Lewis's students are now retired, for the most part, a few continue to exercise their right as senior professors to teach a course from time to time, and yet, in another sense, none of them has retired. They continue to work, to study, and to write. Some continue to lecture and to preach. In every case, they continue to learn.

Many of them wrote to Lewis through the years, and his replies often deal with their continuing questions about their own study and questions about teaching itself. Lewis makes some of his most important comments on teaching in these letters. Brief snippets of these letters may be found in Warren Lewis's edited *Letters of C. S. Lewis* and in Walter Hooper's exhaustive compilation in three volumes, *The Collected Letters of C. S. Lewis*.

Although the contributors to this section are teachers whom Lewis mentored, not all are cut from the same cloth. Some sought Lewis out because of his deep faith. Some sought him out in defiance of his faith. Some became Christians through his influence. Some have never had any interest in religion. Most express some points of disagreement with Lewis over some matter or other, but all express an appreciation for and indebtedness to Lewis for how he helped them develop their minds.

Chapter 3

C. S. LEWIS: SIXTY YEARS ON

Derek Brewer

Asked to comment on Lewis as a scholar and teacher now after fifty years of my own attempts to be such, the first thing to remark is that though Lewis was efficient and conscientious beyond many, and certainly more talented than most, he was not a "professional." He acted as he did primarily because he wanted to do so. He did not have "a job." Most of my academic colleagues have in my lifetime acted from the same motivation. We do not do it for the pay, much as we need the money. This will seem obvious to most of my colleagues but is perhaps less obvious to the outside world of less fortunate people who have to work at jobs which they may well feel only occupy a part of their personalities, or may indeed be unpleasant, only done for financial reward and lack of more attractive opportunities. Of course, ours like every other occupation has aspects which are tedious or less agreeable. Marking essays, conducting examinations, and carrying out many administrative tasks would rank high in many university teachers' and scholars' lists of those aspects of their occupation that are less agreeable. But university teachers and scholars in the Humanities have on the whole agreeable occupations which they would rather do than anything else. Some have even expressed their surprise that they are actually paid, if usually inadequately, for doing what they want to do.

Nevertheless, in comparison with Lewis's heyday, there is a creeping professionalism which does not always seem good. We now have "offices," and office hours, not studies. Our productivity, especially of "research" as expressed in articles and books, is weighed as if in a scale. Our books and essays should figure in a citation index: our footnotes must follow a rigid formula. The study of the Humanities is increasingly (as it seems to me) modeled on professional research in the Natural Sciences. I understand that undergraduates in the Natural Sciences in Cambridge now even have an official "mentor," as opposed to their college "moral tutor" or Director of Studies, or supervisor for weekly sessions.

All this is a world away from the university of sixty years ago. I have been asked, did Lewis consider himself a "mentor"? Was he, for example, in the dinners with Dyson and my friends which I mentioned in my essay of 1979, intentionally "investing himself in the next generation"?[1] A good question because it reveals the huge gap in attitudes between the generation of Lewis and myself of modern times. The short answer is no. Our meetings were thought of by me and my friends as pure conviviality—one might say, in modern idiom, "for fun," except that that much-used modern word itself gets the feeling wrong. "Fun" implies a sort of deliberate frivolity escaping from the serious business of life. It implies a clear division between work and play, profit and pleasure that did not, I think, exist for us. We met as friends and certainly not to "work." There were jokes and cheerfulness, but the things that naturally interested us, and which we often talked about, were also the subjects we seriously considered and felt deeply about; on literature, morality, history, and so forth. I do not think that we talked much, if at all, about politics, certainly never about sport. Nor was there any of that tediously facetious rude banter and teasing that so often passes for conversation in masculine society amongst men who consider real topics unsuitable for social conversation.

Thus although Lewis made his living as an academic, he was not self-consciously "professional." Although as a teacher he obviously tried to convey the truth of his "subject," his conception of the subject was vast, and the essence of his study of it was a high kind of pleasure. Moreover, as I commented in my original essay, he did not value teaching highly nor professed particularly to enjoy the tutorial aspect. I thought then, as I think now, that he was mistaken, that teaching is important and valuable, even enjoyable to teacher and taught, but I never engaged him, as far as I can remember, in explicit debate on the subject. In the latter part of his life, as I also commented, he expressed his pleasure at having taught so many people and in consequence having so many friends younger than himself. But in the years immediately after World War II, he had a very heavy tutorial load. It must have amounted in those years to some twenty hours a week or more. That may not sound much to nonacademic professionals, who note that three terms in Oxford came only to twenty-four weeks a year, fully packed though they were. But when one adds to it the necessary reading and rereading, some academic committees, and recognizes the pull of creative, scholarly, and critical writing, it is indeed a burden. Famous as he became from the forties onwards for his Christian apologetics, he did not conduct tutorials in any missionary spirit. Tutorials in any case, as I commented in my previous essay, were not instructional in any schoolmasterly way, except perhaps for those in Old English. In my own career I tried to follow the same pattern (including the Old English). In the "modern" literature, post–fourteenth century, a tutorial depends on the "student" (as we did not call ourselves) having done a decent amount of work on the agreed topic, which was usually an author's text, and then being ready to expound it. The tutor's job is to respond and where necessary to inform, correct, and extend. In my own career I always felt that it was most unsatisfactory if an undergraduate had been so idle as not to have anything worthwhile to say, and to force me to occupy the time with an impromptu lecture. I could do that, often more easily than responding to a genuine but perhaps (as I saw it) wrongheaded essay, but a tutorial that became a ding-dong argument about the text between tutor and undergraduate was always more worthwhile. One of the advantages of the study of literature is that a conscientious pupil writing in good faith can always have something interesting to say to a tutor (or in Cambridge terms, "supervisor"), even if the tutor is an acknowledged expert, because the pupil is young and has a different experience of the world, different values. Even the pupil's errors become interesting to the tutor, and the more so if the pupil is ready to support them. (I take it that the Natural Sciences are different in this, and that the pupil has to be more advanced in study before disagreeing with the supervisor, because in literary study one reaches the borders of "objective fact" more quickly than in the Natural Sciences.)

My view implies that there is a fundamental equality between tutor and pupil, insofar as they are equally interested, equally concerned to establish the literary truth. The tutor ought to be more learned, etc., but both tutor and pupil are engaged, if at different levels, in the same sort of quest. That at least is how I, and I think Lewis, and most dons at Oxford in those days felt about the business, and how, as far as I can judge, most of my young colleagues in the Humanities still feel.

Perhaps one has to allow here for my own naïveté and interests, which may not have been shared by all. Brilliant men like Kingsley Amis, an exact contemporary, and Philip Larkin a year or two earlier, neither of whom I ever met or heard of in my post-war undergraduate days, would have derided my earnestness, but I think most of my fellow pupils in Magdalen, who almost all happened to be grammar-school boys (contrary to current cant about "elitism"), and most of those I met in other colleges had much the same attitude. Some were no doubt much less earnest than I, and there was the usual amount of foolery practiced by young men (there were alas very few young women whom I knew), but since most of us were ex-servicemen who could hold our drink and would soon need to earn our livings, we might be skeptical but not revolutionary. We were very pleased to be alive and at the university, and felt a certain equality with our elders and betters.

Postwar Oxford was not like Evelyn Waugh's Oxford of *Brideshead Revisited* for most of us, though something of its spirited flippancy survived. It is hard now to convey the atmosphere of Oxford in the immediately postwar years, and it must have been different for many individuals. For many of us it was delightful despite the food rationing, fuel shortage (the winter of early 1947 was desperately cold), and so forth. As ex-servicemen we had been through a just war, survived, and thought we had won. To take an extreme example, imagine the difference for my friends Tom Stock and Philip Stibbe between savage ill treatment in a Japanese prisoner-of-war camp and life and study in an Oxford college. Such suffering still cast dark shadows on postwar life for some, and some never fully recovered, but although there was a leavening of brilliant boys straight from school, like Kenneth Tynan (who himself behaved in a decidedly *Brideshead* style), most of us were young men in our early to middle twenties. There was variation in our seriousness. One of my friends reading English, a married man with children, who had a couple of medals for his bravery in flying unarmed aeroplanes in daylight over Germany during the war, went into his academic examinations quivering like a leaf, and not because he had failed to work. Some of us might criticize the English course (set out, it was said, mainly by Lewis and Tolkien), but there was nothing like the rebelliousness of the late sixties, which with the accompanying or following revolutions in morality, and other changes too numerous to mention, have permanently changed the tone and attitudes of "students." The small proportion of women present should also be remembered.

This is only my personal, very limited perception of a very crowded university at a very unusual time. Ann Thwaite in the preface to her fascinating collection of essays by a number of different people from Robert Boothby (Balliol 1919–21) to Martin Amis (1968–71) remarks how various were the experiences and how little various sets of people coincided.[2] All her contributors are successful, brilliant people, most of whom got "firsts" without apparently much trouble. Ann Thwaite herself illustrates how an undergraduate of wit and intelligence could come to know a great variety of clever, delightful, and later famous people. If I may say so without prejudice to my quite large acquaintance, such was not my fortune, though I did at Magdalen start a sort of literary society (the Lyly—after the sixteenth-century grammarian, who was a Magdalen man, not the slightly later author of *Euphues*). I also in my folly (what will an ex-adjutant not do?) volunteered to become the secretary of the Rugger Club (1946–47) because I was so exasperated at how inefficiently it had been run in the previous year. It was a time-wasting business, getting men to turn out on chilly Saturday afternoons when they were proposing to break promises rashly made on the preceding Wednesday to turn out on Saturday. Providence came to my aid in the great snowstorm and freeze-up which started about 5 January 1947 and lasted until March, and no games were possible. There was a major fuel crisis in the country and huge floods afterwards, but I was deeply grateful.

Perhaps some of the rugger players and certainly several of the
Lyly Society have gone on to distinguished careers, but I myself did
not move in any brilliant circle though I went to the usual kind of
meetings. The novelist Nina Bawden in her excellent account of her
days in Oxford (1943–46) recalls the number of later famous men
she met, but comments on how dreary and busy Oxford became in
late 1945 when all the ex-servicemen returned. I was one of the ex-
servicemen. Few of the essayists in Ann Thwaite's *My Oxford, My
Cambridge* remark on attention to their studies. One, the politician Jo
Grimond, remarks that the education, though excellent, was "unreal."
Of course he got a "first" but complains that no one was taught the
skills of life "to type or mend a motor car, to work or read a balance
sheet."[3] Needless to say, this seems ludicrous to me but illustrates in
part how wide a gap exists between many of the ex-servicemen and
those who came before and after. Alan Coren (1957–60) gives another
example in Ann Thwaite's book.[4] He achieved a first-class degree in
English in 1960, treated the subject with disdain, "screwed," it would
appear, many girls, and went on to research for a year. He enjoyed his
life then and later as a successful humorous journalist. To my regret
I did none of these things, and the reader should notice how unrep-
resentative my account must be, even though the difference between
1945 and 1957 in general attitudes was considerable.

My generation was of course equally far from the Oxford of the
twenties and thirties, though even at that time there was a gap between
the men of Evelyn Waugh's type and the earnest studious men represented by the derided Paul Pennyfeather in Waugh's wonderfully
funny satire *Decline and Fall* (1928). Lewis was different again. Apart
from a year in a public school which he hated, he had been privately
educated. As an undergraduate he had lived in an almost entirely male
society of a kind very different from that of Waugh. Fundamentally
serious-minded, perhaps shy, unfashionably chaste, Lewis might now
be accused of a misogyny was normal enough in those days. After the
war and his recovery from his wound, he seems to have worked in college although he lived at home with his adopted mother and sister (his
adopted mother was the mother of a friend killed in the war). During
the day he might in conversation refer to "my mother," which was at

first a puzzle as somehow we knew that his natural mother had died when he was a child, but he never gave the impression of enjoying domestic felicity, as I noted in my essay.

In this still predominantly masculine postwar society, in which so many undergraduates had already held wartime positions of high responsibility in matters of life and death, no one thought of tutors as "mentors," and in Oxford least of all as tutors trying to mold their undergraduates' minds. For many undergraduates, perhaps, the subject they studied was unimportant, as noted as the impression one gets from such a volume as *My Oxford, My Cambridge*. Although Lewis was not a domineering influence, and as I have noted rather despised teaching, it is nevertheless the case that all four of the undergraduates who attended the parties with Lewis and Dyson also became academics and teachers. It is likely that we unconsciously shared the same kind of academic attitudes. This may be suggested by the obvious contrast between Lewis and F. R. Leavis. Leavis at Cambridge was the very incarnation of a great and influential teacher who certainly aimed to mold his pupils' views. His strong dogmatic personality and literary views were far more identifiable and clear-cut than Lewis's. At one time there seemed to be hardly a grammar school in England which did not have, on its English-teaching staff, at least one identifiable "Leavisite." Leavis refrained from theorizing, but there was a canon of authors whom you must admire, and those you must despise and repudiate. The leader of the admirable was D. H. Lawrence. On the other side were Old English authors, Spenser, Milton, Swift (who receives a swipe in the very last sentence of an essay on Blake), and the later Eliot as a Christian.

This is not the place to measure Lewis and Leavis against each other. Mrs. Joan Bennett, who disagreed profoundly with Lewis but could also qualify her praise for Leavis, once told me that Leavis's teaching of the then most modern authors such as James Joyce (for a time banned in England and the U.S.) was a really exciting and innovatory intellectual experience. One might say that for Lewis such experience came from his reading of the older English authors, especially of the sixteenth century, for whom he had a particular affinity, and whose virtues he opened up. But Lewis had great skill in eliciting some special value for many obscure medieval and often Latin authors, knowledge of whom, for most of us, remains limited to Lewis's sympathetic accounts. He was not afraid to judge on either literary or moral grounds (I have quoted in my earlier essay his passing comment that Marlowe and Carlyle were the most depraved English authors). His objection was on grounds of humanity, against their promotion of tyranny and cruelty (in Carlyle's case presumably his admiration of Napoleon). For Lewis, contemporary history in the case of Germany and Russia was offering current examples of such wickedness, but I never heard or read a political comment by Lewis, and he never said we should not read such authors. There was nothing paranoid about him. His interest was in secular literature, as Kathryn Kerby-Fulton shrewdly points out.[5] He largely disregards the huge complexity of medieval allegorical writing on the Bible and religious texts, just as he disregards, quite legitimately, medieval religious writings in English.

Although from the 1940s onward, Lewis took on himself the duty, as he saw it, of Christian apologetics with some zest, for he loved an argument, there was no malice in it. He respected those he disagreed with. As others as well as I can testify, he never brought specifically Christian doctrine into his teaching (except, I suppose, as it might lead to historical understanding of an unfamiliar point of view, though I remember no example of this). Here he differed from the didacticism of Leavis or, on the other side, the even more vigorous propagation of political Marxist or fellow-traveling, more recently anachronistic feminist views of many of his, and later my, colleagues, especially in Cambridge. (When he gave his Inaugural Lecture, "De Descriptione Temporum," the monthly periodical *Nineteenth and Twentieth Century* brought out a whole number, whose contributors were mainly from Cambridge, composed of essays in opposition to his assumed views. I only wish I had kept a copy of this ephemeral publication.)

Lewis's general attitude to literary study could found no school because it was grounded in a very ancient tradition, often repudiated nowadays especially by left-wing and feminist writers. His attitude could be summed up in Pope's words,

> *A perfect Judge will read each work of Wit*
> *With the same spirit that its author writ*
>
> *Essay on Criticism*, 233–34

though I do not recall Lewis on Pope (he liked Swift), and Lewis would certainly have deplored Pope's Renaissance neoclassical standards. Pope's *Essay*, drawing on ancient sources, expresses a long tradition. A characteristic early-nineteenth-century repetition can be summed up in words used by Macaulay writing of Sir James Mackintosh on the need to understand figures of the past in the context of their time. This applies to thoughts and feelings as well as deeds.

> In order to form a correct estimate of their merits we ought to place ourselves in their situation, to put out of our minds, for a time, all that knowledge which they, however eager in their pursuit of truth, could not have, and which we, however negligent we may have been, could not help having.[6]

The derivative nature of my quotation is itself an example of its general acceptance in a stream of thought, not a "school," to which Lewis (and I) belonged. Lewis repeats the same argument in the splendid first chapter of *The Allegory of Love*, a book which the writing of this essay has led me to look at again (I see that I bought my copy in 1949) with renewed respect, mistaken as I believe it to have been in certain respects. Lewis writes,

> There can be no mistake about the novelty of romantic love: our only difficulty is to imagine in all its bareness the mental world that existed before its coming—to wipe out of our minds, for a moment, nearly all that makes the food both of modern sentimentality and modern cynicism.[7]

Newsome, while quoting the Macaulay passage already referred to, goes on to quote Lewis's warning to historians against "the erroneous doctrine of the 'Unchanging Human Heart'" expressed in Lewis's *Preface to Paradise Lost* and foreshadowed in *The Allegory of Love*.[8]

A great example of Lewis's characteristic turn of mind may be found in his *English Literature in the Sixteenth Century Excluding Drama* (1954). (When I wrote him a letter expressing my admiration of this book, he replied in mocking vein—what a Frank Churchill of a letter writer I was—a reference to Jane Austen's *Emma*. My letter was not intended as flattery—what could I gain from that?—and Lewis was not vain. He had no need for admiration for himself, though it was something he warmly felt for others, as for example Charles Williams and Tolkien.) No one has written better about Spenser and Sir Philip Sidney than Lewis in this book, which is not to say that it is the last word on those authors, but it remains a source of imaginative stimulation and real literary pleasure. A brief consideration of Lewis's writing on a less obviously great poet, Gavin Douglas, gives the characteristic flavor of his work. After an account of Douglas's other poems, Lewis comes to Douglas's great work, *The XIII Bukes of the Enneados,* and apologizes that he must take up the reader's attention.[9] He continues with the problem of overcoming cultural difference, though I doubt if he would have liked that phrase. He remarks of Douglas's translation:

> Its greatness easily escapes modern eyes. The public for which it was intended no longer exists; the language in which it was written now awakes false associations or none; its very original has been obscured first by classicism [he means the Renaissance attitude particularly to the classics of the so-called Golden Age of Latin literature] and then by the decay of classicism. An effort is required of us.[10]

Literature is enjoyable, but enjoyment means effort, like climbing a mountain, though Lewis was no athlete. The exuberance of his personal response to literature both good and bad makes him immensely readable, even if outdated in assumptions. He refers to "the modern reader, whose Latin is likely to be better than his Scots."[11] There are far fewer modern readers nowadays who know any Latin, let alone Scots. More profound is Lewis's innocent choice of the possessive "his." What modern critic would write so unconsciously exclusively? Lewis makes it worse by such a phrase, recommending a particular reading as "once a man's eyes have been opened to this ...,"[12] which cannot but be noticeable even to a reader like me, though it was a common enough stylistic habit sixty years ago. "Man" was the unmarked term for Lewis, and he more often writes "we," but all we can do here is to refer to his own historical comments on Douglas's own "quaintness" and adjust our minds and imaginations accordingly. He was a product of his own time, writing in an environment dominated by masculine values, though those included deep respect for women as well as occasional jests at their expense. He had his own special version of that, the value he set on chastity and marriage. In this he is purely Spenserian and Miltonic, in conformity indeed with religious and social convention, but with an unusual intensity for a literary critic and quaint indeed today. That said, one cannot but admire his fullness of information, his verbal energy, the generous sweep of literary reference both to the classics and later English literature, his firm judgments based on close textual but literary reading. And this was what Lewis's tutorials were like.

In all this there is a sense of personal enjoyment of literature and sheer pleasure in reading which nowadays looks "unprofessional" and perhaps even—a condemnatory word—belletristic. It is unashamedly personal. Yet it is saved from uncritical and uncontrollable subjectivity by the corresponding attempt to submerge itself in the "other," the work itself, independent of purely contemporary concerns. Such submersion of the self is never completely possible. Lewis would have agreed that one cannot jump out of one's own skin, be a complete critical chameleon. We remain of our own time.

The relation of Lewis's teaching and criticism to his Christian apologetics was indirect. He accepted classical writers as pagans but made the point that pagans had a natural sense of religion. With this he could sympathize, and he had been well educated in a classical tradition which, though he criticized its Renaissance distortions, was nevertheless also soaked in the Christian tradition which it had in part formed. As his teaching and writing were based mostly on texts from a Christian environment, however changed in many ways, there was no need for polemics in teaching. The key words of Oxford teaching, as I understood it when I was young, were *understanding* and *appreciation*. They were based on close study of the historical meaning of words. He was very different from such a Cambridge critic as Sir William Empson, genius as he was both as a poet and critic, who was content to interpret words in senses which are not recorded until much later than in the work in question, and who had a strongly partisan object to some historical subjects, like Milton's God. In the same way some modern critics much object to the high valuation of virginity in Chaucer's *Physician's Tale*. Her father would have done much better to have let her be abducted, enslaved, and raped than to have killed her. Since the father's action is condemned, the poem is judged to be bad, and the Physician who is represented as retelling this ancient folktale is judged also to have been a bad doctor. Lewis had the advantage of a strong historical sympathy with such ancient virtues as virginity.

Lewis's role as a Christian apologist in person appeared most vividly in wartime and postwar Oxford in the Socratic Club, mentioned in my earlier essay. As everyone knows it was well attended by undergraduates, as they used to be called ("students" is the ubiquitous modernism which has a quite different aura of association). I do not know the background of its organization. The chairman, and I suspect moving spirit, was an earnest lady, Miss Stella Aldwinckle. Lewis must have been some sort of president but I do not recall any kind of formal organization, membership, subscription, nor, of course, refreshment. People simply went along on the usual evening, whenever that was, and various speakers of different views came along to talk on some religious topic. It usually fell to Lewis to open the discussion, especially if the guest were an atheist, though sometimes Christians provided problems. At one stage after such an occasion I had a tutorial on the morning immediately after the meeting of the Socratic, and Lewis greeted me with the words, "Well, save us from our friends." But we only touched on the subject, as I wished to get on with my essay. In general I formed the impression that Lewis much disliked the meetings but went along as his Christian duty, should explication or defense be required. This is how he fell to the onslaught of the formidable Miss Anscombe which so upset him, as described in my earlier essay.[13] He was distressed, as I think I may use so strong a word, not so much by defeat in argument as by realizing that he had got his own argument wrong—it was about miracles, and I forget the technicalities.

As to his influence in general, I have to confess that I did not, do not, much care for his religious works. I do not object to the religious allegory of the Narnia books, though I did once diffidently criticize in conversation with him the Malorian flavor of the final part of the first of them, *The Lion, The Witch and the Wardrobe*. He did not agree with me, of course. In a similar conversation about his autobiographical account, *Surprised by Joy*, we remarked how very differently different critics valued the same work, and to this extent he took adverse criticism pretty calmly. I did not much care for the undue literalism of some of his religious writing, but on the other hand, his sermons, such as "The Weight of Glory" and "The Inner Ring," still seem splendid to me. In the latter he comments that his only standpoint in such matters could be that of "the middle aged moralist," since of the three traditional enemies of mankind, "The World, the Flesh and the Devil," he had had too much to do with the Devil (a joke about the success of *The Screwtape Letters*, much liked by those of us who like that kind of thing), was too middle-aged to talk about "the Flesh" to a young audience better acquainted with it, and so discusses "the World" in terms of the dangers of what might nowadays be called "the Old Boy Network," or, less facetiously, the corruption of influential groups and parties of all kinds. It was an appropriate expression of what might be a lonely integrity, Christian but not only Christian.

True as the message is, and remarkable as Lewis's insight into some aspects of human nature is, he was not a worldly man. He was too generous, too disinterested, too socially clumsy, and even in academic life, too naive. I have told how he misunderstood (to some extent) the implications of expanding the numbers of the College. He once told me that a confidential reference (say, for a pupil) would always be strengthened if it contained some small item not entirely to the candidate's credit. He thought thereby the honesty of the reference would be more obvious. In fact, my own experience of many committees before my retirement was that a referee's least hesitation was normally enough, in the large numbers of applications, to provide a reason for throwing out at least that application. On the other hand, in an open reference he once gave for me, he commented that I had good health. That would read today, and doubtless did then, as a friendly referee seeking desperately for something favorable to say.

Despite this kind of unworldliness, and little love for much that was modern, there were some aspects of his thought that would have chimed with some apparently modern movements. Animal rights, for example, despite the paradoxical cruelties of some extremists, would surely have attracted his sympathy. "Kindness to Animals" in England goes back ultimately to some folktales but took on strength in the second half of the eighteenth century, an aspect of Romanticism. The word and idea of "vivisection" is first recorded in 1701, but there was from the eighteenth century a slowly growing objection to it on humanitarian grounds, and on the grounds that human medicine should not benefit from animals' pain. "Kindness to Animals" develops more strongly from children's literature as an offshoot of Romanticism around 1800 and becomes a force in the nineteenth and twentieth centuries. Lewis might well be thought a belated Victorian Romantic. He even somewhere talks about the possibility of some dogs, if loved enough, being admitted to heaven, though I never knew him to own a dog or even (like Dr. Johnson) to cherish a cat. Lewis's novel *That Hideous Strength*, one of his famous science-fiction novels, attacks the dehumanized science that seeks absolute control over men's lives and is strongly influenced by his hatred of antihumanistic totalitarianism as expressed in some kinds of science. Towards the end of the novel, in chapter 16, we see how the scientists can only speak nonsense and kill each other, and the caged animals kept to be experimented on break out and exact a terrible, violent revenge. The episode is written with a terrific gusto that some people find repellent, revealing a streak of violence in Lewis's own imagination of which they detect traces in other books. Some violence may have been there in so ebullient an imagination, but it is neither morbid nor obscenely detailed, and there was nothing like it in Lewis's own life. (Dr. Johnson at one period had himself chained and beaten. Proust in his section on "Sodom and Gomorrah" describes a good deal of such behavior in his *Remembrance of Things Past*. Nobody thought of such matters in the case of Lewis, though one malicious later contemporary speculated on whether he had an affair with Mrs. Moore, his adopted mother. The same critic tried to prove incest between Wordsworth and his sister Dorothy. Both seem absurd to me.)

Another modern movement with its roots in the nineteenth century or earlier with which Lewis would surely have sympathized is the desire to preserve what is left of the English countryside. With

Greenpeace, on the other hand, I suspect he would have disagreed. He hated war, and the destructiveness of so much science, but he was never a pacifist. Granted that he would support the good, he was, as I earlier noted, an almost complete pessimist about the forthcoming destruction of the world (or as one might now say, the environment), whether from nuclear war or the irresistible advance of technology and human greed. It is not surprising therefore that when, a few years ago, long after his death, I suggested that Madgalen College, Oxford, should buy some letters by him that were up for auction, I was told that he had not been very well liked by the Fellows and there was no wish to gather an archive or mementoes of his long Fellowship — he the most famous Fellow of the College in its more than five hundred years of history. This was in contrast with Magdalene College, Cambridge, where he was, I am told, well liked. Perhaps such jokes as the Penitent and Impenitent (Magdalen[e]s) went down less well in Oxford. In Cambridge, as I have remarked, his election to the Chair of Medieval and Renaissance Literature provoked an outburst more on antireligious than scholarly grounds. I never heard of any dislike expressed in the English Faculty, but I was not there at the time, and I have noted in my earlier essay his acceptance of Dr. Leavis. (Whether Dr. Leavis accepted him is another matter, but I know no record either for or against.)

From 1949, when I was appointed to the English Department at Birmingham University, I necessarily saw less of him, and I have already recorded my few contacts. I was on friendly terms but never one of his closer circle, the so-called Inklings. Of course, I had been influenced by his work and personality, both of which I liked and admired. His influence was general in that it was an unself-conscious, ancient, larger tradition of which I have written above. It was more particular in that it led me towards an interest in medieval literature, especially of the vernacular kind. Since the influence was general I floundered a good deal when I began my "research." It was really not a concept that flourished in those early days in Oxford. I was not clever enough to think of a specific topic. In general, as I have written before, in the English School in Oxford it was felt that you should either get a "first" and a Fellowship in a college or disappear into the outer darkness of the world in general. School teaching, which I had always considered a possible alternative, was despised. Indeed, a number of my contemporaries hung on for a bit in the margins of that small world until we got jobs in other universities — Philip Larkin, Kingsley Amis, John Wain, Anthony Thwaite, to name a few — and they made great reputations for themselves as poets and novelists rather than as scholars and critics. None of these were at Magdalen or influenced by Lewis. They might well have found him repellent, and (with the exception of Anthony Thwaite, the youngest of those mentioned) his religion ridiculous. He thought highly of Kenneth Tynan, but Tynan shows no influence, to say the least. Before the war John Betjeman would have been perhaps the best-known of his pupils, but Betjeman was said to have detested Lewis. Though I was undoubtedly influenced by Lewis, my first book was on Chaucer (1953), in whom Lewis was not much interested. When I came to write on Chaucer I soon realized that almost everything written about "courtly love" and its "code," which goes back to the work of W. G. Dodd's *Courtly Love in Chaucer and Gower* (1913), was considerably mistaken, and I think I was one of the first to say what later became a commonplace. Lewis's *Allegory of Love* was in fact widely influential over scholars in related disciplines, whether one agreed in detail or not. Amongst his immediate pupils who wrote on medieval English literature were J. Lawlor and R. T. Davies.[14] More widely spread were those who might differ from, yet who profoundly respected Lewis's work. The brilliant American critic E. T. Donaldson, whose first important book was on *Piers Plowman* and who invented the "Narrator" as a critical tool for analyzing Chaucer's writing, came from the New Criticism school of Yale, yet once said to me personally he would have "given an arm and a leg" to have written *The Allegory of Love*. The English critic John Bayley, most recently known as husband and widower of Iris Murdoch, wrote *The Characters of Love* (1960), of which the first chapter, on "The Code of Courtly Love," is based on Lewis's book. The same diffuse yet subtle and far-reaching influence has been exercised by Lewis's book on the sixteenth century. All this is independent of the influence of Lewis's Christian apologetics, of which there are far more expert expositors than I. In respect of the influence of his writing on secular literature there would be no lack of controversy, but that would not have disturbed or upset him. Yet in the end the secular and the religious writings, however various and controversial, are part of the same eager sympathetic imagination. Lewis's magnificent response to many medieval authors and in particular to Spenser and Sidney, even Milton, was due to the continuity of his religious understanding of them. Paradoxically, this was that of a Christian Humanist, though he criticized the Humanists of the sixteenth century for their unhistorical rigidity in exalting some aspects of Latin Classicism. He was by no means mistaken when he described himself as an example of Old Western Man.[15] As he foresaw, those of us who follow him, however old-fashioned some of us may be, however sympathetic, open-minded, and learned, are inevitably different and more modern. Take him for all in all, he was a man the like of whom we shall not see again. But his influence will be long to fade.

Chapter 4

GOOD COLLEGE MAN

Peter C. Bayley

The Collected Letters of C. S. Lewis, Volume 1, edited admirably by Walter Hooper, is almost a thousand pages long. I don't often read very long books nowadays, but I found these letters inescapable: discovery, fascination, illumination on every page. They cover an enormous range, of knowledge, of enquiry, of ideas, almost, one might say, anything and everything. His mind is always questing and questioning, imaginative and challenging, and the energy of the writing sweeps the reader along irresistibly. He seems incapable of writing a dull sentence. There are good jokes, learned wit, brilliant characterizations and descriptions, a delight in idiosyncrasy—and deep human concern.

Professor Bayley kindly submitted the following article, which he had originally written for the *University College Record* (October 2001), but the accompanying letter goes beyond the article and should be read as an extension of it. The original essay comprises Bayley's discussion of Lewis as a teacher in the context of reviewing Walter Hooper's recently published *C. S. Lewis, Collected Letters*, vol. 1.

Dear Professor Poe,

Thank you for your letter of 2 September. I think I haven't anything further to say or write about my admired tutor in the way of expanding on what I wrote for CSL at the Breakfast Table.

However, on reflection it occurred to me that something I had written about his being an Oxford tutor (as opposed to what they all seem to want to be today: merely a lecturer and/or professor): i.e. pater familias, "don", knowing undergraduates personally because of the tutorial system and the expectation of college that "the dons" would carry out offices & responsibilities incl. the running of the college, which meant really knowing virtually everybody & not just one's own pupils, might possibly be of interest. I was at various times at Univ Junior Dean, Camerarius (responsible for furnishings, decoration etc internally) Keeper of the College

Of great interest, naturally, was to me the discovery of something I hadn't known about him when I was a freshman pupil of his in 1940. (Univ. had no English Fellow, and Lewis kindly took the very few who read the subject.) Challenging, friendly, formidable, engaging tutor though he was, I did not know him well enough to realize the strength of his commitment and devotion to the ideal collegiate life. As I fear some threat to the College idea in a huge world-class university committed to science, expansion, and research, I thought to concentrate on that aspect of Lewis's life here.

I count it a glory for Univ. that he came to us, and a fault that the College didn't make him a Fellow. He came up in Hilary Term 1917. He had been advised to choose New College in the Classical Scholarship. The Master, R. W. Macan, snapped him up with a scholarship, "New College having passed you over." He only had two terms, for although as an Irishman he was exempt from conscription, as an Ulsterman he chose to enlist. He was commissioned into the Somerset Light Infantry in September 1917, was fairly severely wounded by shell-blast, in hospital for months, and demobilized at Christmas 1918, returning to Univ. in Hilary Term 1919.

He had found Univ. delightful enough before; now it was very heaven. A. B. Poynton "is an exceptionally good tutor, and my visits to him are enjoyable as well as useful."[1] He is made Secretary of the Martlets, then an exclusive literary club limited to twelve members and usually attended by some Fellows. One week, he writes to his

---

Buildings responsible for the "fabric" — stonework, roofs, repairs, renovations etc etc Tutor for Admissions, Domestic Bursar — responsible for the domestic economy, college servants, Hall & Chapel etc etc; & for 21 years I edited the annual College Record (for which I wrote this small piece) oh, & Librarian. Although I don't think Jack did many college jobs, he certainly did his stint on committees, and especially when Vice-President of Magdalen. But of course he was writing great works & great articles & I was only writing little things.

I don't suppose this will be at all to your purpose, though it does perhaps a little illuminate the influence of Lewis on many (not only his own pupils at Magdalen) & "the role he played in the formation of the next generation" by donnish availability.

All good wishes
Yours sincerely
Peter Bayley

father in Belfast, he is reading the lesson in Chapel, saying Grace in Hall, writing a paper on Morris, finishing the *Iliad,* and dining with the Mugger (Master Macan).

His First in Honor Mods in 1920 and in Greats in 1922 were followed by a First in English in 1925. The College got him to substitute for E. F. Carritt in Philosophy while the latter was teaching at Ann Arbor, Michigan. Encouraged by G. H. Stevenson ("honest fellow, whom nature intended for a farmer: by which I mean no depreciation of his scholarship but an appreciation of his character") who averred, "It will be a scandal if you don't get a Fellowship at this College or some College soon,"[2] he tried for four or five Fellowships in Classics and in English, and embarked on a D.Phil., increasingly "anxious about being adrift and unemployed at 30."

Then at last came success: a Fellowship in English at Magdalen in 1925. A letter to his father that year expresses a momentary regret "that when the opening came it did not come at Univ. I shall never find a common room that I did not like better," and goes on with a wonderfully interesting defense of his desertion of philosophy and remarking on the differences between the studying and teaching of Philosophy and English.[3] He acknowledges, "If I had the mind, I have not the brain and nerves for a life of pure philosophy. A continued search among the abstract roots of things, a perpetual questioning of all that plain men take for granted...."[4]

A couple of years later he wrote to his father, "... a very good evening the night before last ... my newly acquired right of dining at Univ.... Poynton, the Fark, Carritt and Stevenson ... were all in that evening and it was delightful to revisit the whimsical stateliness of that particular common room. There's no getting away from the fact that we at Magdalen are terribly 'ordinary' beside it. We are just like anyone else: there, every single one of them is a character part that could be found nowhere outside their own walls."[5]

Univ., of course, now crops up much less often, but the impression the College had made on him was clearly great and lasting. Magdalen he found not only less idiosyncratic and various but also less admirable. The societies, the sociability, the easy association of dons and undergraduates (not to mention the scouts), the friendliness, almost the familial feeling, of small Univ. had little counterpart at Magdalen: considerably more than twice as big in numbers both of dons and undergraduates.

Besides, Lewis found that Magdalen was "a very curious place": there were no undergraduate societies.[6] They had been proscribed at some stage during the long presidency of Warren, "an act which was then necessitated by the savagely exclusive clubs of rich dipsomaniacs which really dominated the whole life of the place.... When I came I found that any Magdalen undergraduate who had interests beyond rowing, drinking, motoring, and fornication, sought his friends outside the College, and indeed kept out of the place as much as he could."[7]

Lewis set about remedying the situation with one or two others, K. B. McFarlane the medieval historian his chief ally; Lewis had already started a play-reading group which met in his rooms after dinner. He had also started what came to be called his "Beer and Beowulf" evenings: a class, as it were, meeting after dinner at 8:30 once a week and reading Anglo-Saxon with him. "The actual work is usually done by half past ten: but they are comfortably by the fire and like to sit on and talk"—and the beer-jug circulated.[8] After a while, with McFarlane he got their colleagues to "agree to the relaxation of the rule against societies," very carefully picked out men they thought suitable and founded a society called the Michaelmas Club.[9] When one considers how much Lewis gave to Magdalen in these ways and when one notes his regular ordinary tutorial commitment—many days teaching from 9:00 till 1:00 and from 5:00 till 7:00, and from 9:00 till 1:00 on Saturdays, a weekly total of up to twenty-four hours, one can only marvel. (This sort of regimen was not uncommon: being the sole Fellow in English at Univ. I normally did something approaching his tally for a number of years. Of course there was no *pressure* either for research in Arts subjects or for publication, though most of us did in fact do both.)

Lewis thought, we all thought, the social, sociable, pastoral aspects of the job of vital importance, the very essence of Fellowship, and enjoyed without embarrassment or reproach a seemly society of three orders: dons, undergraduates, and College Servants, each of which shared similar feelings of belonging, of loyalty, and of duty. There are many signs that the collegiate idea (and ideal) is under serious threat, and oldsters like me cannot but be anxious, and cannot resist running the risk of boring their youngsters by celebration of old days and ways.

Chapter 5

THE ART OF DISAGREEMENT: C. S. LEWIS (1898–1963)

George Watson

I first encountered C. S. Lewis on a lecture platform in Oxford in 1948; and I was only there, as I vividly recall, because I had been told not to go.

To study at Oxford is to listen to benevolent advice about lectures, among other matters, from a college tutor. Mine was a young man of radical views who had little confidence in Lewis, who was then, as he remained, a highly controversial figure. His implacable conservatism, during the postwar socialist government headed by Clement Attlee, hardly mattered, since Oxford thought its own affairs easily more interesting than national politics. But he had recently engineered the election of an obscure chaplain from his own college, which was Magdalen, into the chair of poetry, and against the nomination of a reputable scholar called E. K. Chambers, in a coup not lightly forgiven; and his lectures on medieval and Renaissance literature, which were European in scope, were thought by some too wide-ranging to be helpful. They might even confuse me. "If I hear you are going to Lewis," my tutor said, "I shall have serious doubts about you." So I went.

The event was in many ways a surprise. For one thing, there was an enormous audience. For another, the short, stocky figure on the platform looked less like a wit than a pork butcher of hearty disposition with

Reprinted by permission from the *Hudson Review* 48, no. 2 (Summer 1995), and with the permission of the author. Copyright © 1995 George Watson.

a loud, booming voice. The voice was used in unexpected ways. Instead of talking fast and soft, which was the Oxford mode, Lewis talked loud and slow, on or off the platform, in a deep velvety tone. You could have taken dictation from his lectures, and some (including myself) did. I still have the notebook based on his "Prolegomena to Medieval Literature" and "Prolegomena to Renaissance Literature"—Lewis knew Greek as well as Latin, and loved exotic English words based on Greek—and after nearly half a century I find my notes set out, like the lectures themselves, in a severely segmented way, with numbered sections divided into lettered subsections and still smaller subsections. That was the first thing I ever learned from him: that even ideas can be tidied up to look like a salad rather than a stew. He hated mishmash. "The very seas would lose their shores" was a quotation from Ovid he was fond of, and he was much given to dividing ideas and keeping them apart. "Distinguo" was a favorite word of warning, accompanied by a raised forefinger. The perennial philosophy of Aldous Huxley he used to deride by saying, "Christianity and Buddhism are very much alike, especially Buddhism." Lewis thought ideas should have space around them to breathe; he was instinctively suspicious of easy reconciliations. In fact he once declined to contribute to a Festschrift I edited for Basil Willey, *The English Mind* (1964), on the highly principled ground that philosophy and literary criticism should be kept apart. In the courteous letter in which he declined, I need hardly say, he quoted Ovid in the original.

His expositions were above all lucid, but it was only years after hearing him lecture that I realized how that lucidity had been achieved. I remember calling on him in the early sixties, as a Cambridge colleague, while he was writing *The Discarded Image* (1964), working with a steel pen dipped in ink. That seemed symbolic of the book. He handed me the lecture-notes for his prolegomena, out of which he was composing, and as I nervously turned the pages of a battered little notebook under his watchful eye—it was a very intrusive act I was performing, after all—I saw that it was laid out in sections and subsections on the left-hand side, with the right-hand side neatly peppered with quotations from the medieval schoolmen and early modern authors like Shakespeare, Bacon, and Sir Thomas Browne, culled from his reading over several decades. It was a moment that taught me a lot about scholarly method: a pocket notebook one could travel with, with headings on the left and accumulated instances on the right; and as I came away I realized there was no other way by which such lectures could have been assembled.

Writing was Lewis's life, in the sense that he was always writing when he was not doing anything else. He was endowed with whatever it is that is the opposite of a block; and his books, including the posthumous collections, easily outnumber the years he lived, which were sixty-five. "Have you never found it difficult to write?" I once asked; and he looked puzzled, his answer suggesting that the question had not been altogether understood. "Sometimes," he said, "when I come back in the evening after dinner, I tell myself I am too tired and shouldn't write anything. But I always do." So putting prose on paper was a profound addiction. The most articulate being I have ever known, he loved to talk about the sheer mechanics of turning thoughts into sentences. "I find I want to begin every paragraph with 'It would be difficult to exaggerate . . . ,' so to break myself of the habit I am going to start the next paragraph with 'It would be difficult to exaggerate, but I'm going to have a jolly good try.'" Writing was so much a mode of life that you felt that his highly deliberated utterance, in conversation as well as in lectures, had been progressively achieved by pacing his thought down to the speed of longhand writing. After all, I never knew him when he was young. He may once have been a quick-talking youth.

Perhaps, before I go further, I should make an avowal of a modest and personal kind. Though I loved Lewis, I could not without presumption call him a friend, since he was almost thirty years older than myself. Nor did we share many opinions or daily habits. As a colleague in Cambridge, to which I moved in 1959, five years after he did, he advised me cheerfully on arrival about where to take country walks; but we both preferred to take them alone. He sometimes urged me to join him in drinking draught Guinness at the Pickerel, a pub opposite Magdalene College, where before he lost health and appetite he found high table dinners too late; and I regret to this day I never went—out of an indifference to stout, it should be said, never to his company. "A very good drink," he assured me warmly—it was the only Irish thing I ever noticed about him—and I only wish I could have agreed with him.

But there are more important matters than drink. Lewis was a Christian conservative from around the age of thirty, which is to say before I knew him; and since I am neither one nor the other, there was never any question of a doctrinal influence. If I was not exactly a friend, still less was I a disciple. That in no way altered my sense of admiration and affection. He was much given to writing and uttering witty homilies embodying views I respected rather than shared, and this proved an embarrassment to neither of us, since we both thrived on dissent. In fact I doubt if he would have known what to do with agreement, any more than I would. That is not an attitude I owe him, since I have always held it; that the stuff of good conversation is polite and animated disagreement. The best teacher I ever had, and the best colleague, he did not ask or expect me to share his convictions. It is a point to return to.

Oxford was a cold, hungry place after 1945, and my chief contact with Lewis was not in classrooms but at evening meetings, for the simple reason that poverty made it hard to heat a room. Life in England before central heating was dominated by a coin-box attached to a gas-fire, and a lack of coins could drive you out on winter evenings, and even on autumn and spring evenings, to societies like the Socratic Club. It was there that I really came to know Lewis. He was the president of a body which, despite its pagan name, was undoubtedly Christian in impulse; and its organizing secretary, a formidable South African spinster called Stella Aldwinkle, who was rumored to be writing an unfinishable thesis about divine providence, was a passionate advocate of something she called Advanced Adult Theism. I never discovered what that was; but I discovered, as I sat by the fire, a good deal else. The Club justified itself by keeping me warm, and it justified its name by Lewis's behavior in it.

He, at least, was Socratic, though a Socrates with a sense of fun. One evening Miss Aldwinkle read the minutes and asked if they might be signed as an accurate account of the last meeting, and all hands went obediently up, including Lewis's. She rounded on him. "How,

Mr. Lewis, can you express an opinion about the truth of the minutes when you were not present at the last meeting?" "That, my dear," said Lewis, "is because your reading has transformed my concept of the truth itself." The main business of the meeting, however, was desperately earnest and was usually concerned with a large moral issue; and if Lewis did not read the paper himself, he was often the first to speak in discussion. His manner might be described as politely merciless. I am now possessed of more philosophical understanding than I then had, and realize with hindsight that I was listening to a highly individual hodgepodge of Victorian positivism, which Lewis had imbibed as a boy from a Scottish tutor in Surrey—he has told the story in his memoir *Surprised by Joy* (1955)—and then partly or largely rejected; with it came the remains of a Hegelian training as an Oxford undergraduate and the Christianity of a convert, with all a convert's passion for analysis and self-examination. No dogmatic stone was to be left unturned, nor did he have any use for unexamined propositions. His interventions were often directed against false reasons for true belief, and it hardly mattered if such reasons were advanced by believers or nonbelievers. "That is not why I believe in such-and-such" was a characteristic opening. He was endlessly counter-suggestible. "That is not why I became a Christian," I recall his saying once. "When I was studying philosophy in Oxford, German Idealism was the thing, and it sometimes bordered on solipsism or mere self-exploration. We were often warned against that. Do not go down that dark tunnel. So I went down it, and found God."

To know Lewis as a teacher was to know him as a colleague, and I never observed any difference in his behavior to old or young. Questions of inequality hardly arose, since his interest was in a point made or not made, not in whoever had made it. I can only speak from personal experience, but my sense of him was that he was interested in what you said rather than in you. When he sat on the committee that appointed me to lecture in Cambridge in 1959, we had a delightful conversation in his college room, which was as spartan and uninteresting as the one in Oxford. One hardly associated him with a visual sense, except for landscape. The first thing you saw, as you entered, was an ancient battered bathtub standing abruptly in the middle of a tiny hallway, and the only decoration I recall in his sitting room was a cheap reproduction over the mantelpiece of Michelangelo's creation of Adam from the Sistine Chapel. "I am in a Warburgian state of mind," he would explain sonorously, meaning he had acquired a sudden interest, in the style of the Warburg Institute, in the connections between Renaissance poetry and painting through rereading Spenser's *Faerie Queene*. In an interview at which he was supposed to form an opinion about appointing me to lecture—our first meeting in several years—he appeared wholly indifferent to that question, which was not even mentioned, but highly interested in a story I had just read in a newspaper. In 1959 a magistrate who had harshly sent a poor widow to jail for secretly doing part-time work while drawing a state benefit had died a day or two later of a heart attack, his sudden death being represented in the London tabloids as an act of God; and Lewis slapped his thigh appreciatively when he heard it, though it had been headline news for several days, and exclaimed, "That illustrates something I have always believed—that it is no use reading newspapers. If anything interesting happens, someone will always tell you about it." I do not imagine the incident had any bearing on my appointment, which in fact I cannot explain on any ground whatever. As I left the room with the Faculty chairman, I heard him remind Lewis of the meeting of the appointments committee a few days later. "I don't have to bother with that, do I?" Lewis said mildly. "Oh yes, you must come, Clive, you must," said the chairman. Appointments are notoriously that part of academic administration that academics take seriously—sometimes too seriously—but by the age of sixty Lewis had lost his taste for such matters. "How can people get interested in such things?" he asked me reproachfully a year or two later, when I told him I was on my way to Oxford to vote in the election of a Chancellor of the university. He had left all such enthusiasms far behind him.

His twin passions by then, apart from literature itself, were people and arguments, but he did not often make the mistake of confusing them. Good people can believe in wicked things, as the present century has abundantly proved with idealistic doctrines like race war and class war. Lewis could be polite, even friendly, to such people. What aroused his trenchancy was evil opinion. A capitalistic robber baron, he once told J. B. S. Haldane, the Communist scientist who had acclaimed the Soviet Union for abolishing Mammon, is at least better than an Inquisitor, since greed is easier to satisfy than dogmatic certainty; "Men do not become tyrants in order to keep warm" was a favorite dictum of Aristotle on his lips. He believed in democracy and private enterprise for the most grudging of all reasons: though they are much less than good, every other system is worse. One Cheer for Democracy might have been his slogan. He had once lived unhappily as a school boarder, he told Haldane, in "a world from which Mammon was banished" and where favors were gained by cringing servility or brute force. "It was the most wicked and miserable I have yet known." The analogy between communism and an unreformed boarding school is instructive, but the point is potent without being offensive; it is about communism, not about a Communist called Haldane. Lewis reviled many dogmas but seldom, to my knowledge, those who held them. Perhaps his most astringent remark, which I know only by report, was made about Attlee during his premiership, but then it should be remembered that it was made by somebody who never read a newspaper and was proud of it. "It cannot be doubted that Mr. Attlee is an agent of the Devil."

The limits of his malice were reached quickly, however, in conversation, by a wry smile and an agreement to differ. He was not wholly displeased to recall an incident at the high table of an Oxford college when an American visitor, mistaking the political historian A. J. P. Taylor for the art historian he had expected to sit with, repeatedly discountenanced him with questions about the history of art. "Don't know anything about it," Taylor replied, a sturdy Philistine, in increasing exasperation. Not that Lewis's dislike for everything Taylor stood for can ever have been in any doubt. Or vice versa. They were like chalk and cheese. "Lewis never talked about religion in the college," Taylor once acidly remarked. "We didn't want to hear it, for one thing."

When Lewis came to a chair of Medieval and Renaissance English at Cambridge in 1954—a post he was the first to hold, and which he had accepted on the second offer at Tolkien's insistence—he found a School of English dominated by no single figure, as I. A. Richards had come near to dominating it before his emigration to Harvard in 1939, but rather one racked by conflicting heresies almost as bitter as those of the early Church. The chief heresiarch was F. R. Leavis, who was three years older than Lewis and belonged to the place by birth as well as by election. His cult then stood at its highest; he was Cambridge English personified. The two men had next to nothing in common, but it is worth putting on record that they were always courteous to each other, and in a manner so elaborate that when they sat on committees one was reminded of the formality of a tea party before the First World War. This was Edwardian decorum at its best, and both men belonged to a generation for whom courtesy in that style was a mark of distance. Lewis in those days was supposed to represent the past, Leavis the future; and nobody would have guessed, nearly half a century on, that Leavis would be an all-but-forgotten name and Lewis the object of a vast and ever-increasing international cult. That would no doubt have surprised Lewis, and Leavis still more.

I never heard Lewis speak ill of Leavis, but then he plainly preferred not to speak about him at all. It is clear he found little virtue in his writings, and the high-minded priggery of that kind of agnostic mind was never to his taste. "Oughtn't the word 'serious' have an embargo slapped on it?" he once proposed to Kingsley Amis; instead of meaning the opposite of comic, he complained, it had come to mean good, or "literature with a capital L." It is easy to guess whom he was thinking of. I once asked him directly what he thought of Leavis. He looked very grave, as if fearful of being quoted; and then, in a half-mocking tone, he said in a low voice: "I think he's saved." I asked why. "Because," he replied with what appeared to be complete gravity, "he isn't interested in money." "So you think you may meet at the Last Judgement?" I asked, steering us out of embarrassment. "If our names on that occasion are taken in alphabetical order, yes," he said, and the exchange broke up in a laugh.

To his colleagues, myself included, Lewis was endlessly kind. His successor-but-one, John Stevens, has told how, as a young Fellow of Magdalene with medieval interests, he felt it was high time he learned Old as well as Middle English; Lewis agreed with him and devoted a whole evening of every week for a term to reading Anglo-Saxon together. In conversation his dissent, though forthright, was polite, and all the more formidable for an exceptional memory. He did not admire the novels of Henry James as much as some did, and when asked if he did not even like *The Portrait of a Lady*, he replied, "Don't you think there is something absurd about the tea-party conversation in the first chapter?" and then quoted it from memory. He did not always persuade, and may not always have wanted to persuade; much of what he said smacked of a spot-the-fallacy test. But he always had his reasons and knew how to deploy them, and they were backed by a formidable literary memory that included prose as well as verse. I remember, with gratitude, the letters he sent me about a book I had just written called *The Literary Critics* (1962). I still have them; and they still strike me, as they did then, as models of a critical engagement at once devastating and urbane. Perhaps it is fortunate that he was charming, all things considered, since his fondness for the put-down could be alarming. I once told him, as he was about to read a paper on Jane Austen, that I did not know he was a Janeite. "That is rather like saying that somebody who likes bread-and-butter is a bread-and-butterite," he snapped back. There was no answer to that. I have still not thought of an answer to that.

His intellectual life was far odder than has yet been realized, and in a recent book, *Critical Essays on C. S. Lewis* (1992), I have tried to explain why. He was only partly a coterie man, though he belonged to a literary group called the Inklings that included Charles Williams, down to his early death in 1945, J. R. R. Tolkien, and Owen Barfield. But with all his faculty for friendship, Lewis was seemingly self-sufficient, or as nearly so as a human being can be: he enjoyed company, that is, but you never felt he needed it. Like Tolkien, he never visited the United States. The world came to him. When you visited him in Cambridge, in his college room, he would greet you warmly and talk enthusiastically; but he had laid down his pen to do so, and you did not doubt he had lifted it again before you had left the room. His love for his American wife, Joy Davidman, in his last years was touching; but when he invited me to lunch in Cambridge, on one of her rare visits, it was not quite as I had expected.[1] I have lived in New York among Jewish intellectuals, and there is a stereotypical instance of one in the film just made about their marriage called *Shadowlands*. What I met was a frail, distinguished, soft-spoken being, supporting herself on two sticks—above all a woman of letters. There was nothing brash about her. In fact, Lewis was noisier than she, by far. Perhaps I too was surprised by Joy, on the only occasion I met her. I am certainly surprised by what filmmakers have made of her.

In many ways Lewis was a man out of sequence. He had fought as an adolescent in the First World War, on the Western Front—it was an experience he spoke of, if at all, only in muted horror—but he had no other direct acquaintance with the dire events of the century, and the war seems to have done little more than confirm his dislike of foreign travel, though he was a master of languages, modern as well as ancient. This paralleled his intellectual interests. His contact with Freud and Marx, for example, was purely adversarial. Nor was he a party man—merely a conservative in a general sense of the term—and though an Anglican he disdained distinctions like High and Low. Intellectual fashion existed only in order to be tested and refuted. He was almost the only being I have ever known who read the great Italian epics, like Ariosto and Tasso, as a private diversion, and his academic pursuits were out of sequence in a similar way. He pursued narrative theory as early as the 1940s, in some notable papers posthumously collected in *Of This and Other Worlds* (1982), at a time when no other critic in the Western world, to my knowledge, was pursuing the matter at all. But I have never heard him called a critical theorist, and we are only now emerging from a period of intense interest in literary theory which treated him as if he never existed. He was fascinated by meter as few are or were, and once told me proudly that a French critic had commended him for an interest, unique among Anglo-Saxons, in the formal properties of literature. His contribution to response-theory, as it came to be called after his death, never struck me as one of his more rewarding concerns, but he proposed something rather like it as early as 1939 in *The Personal Heresy*, a controversy with E. M. W. Tillyard, seven years before Wimsatt and Beardsley published a celebrated article on the intentional fallacy in *The Sewanee Review*; and he pursued his strange and (I think) misguided vendetta against authorial intention years later in *An Experiment in*

Criticism (1961). It is characteristic of his after-reputation that modern response-theorists pay no attention whatever to these works, no doubt because his fame as a nostalgic, an enemy of Modernism, would have made him a damaging and unfashionable ally. We think of theory as avant-garde, and he was never that. He did not even share the views of friends like Tolkien in matters concerning literature or religion, or not always, being content to understand the fruitful nature of their disagreements. That is a world away from the narrow dogmatizing of other theorists before and since.

But then agreement would have spoiled the game, and Lewis in debate tried to keep disagreement going for as long as he reasonably could, and sometimes for longer. If I were ever to be asked what I learned from him, that would be my reply: the art of disagreement. It is hard for me, by now, to disentangle his mind from mine. I loved argument before I knew him, but knowing him helped me pursue it with firmer purpose and better grace. His mind, unlike his figure, was elegant, as if he used language to compensate for other lacks. "He makes every occasion so agreeable," I remember another Cambridge colleague, L. J. Potts, remarking with emphasis when I mentioned his name. He had vigor without venom; he was generous.

Perhaps his shade can still teach, since heresy-hunting has not vanished from academic life with the demise of Leavis's *Scrutiny* or the fading of Marxism. Extravagant phenomena like radical feminism and political correctness will no doubt go the way of Leavis and of Marx—"With eager feeding food doth choke the feeder"—but there is still enough of a steady, sober diet of intolerance to disquiet. It seems to be widely assumed, that is to say, that to extol an author is to endorse his views; often, over the years, I have been earnestly assured on praising a work that it was wrong about this or wrong about that. Some years ago—to give an instance—on announcing a course of lectures on George Orwell, I was told by more than one colleague that I labored under a regrettable illusion, since Orwell had been mistaken. The notion that a mistake might be worth discussing is still not part of the common wisdom of the age. (The proposition is not reversible, by the way, and I do not mean to imply that all mistakes are worth discussing, or that only mistakes are.) It is still not as widely understood as it deserves to be that we *need* bad arguments, if only because without bad arguments, there would be no good ones.

Tolerance in that style, or any other, can easily be derided as facile or wooly. Lewis made it harder to do that. No one who knew him, no one who has read him, could think him facile or wooly. He knew truth mattered. His mind was tough. That he could draw so freely on the affection of those who disagreed with him, among many others, is the tribute he deserves above all to be paid.

Chapter 6

C. S. LEWIS: PERSONAL REFLECTIONS

W. Brown Patterson

I had the privilege of studying at Oxford — "reading English," as the Oxford vernacular has it — under the eminent writer and scholar C. S. Lewis. This was no accident. When I was a senior at the University of the South in Sewanee, Charles Harrison, my adviser, told me that two of the leading scholars of the English Renaissance were Douglas Bush at Harvard and C. S. Lewis at Oxford. He encouraged me to think that I would have a chance if I applied for a scholarship to Harvard or Oxford for further study. As it happened, I had the privilege of going to both universities and of studying under both men. In 1952–53 I was at Harvard under an American Council of Learned Societies First-Year Graduate Fellowship. In 1953–55 I was at Oxford on a Rhodes Scholarship studying under Lewis at Magdalen College. My essay in connection with my Rhodes application made a case for going to Oxford for precisely this purpose. I said that I wanted to have tutorials with the author of *The Allegory of Love: A Study in Medieval Tradition,* because he was a literary scholar who dealt with writers and texts in their historical and cultural setting. I also said that I wanted to study under a man whose views on the importance of religion and moral values were very consonant with — but much more highly developed than — my own.

C. S. Lewis is known for three major accomplishments. His Christian apologetics in the form of broadcast talks and various books in the course of World War II and during the postwar period made him one of the best-known writers on Christian subjects of our time. His children's books, the Chronicles of Narnia, reached a vast audience and continue to appeal to hundreds of thousands of children and their parents. His scholarship in Medieval and Renaissance literature made him one of the preeminent literary historians and critics in this field. There are also books, articles, and various literary contributions that do not fit neatly into these categories. His prose fiction for adults, including his science-fiction trilogy, beginning with *Out of the Silent Planet*, his *Pilgrim's Regress*, and his *Till We Have Faces* continue to find many readers and are treated as significant works by critics. He also published a fascinating spiritual autobiography, *Surprised by Joy*, a number of poems, and various critical articles. A considerable number of books, drawn from papers that Lewis left on his death in 1963, have been published in recent years.

For two years—or, rather, most of two years—I had a weekly, hour-long tutorial with Mr. Lewis, as he was called, during his last years as a stipendiary Fellow and tutor in English Language and Literature at Magdalen College. He and his colleague J. A. W. Bennett, also a distinguished medievalist, each had me for an hour a week. Under their guidance, I wrote essays on broad subjects, based on primary texts they assigned, with whatever help I could get from the lectures given up the street in the Examination Schools or in various colleges—Balliol, Merton, and New College, among others. Lectures at Oxford, which were announced each term in a thick, folio-sized schedule, were strictly voluntary. No attendance was taken or tests administered. The whole focus of my week's work, especially the nights before my tutorials, was on the essay. My essay was, in fact, the main item on the agenda for each tutorial. It is hard to imagine a system more exactly opposite to the prevailing one in American colleges and universities. Instead of listening to a professor lecture for an hour at a time three times a week, and later trying to remember as much as possible about what he or she had said when it came time for a test or examination, the emphasis at Oxford was on the student and the development of his or her ideas.

The first thing that happened in a tutorial with Lewis was that I would read my essay—on a topic like Shakespeare's tragedies or Donne's love poems or Swift's *Gulliver's Travels*. My tutor's head — indeed, much of the small sitting room where we sat — would be wreathed in the smoke from his pipe, so it would be hard to know what he was thinking. He would interrupt frequently to ask me to read a sentence again or to expound on a point further. Finally, after the ten or fifteen minutes it had taken me to read my composition, he would begin his critique. He could quote back to me sentences I had just read, which he commented on for style as well as content. I once used the word "fortuitously" to mean "fortunately." He reminded me that it meant "by chance" and convinced me that "we" should not let the word change its meaning to something for which there was already a perfectly good word available. He would agree or disagree with me as he thought best. But in all his criticisms he sought to lead me to strengthen an argument, to express an idea more clearly, or to anticipate a difficulty. All of this was aimed at improving my way of understanding the texts and expressing my point of view. Unless I asked him directly he would not elaborate on his own views, let alone try to impose them on me.

An approving word from Lewis — as came, for example, in a session on sixteenth-century English tragedy — was something that made my efforts seem entirely worthwhile. I was very much aware that I was presenting my half-baked ideas to a world-class scholar, and as a result I tried to advance an argument that was as tenable and persuasive as possible. I ventured to suggest that a tragedy in Elizabethan England had a different quality from the tragedies of ancient Greece, partly because Christians thought of death, at least for the faithful, as an entrance into larger life. The ancients seemed to have no such hope, with the result that death seemed a stark and fearful alternative to earthly existence. We talked about several plays of Shakespeare and Sophocles, and he seemed surprisingly taken with my distinction. One thing he did not like was an argument or an expression that was pretentious or too technical. I once adapted a term paper I had written at Harvard for my tutorial essay. It was full of definitions and critical terms — allegory, symbolism, myth, analogy — and quotations from critics, including Lewis himself. He did not like it at all. He preferred a paper which developed two or three ideas with quotations from the literary texts themselves and which contained hardly any references to secondary sources.

The tutorial has seemed to me ever since the ideal way to teach. The student has to take the initiative, master the texts, present ideas—and then refine them in the light of the comments of an established scholar. Also, there is nothing like having to write one's ideas down and read them aloud before a person whom you want to convince, to improve one's literary skills. After two or three terms at Oxford, I wrote a several-page-long letter to Charles Harrison at Sewanee proposing that the entire curriculum at my alma mater be converted to the tutorial system. He was, by then, Dean of the College, and I know from his reply that he gave my letter to Edward McCrady, the Vice-Chancellor, to read. Needless to say, the entire curriculum was not changed—in many respects it remains today much as it was then—but it happened that the Brown Foundation Tutorial Fellowships were instituted a few years later to bring outstanding scholars to Sewanee for stays of up to a semester, and a Junior Tutorial (a small seminar to be taken in the junior year, requiring a weekly essay of every student) is a part of the major in the History Department.

One of my hopes in going to Oxford was to be able to discuss with Lewis the religious and moral questions of the kind he had so provocatively advanced in a series of books which I had discovered at Vade Mecum, the church camp I attended in North Carolina. These books included *Christian Behavior* and *Beyond Personality*. He was happy to do so in the weekly sessions we had, as long as the questions were related to the subject of the week. His was a very down-to-earth, commonsensical view of such questions. He took Christian tradition and the Scriptures very seriously. He also felt strongly that certain ideas and values could only be understood with reference to a standard, a "way" which virtually all civilizations agreed on. This was, as I came to understand it, a "natural law" point of view. He had little time for theologians who were urgently trying to be responsive to changes in society and knowledge in what later came to be called a "trendy" way. His was a Platonic point of view that the basic human search was for ideas and values that were eternal. To call him the most successful of mid-twentieth-century apologists for the Christian faith in the English-speaking world, which is true, is to state a paradox. He specifically rejected the apologists' usual technique of stating the Christian faith in terms appropriate to the culture of the age. What he aimed at doing was to present the agreed-upon doctrines of Christian tradition in language and images intelligible to ordinary people. His examples were often strikingly homely, suggesting that he was a keen observer of how people actually lived. It seems appropriate that his own conversion to a belief in God was while he was deep in thought during a ride on a double-decker bus ascending Headington Hill in Oxford.[1] I have ridden the descendants of this bus many times, during sabbatical leaves in Oxford, and I cannot imagine a more mundane sacred place.

During my second year at Magdalen, when, incidentally, I lived on a staircase in New Buildings only a few yards away from the rooms in which my tutor spent his days, Lewis accepted the position of Professor of Medieval and Renaissance English Literature at Cambridge University. But he did not move to Cambridge at once. In fact, he never moved his permanent residence from Headington Quarry; he simply spent several days at a time in Cambridge, where he lectured, supervised graduate students, and resided as a Fellow at the Cambridge Magdalene—with a final "e." Fortunately for me, and for his other students at Magdalen, Oxford, he continued to give us tutorials for the Michaelmas and Hilary terms. He encouraged me when I showed an interest in going to a theological seminary, and he wrote a letter of recommendation for me to the Episcopal Theological School in Cambridge, Massachusetts, where I entered in the fall of 1955. Soon after I arrived at ETS a professor there commented with arched eyebrows that I had been recommended for admission by C. S. Lewis —and proceeded to tell me where he differed with Lewis on several theological issues.

The experience of studying at Oxford under C. S. Lewis was important to me in ways which I came to understand more fully as the years passed. Thinking through literary, moral, and religious questions helped me to sort out my own ideas and values. Receiving his criticisms and advice on my essays certainly helped me to become a more effective writer. More than anything else, conversations with him gave me confidence in my own abilities. I remember once spending half an hour with Lewis and a friend and benefactor of mine from the United States—Kenneth I. Brown, Executive Director of the Danforth Foundation (who had asked me to arrange this meeting). I somehow found myself trying to explain why the University of the South, which then had an enrollment of about five hundred students, all men, called itself a "university." I chose to argue that the undergraduate program at Sewanee was based on the course of studies at the medieval universities, which had its roots in antiquity and was constantly being revised as a result of the ongoing investigations of contemporary scholars. I said that it was this kind of education that John Henry Newman had described in his great work *The Idea of a University*. (I had read Newman's book in preparation for a debate at Sewanee on the value of a liberal arts education.) Lewis liked my argument. He did not actually agree, but he said enough to show that he took what I said seriously.

Lewis was a complex person, as we all are, and not everyone at Oxford saw him in the same light I did. The Dean of Divinity at Magdalen during the years I was a student there has written of Lewis:

> With his vast erudition, and the certainty of his own convictions, Lewis was formidable in conversation, as well as in argument in which he delighted to prevail, when the put-down, even knock-down demolition of another's case was a tactic which he used with great effect.[2]

Another colleague of his at Magdalen in those years describes him as having been notoriously absentminded or perhaps negligent in keeping appointments and honoring engagements. Lewis's one year as Vice-President at Magdalen—this is an office that rotates among the Fellows—was apparently not a success. This colleague has written:

> It is a function of the Vice-President to allot rooms for meetings or private entertainment. Lewis carried a little diary in which he sometimes entered the arrangements, more often not. Consequently two societies might find themselves holding lectures simultaneously. The efficient kitchen staff usually

sorted out conflicting dinners. His brother Warnie [the historian W. H. Lewis, who lived with him] tried to organize his engagements.[3]

On one occasion, a dinner guest, a bishop of the Greek Orthodox Church, apparently arrived at Magdalen an hour late, after dinner was over, due, apparently, to a mistake in Lewis's letter of invitation. After some awkward exchanges between them, Lewis was finally persuaded by one of his colleagues to take the hungry and frustrated prelate to the nearby Eastgate Hotel for a late supper.[4]

My own impressions of him were rather different, as I have tried to indicate. I can picture him easily as I first saw him. He was out for a walk along the college "water walks" by the Cherwell River. He was wearing baggy trousers—corduroy, I think—and a shapeless tweed jacket over a loosely fitting sweater. On his head was an old tweed hat with its brim turned down. His shoes were heavy brogues. I identified him—to myself, of course—as one of the gardeners. (This was my second mistake of the day. The first was in thinking that the neatly dressed, tall, handsome man in the Porter's Lodge was the President of the College. It turned out that he was the Head Porter.) Beneath Lewis's bluff, hearty, and inelegant appearance was, I soon found, a man of uncommon intelligence, vast enthusiasm for books and learning, and a deep, sometimes mystical devotion to the God he had come to know.

My own career did not follow the course Lewis and I both assumed it would when we first met together. Instead of returning to Harvard after my two years at Oxford to continue working towards a Ph.D. degree in English there, I enrolled for a B.D. degree at the Episcopal Theological School in Cambridge, Massachusetts. I wanted to learn as much as I possibly could about the Bible, the biblical languages of Hebrew and Greek, the history of the Christian Church, and Christian theology. After three years of study, followed by ordination in the Episcopal Church, I went back to the Harvard Graduate School for a Ph.D. in a program called History and Philosophy of Religion. My graduate courses were mostly in history, and I had as my thesis adviser the historian W. K. Jordan, who wrote extensively on the development of religious toleration in England in the sixteenth and seventeenth centuries. As a scholar, I found my vocation in investigating the ways in which religion and politics were related in early modern Britain and Europe. Not all of the subjects I have researched and written about are likely to have been of interest to Lewis. But they all, I think, illustrate a point frequently made by him in his lectures and tutorials at Oxford. That is, that no one can understand adequately the men and women of medieval and Renaissance Europe without a firm knowledge of the Christian ideas that pervaded the culture of those centuries. As a teacher I have found that the surest way to lead students to a knowledge of the past and its significance is to get them to write essays and research papers dealing with historical events, persons, texts, and ideas. By writing, they gain ownership of some part of the subjects they read about and hear discussed in class. I try to teach students to write effective compositions in large part because it enables them to think clearly and critically and to retain what they have learned through their own efforts. In this approach I am aware that I am drawing heavily upon what I learned from Lewis as a result of going to him for weekly tutorials.

C. S. Lewis seems to me to have three distinguishing characteristics as a writer, teacher, and Christian theologian.

1. Doggedness: Lewis resolutely upheld those ideas and values he believed in. He stubbornly resisted Christianity before his conversion. Afterwards he was just as stubborn and persistent in its defense. What he defended, moreover, was no fashionable or trendy version; it was the solid heart of the matter. He defended his critical ideas about English literature in the same way. He was, after all, by birth and upbringing, a northern Irish Protestant.

2. Imaginativeness: Lewis had a vivid, almost wild imagination, which he harnessed to interpret the sometimes strange, exotic, remote territory of the European Middle Ages and to create the lands of Narnia and the extraterrestrial life of his science fiction. His Christian faith became the organizing principle of much of his work, and he defended Christianity with great skill, but his faith was at bottom the faith of a poet, a storyteller, a magician in words. He was, of

course, from Ireland and had a keen appreciation of its topography and society.

3. Humanity: In everything he wrote, Lewis was deeply aware of how ordinary people lived, what they thought, and what they were looking for in life. This is what makes his Christian writings so accessible and so influential. Lewis was not an aristocrat, nor was he an intellectual snob. He never liked the role of a celebrity. He could talk to you and me in our everyday language and understand us. Late in his life, after my time in Oxford, his humanity seems to have been further enhanced by the love that he and Joy, the American whom he married, shared with each other. Lewis was able to be a friend to thousands during his lifetime by his teaching, his lecturing, and his extensive correspondence—as he still is through the many books he wrote. To use his own term, he was a "mere" Christian.

Chapter 7

C. S. LEWIS: SUPERVISOR

Alastair Fowler

How C. S. Lewis came to direct my doctoral research calls for explanation. When I graduated from Edinburgh University in 1952, research awards encouraged me to go on to Oxford. But which college? Information to inform the choice was then not easily available. Eventually, after a false start and several interviews, I was accepted by the English faculty and by Pembroke College. About Pembroke I knew nothing except its small size. It turned out a happy choice; the vice-gerent was a historian, R. B. McCallum. He had worked on John Calvin and was interested in my proposed topic, Protestant defenses of poetry. We agreed, against the general misconception, that Calvin's views on literature were liberal-humanist. McCallum advised me to approach the supervisor I wanted rather than wait to have one assigned to me.

The exciting thing about Oxford to me then was the novelist Charles Williams; he must supervise my dissertation. Confident that biographical criticism was irrelevant, I had failed to register the fact of Williams's death in 1945. Well, then, if Williams was unavailable, how about his friend C. S. Lewis? For years I had enjoyed *Out of the Silent Planet*, and *The Allegory of Love* was a high point of my Edinburgh reading. Yes, Lewis must be my supervisor. But here a new difficulty arose. Lewis was averse to supervised research; like many dons then, he considered it unlikely to improve literary studies. (Of the three kinds of literacy at Oxford—literate, illiterate, and B. Litterate—he

This essay is reprinted with the kind permission of Alastair Fowler. It originally appeared in *Yale Review* 91, no. 4 (October 2003), 64–80.

preferred the first two.) He so often refused to direct research that it is hard to think of exceptions at Oxford, apart from those who, like Peter Bayley and Henry Yorke (the novelist Henry Green), were already his pupils. Only Catherine Ing, M. M. McEldowney, and Mahmoud Manzalaoui come to mind. When Lewis taught graduates from other universities, he usually prepared them for a second undergraduate course. Being married and poor, I had no leisure for that.

When I wrote to Lewis, he politely excused himself; supervision was to him *invita Minerva* (uncongenial). Very well, he would have to be persuaded. McCallum undertook to write; as a member of Lewis's Inklings group, he knew him well. And he suggested consulting Henry ("Hugo") Dyson, an old friend of Lewis's. Dyson, possibly Oxford's sharpest literary critic at the time, was the kindest of men and most uproarious — capable of shouting across the street, "All right for money, Fowler?" He muted his ebullience when I asked his help, and hesitated before writing Lewis a pleading letter — conscious, perhaps of asking a large favor? Summoning joint memories to appeal to?

Armed with Dyson's note, I approached the seat of the spokesman of Old Western culture; through Magdalen lodge, round the cloisters in the shady Old Quad, and suddenly out into a bright vista of the eighteenth-century New Building with its wisteria swags, patently regular against the enormous trees of the Deer Park. Climbing the wrong stairs, I trod the bare, scrubbed boards of Top Corridor smelling of freshly moistened wood and descended Lewis's staircase. With some sense of occasion — not nearly enough — I knocked and a voice said, "Come in." I crossed a large threshold into a north-facing room with a view of the Deer Park ("the Grove"): a sitting room with no one in it. I was nonplussed until a hearty summons from an open doorway directed me to a smaller sitting room looking south to the rest of the college. Here the great man defended the rampart of a desk. While he read Dyson's note I took in the room's cream paneling; its cliffs of shelved literature (fewer books than Dyson's); its huge floral-patterned Chesterfield; its large, dim reproduction of Botticelli's *Mars and Venus* (one of the pictures Lewis most cared for when he first visited the National Gallery in 1922). He reread Dyson's letter, pondered, and — relented. He would take me on. Why? Had Dyson called in some indisputable debt? Did I seem a potential Boswell to Lewis's Dr. Johnson?

For our first meeting I was to write on the sources of defenses of fiction. I must have looked at a loss, for he started me off by jotting down a dozen or so authors and titles, mostly Greek or Latin: Plato, Plotinus, Philostratus, Dio Chrysostom. Fracastoro's *Naugerius*, Philip Sidney's *Defence*. History of ideas, without the name. The tradition of imagination's access to metaphysical truth—the same tradition (assimilated from Owen Barfield) that Lewis would trace in the Sidney chapter of his volume in *The Oxford History of English Literature*, published a couple of years later. The assignment would make me show my paces on ground fresh in Lewis's memory. His *OHEL* volume, just off his hands, summed fifteen years of work; so he was deeply read in sixteenth-century writing without being inaccessibly specialist.

A great teacher and a great writer need not be an efficient supervisor. Lewis was too permissive and left me to get on with things. Perhaps this was deliberate; he was to follow a similar method during his early years at Cambridge, where he supervised David Daiches, Roger Poole, and others. Lewis never insisted I should begin by reading secondary sources. He never insisted I should compile a preliminary bibliography. He never insisted on anything. On the wild assumption I shared his own powers, he gave me so much rope that I tied myself into a ramifying topic that took five years to escape. Yet he gave generously of his time, unlike most supervisors in those days, who were content to see a research student for a few minutes a term. Lewis spent more than twenty hours exploring the vast wildernesses of my ignorance. And this was in the same overfilled terms when he fell in love with Joy Gresham and made his move to Cambridge. I must have been a great nuisance to him; even as graduate students go, I was raw. Yet, affirmative as always, he found more than duty in our shared interest, for we were soon on a basis of disparate equality. Our meetings were opportunities for both to clarify ideas of the sixteenth century. In fact, he offered something far better than efficient supervision; he opened windows to the *aer purior*, the expanse of intellectuality.

For he talked like an angel. My idea of how angels might talk derives from Lewis. His prose is brilliant, amusing, intimate, cogent;

but his talk was of a superior order. It combined fluent, informal progression with the most articulate syntax, as if, somehow, it was a text *remembered*—and remembered perfectly. The steps of his argument succeeded without faltering, with each quotation in the original tongue, well pronounced. To keep up his half-dozen languages, he belonged to reading groups—J. R. R. Tolkien's Kolbitar for Norse, the Dante Society for Italian, another group for Homeric Greek. Add an extraordinary memory, and you can see how any situation was for him accompanied by a full-voiced choir of verbal associations. "Probably no reader," he writes, "comes upon Lydgate's 'I herd other crie' without recalling the *voces vagitus et ingens* ["voices and a great wailing"] in Virgil's hell." For this assumption, Lewis has been called "bookish"—a dumbed-down response. Of *course* he was bookish; hang it, he tutored in literature. Even standing on the high end of a punt in a one-piece swimming costume with a single shoulder strap, about to dive, he had time for a quotation, half-heard over the water, something about *silvestrem*. Was he teasing me for reclining at ease in my punt—*tu patulae recubans sub tegmine fagi / silvestrem ... musam* ("you lying under the shelter of a beech [ponder] the sylvan Muse")? His allusions, not remotely elitist, were to familiar passages. In those days you were expected to recognize *Aeneid* book 6 or the opening of Virgil's First Eclogue. Similarly with Old English: Lewis had pages by heart but mostly stuck to the high points: *Thas overeode, thisses swa maeg* ("These things I got through; so I may this"), or *Hige sceal the heardra* ("Resolve must be the harder [as our force grows smaller]").

Lewis's marshaling of knowledge might have been overwhelming if it had not been such fun. Here was someone who loved literature as much as I did, but knew the *auctores* and how to draw on them. And he was no mere conduit of sources but could put ideas in the historical philosopher's long perspective. On 26 February 1953, I asked him to explain the puzzling metaphysical dichotomies between form-substance and form-matter. He defined them at length extempore, soon going beyond my comprehension. Sixteenth-century confusions of terms needed more detailed analysis than I was ready for. Yet the explanation, which he reverted to in his Spenser lectures, was lucidity itself.

Lewis opened such abstractions with an apparently natural ease. His forthright, single-minded progressions, although rapid, were unlike Tolkien's bubbly effervescence. (I remember Tolkien as a disconcerting conversationalist; he had a habit of distributing speech between several quite different strands—botanical and linguistic, say—and keeping them all in play, as in the *entrelacement* of a medieval romance, so that you had to keep track of earlier turns of conversation.) It would never have occurred to Lewis to affect finesses of speech in the manner of some dons of his generation. Not for him the exquisitely offhand *sprezzatura* of Lord David Cecil. What Lewis said, however surprising at first, most often came to seem plainly right. This forthrightness (which sometimes raised southern English hackles) comes out in his labeling of the sixteenth-century "Drab" style.[1] It gave him little pleasure, so he said so.

He had almost no small talk; he was courteous but dialectical and sometimes combative. Like his model Dr. Johnson, Lewis was "a very polite man," Claude Rawson remarks, only in self-ignorance. But I think he knew his shortcoming well enough. He generally followed the adversarial system, and not always quietly. Exulting in victory, he argued closely on until his adversary was crushed or ridiculous. For some reason, this method of conversation did not win universal popularity. It has been called verbal bullying, and A. N. Wilson connects it with Lewis's pleasure in fantasies of whipping. This connection seems facile. Outward bullying need not imply inner sadism, and sadistic fantasies may be enjoyed by quiet folk. When he was thirty-five, Lewis wrote about his bullying manner to Arthur Greeves in different terms: "a hardened bigot shouting every one down ... is what I am in danger of becoming." By the time I knew him, he usually remembered to avoid bigotry. His contentiousness was joy in debate; he never bullied me.

As to bullying pupils, the witnesses differ. Some who knew him well, like George Sayer, remember him as never bullying. My guess, though, is that a few pupils were bullied, and rightly so. Nowadays, of course, all students are sober and industrious; and if not, they have the right to remain silent in tutorials and idle outside them. Last century things were different. Faced with blockish inertia or faking of essays or lazy superiority to work or lack of interest in justifying a place at the university, Lewis may well have judged a little bullying in order. Unless students worked hard enough to remember a text, they were unteachable. He did not get on, for example, with John Betjeman, whom he judged an idle, mischievous social climber. (I was to fail as badly with Michael Palin, who turned out well later in life but is on record as having learned nothing from my tutorials.)

Those who called Lewis bully and brute probably included some who shrank from discussing matters of substance. The fifties was a decade of furious exits, slammed doors, demands for "apologies in writing." Heavies like Iain Macdonald hectored their juniors unmercifully. I shall not forget my own fear in case it came out that I had given way to the contemptible weakness of consulting what Macdonald called a "trick-cyclist." Helen Gardner then had the reputation of liking tutorials to end in tears. I can believe it, for I heard her at a student society question the speaker so insistently ("Have you actually *read* the novel? Have you read the last chapter? Are you trying to tell us that ...") that the woman under interrogation broke down. Fierce duels like this doubtless helped to maintain academic standards; it was dangerous not to know the text. But Lewis was not given to ferocity of that sort.

Often enough, though, he had to defend himself against Oxford's anti-Christian orthodoxy. One of these "humanists," H. W. Garrod, the Keats editor, knew how to welcome a guest to Merton: "Ah, Lewis. Aren't you the man who thinks the Holy Ghost has balls?"—not the gentlest way to remind anyone of the Athanasian Creed. Lewis's challenges were less rudely ad hominem, but sometimes sharp enough. When one graduate pupil brought a poor essay, Lewis is said to have torn it silently into the wastebasket. A devastatingly impersonal learning experience. Lewis didn't always know when he hurt. To me, he was more amiable; he would enjoy the escape from repetitive undergraduate tutorials. These cost him much energy—some of it probably going to hide a long-accumulated dislike of tutoring uncongenial pupils in disagreeable subjects outside the English School. Anyway, we got on well; Lewis seemed always on the verge of hilarity—between a chuckle and a roar.

Very occasionally, we had disagreements. One of them concerned Charles Darwin; Lewis saw the theory of natural selection as threatening religion. My education had been on the science side, leading to a year in medicine at Glasgow University; I thought I knew quite a bit about genetics. Probing my views on evolution, Lewis rehearsed an argument from Philip Gosse's ill-fated *Omphalos*. "You talk about fossils. How do you know God didn't put the fossils in the rocks?" Lewis would assume I had read enough Gosse to see the wit of using the Victorian's subtle compromise to test the crude positivism of modern science. Or maybe he was trying out the old argument as one might casually heft an ancient but serviceable mace. Anyhow, I was furious. How could he ignore the evidence of the geological record? Or was that a plant too? Did God often lie to us? And so on. I grew as red as Lewis himself. But he nimbly reined in, avoiding the threatened collision; he never lost his temper in debate.

Full of my "liberal" assurance that there could be no conflict between religion and science, I dismissed Lewis's question as willful obscurantism. If he was determined to set religion against Darwin, surely he could have found a better argument. He might have gone to the *De Genesi*, say, for Augustine's doctrine of gradually ripening seeds of creation. Many years later, when I read *Omphalos*, I was ashamed to find that Gosse had anticipated exactly the objections I made to Lewis in my ignorance. Gosse is sometimes misrepresented as arguing that fossils were inserted to test faith, whereas in fact he revered the fossil record as revealing, without deception, God's laws of biological development. To reconcile this with biblical chronology, Gosse speculated that fossils "may possibly belong to a prochronic development of the mighty plan of the life-history of the world." Lewis must have realized I didn't know *Omphalos* and could have crushed my argument by pointing this out; but the "bully" was too kindly for that. After my outburst I was less in awe of Lewis; his opposition to Darwin came over as simplistic. More recently, I have begun to see that evolution is more complex than it seemed then. All the same, I still think Lewis failed to enter the world of modern science, probably through not grasping its mathematical character. He had so little grasp of mathematics that he could never pass the elementary algebra in Responsions, the Oxford entrance exam.

When I wrote Lewis in 1961 about interesting ideas in Teilhard de Chardin, Lewis replied, accusing me, at least half seriously, of "biolatry": "You talk of Evolution as if it were a substance (like individual organisms) and even a rational substance or person. I had thought it was an abstract noun." He conceded "there might be a sort of *daemon* ... in the evolutionary process. But that view must surely be argued on its own merits?" Well, Teilhard had done just that; so it looked as if Lewis had not read *The Phenomenon of Man*. Then it dawned on me that Lewis was not much interested in science. He had read Greats and like many philosophers — Richard Rorty is a recent instance — was content with general ideas about the philosophical errors of scientists. About the actual character of scientific thought, Lewis knew very little; he had painted himself out of the scientific world picture.

Jenny and I rented an attic at 2 Church Walk in North Oxford, the same house where the Spenserian Rudolf Gottfried stayed. From there I cycled to Magdalen for supervisions. Often Major Lewis sat typing in the large sitting room and directed me through to his brother in the smaller room. One winter morning I got there frozen; Lewis, wearing a dressing gown over his clothes, was engrossed in *Astounding Science Fiction*. Conversation turned to fantasy; I confessed I was trying to write one myself and had got blocked. He made me describe the setting (a paraworld with a slower time lapse), then said, "You need two things for this sort of fiction. The first you already have: a world, a *mise en scène*. But you also need a *mythos* or plot." After that, Lewis was always keener to know how *The Rest of Time* was coming along than to read the next installment of dissertation. This was gratifying, of course, yet somehow depressing to a would-be academic author. But it was an article of faith with Lewis that writing fiction could never conflict with studying literature. Not that he always wrote without difficulty; sometimes he had to set a project aside for a long period. He showed me several unfinished or abandoned pieces (his notion of supervision included exchanging work in progress); these included "After Ten Years," *The Dark Tower*, and *Till We Have Faces*. Another fragment, a time travel story, had been aborted after only a few pages.[2]

Getting to the "other" world was a particular problem, he said; he had given up several stories at that stage. His unfamiliarity with scientific discourse may have played a part in this. The vehicles of transition in *Out of the Silent Planet* and *Perelandra*, although suggestive in other ways, are hardly plausible as scientific apparatus. In the Narnia stories Lewis turned to magical means of entry: teleportation rings from E. Nesbit and Tolkien, or else a terribly strange wardrobe.

Once fully started, Lewis quickly wrote a more or less final version, like Anthony Trollope. Unlike Henry James (or Tolkien), he never drafted and redrafted. Nevill Coghill might have to make ten or more drafts of anything for publication; but when things went well Lewis would write only a rough copy and a fair copy (with one or two corrections per page). And that was it, except for scholarly books like the *OHEL* volume, which were tried out first as lectures. Even the final version would be in longhand; Lewis thought a noisy typewriter dulled the sense of rhythm. Fortunately, his writing was legible enough to go straight to the publisher, unless Warren typed it out. Obviously, composition was not so fast as writing; before committing to paper, he must have composed each work in his head, retaining it by some "power of memory" (as Tolkien called Lewis's retentiveness of the spoken word). Lewis's fluency suggests that he composed in paragraphs, as Robert Louis Stevenson did, and Edward Gibbon in his covered acacia walk. Others of Lewis's generation similarly revolved ideas while walking; the rhythm assisting them, perhaps, to develop expansive themes. Erwin Panofsky wrote much art history in Princeton's woods, returning from a walk with paragraphs finished to the last full stop. He recited installments to a friend who noticed, after a break due to illness, that Panofsky had lost his place and was repeating, word for word, a passage already imparted. And he was not only word perfect but *punctuation* perfect.

The flow of Lewis's writing and speaking had much to do with this remarkable memory. Memory feats were common enough in Oxford then, especially among classicists. Edgar Lobel the papyrologist and fungiphage, to mention one, modestly denied having Homer by heart—but added, "Mind you, if you said a verse I dare say I could give you the next one." Lewis could have claimed much the same of *Paradise Lost*. Kenneth Tynan, whom Lewis tutored, tells of a memory game. Tynan had to choose a number from one to forty, for the shelf in Lewis's library; a number from one to twenty, for the place in this shelf; from one to a hundred, for the page; and from one to twenty-five for the line, which he read aloud. Lewis had then to identify the book and say what the page was about. I can believe this, having seen how rapidly he found passages in his complete Rudyard Kipling or his William Morris. Tynan's anecdote usefully suggests the sort of memory involved; not memory by rote (although Lewis had plenty of that) but something more like the Renaissance *ars memorativa*, depending on "places" in texts. It was not principally *memoria ad verba* but rather *ad res*—memory of the substance, aimed at grasp of contents through their structure. Lewis's annotations of his own books show him continually charting formal structures and divisions of the work. When he offers himself in "De Descriptione Temporum" as a specimen of "Old Western culture," he could have validated this on the basis of memory alone. But we ignored him; and now that detailed knowledge of texts is neither pursued nor examined, an essential method of cultivating and testing literary competence has been abandoned.

Endowed with such a memory, one might expect Lewis to have lectured extempore, as he was perfectly capable of doing (and did, in the informal situation of the Socratic Club). But the lecture notes for his Cambridge Spenser lectures reflect a more complicated procedure, which may have had something to do with his habit of using successive lecture series to work up material for a book. In these notes, quotations are written out in full—even passages one might expect Lewis to have had by heart. These would serve as memory prompts, and to indicate where the script was to take over from improvisation. For the main body of the lecture, by contrast, only a skeletal argument is provided; a sequence of logical divisions and conclusions. Each element has its letter, almost as in formal logic: "Simplicity A ... Sophistication A ... Simplicity B ... Sophistication B"; or

a. B[ritomart] > < Radigund
b. B[ritomart]—Artegall relation > < Radigund Artegall relation.

Sometimes the manuscript signalizes the "lead-in" to some joke or *coup d'amphithéatre*. These were prepared for long in advance; as Derek Brewer puts it, "The fuse might be lit several minutes before the actual, yet unexpected, explosion." Altogether then, the lecture notes are no more (and no less) than *aides-mémoires* for trains of thought serving as armatures for his improvisations. However closely logical the progressions might be, their rhetoric was conversational, albeit with a certain dramatic heightening. I heard part of the "Prolegomena to Renaissance Literature" series (drawn from his 1944 Clark Lectures and already written *OHEL* volume, and trying out for *The Discarded Image*); my impression was of avuncular informality. At times, "Uncle Lewis" seemed hardly to be performing but rather exploring a thought for the first time. And so far was he from standing on ceremony or authority or superior learning that he started his lecture as he came through the door and finished it as he walked out. He was a popular and (not at all the same thing) *good* lecturer — lecturing sometimes to an audience of three hundred or more. He towered above his colleagues in the English faculty — at a time, admittedly, when lecturing standards were not high. His resonant voice suited the rostrum; he was always easily audible (something that could not be said of Tolkien).

Lewis's innate memorial powers were developed by education, first at school and then with his private tutor William Kirkpatrick. At Oxford they were strengthened by having to depend on the Bodleian Library rather than on his own books. In the 1940s, Lewis's personal library struck Brewer as meager. Later, when he bought more largely and accumulated about three thousand books (still not large by modern standards), his reading habits had become ingrained, and he continued to rely on memory. Often he used books almost in the medieval way, as memory prompts.

Literary memory depends on use: it must be frequently refreshed. Even a "photographic" memory like Frank Harris's needs refreshment, to keep out "creative" errors. Lewis had almost total recall of words (he remembered new vocabulary after once looking it up in the dictionary), yet he had to go over texts frequently — sometimes immediately before a tutorial. Consequently his reading and rereading were astonishingly copious. Reading habits, of course, were different in the fifties; I used then to read ten hours a day. Lewis, who read far faster, read with surer grasp, and read whenever commitments allowed—read even at mealtimes—read prodigiously. He kept a record, to know when a text needed rereading (unless it was a case of "never again!"). Some quite minor authors were reread. A copy of *The Worm Ouroboros* he lent me was inscribed "Read for the first time ... read for the second ... for the fifth time," with dates. And E. R. Eddison was neither a canonical author nor a person Lewis found very congenial.

Lewis managed to cram copious reading into his busy life by not making a task of it. He told his pupils, "The great thing is to be always reading but never to get bored—treat it not like work, more as a vice!" Following his own advice, he pursued congenial literature with passion (pleasure is too weak a word). As for uncongenial works, a few minutes a day would get him through. His tastes became more catholic with maturity (he reached out latterly even to drama); but he always read selectively rather than systematically. If a major work like Abraham Cowley's *Davideis* bored him, he set it aside. What he read, however, he read more deeply than most. He led me to see that coverage—complete knowledge of literature—can never be attained. Rising from a thirst to range over it and take in all that is delightful, good reading has to work by sampling, exploring, and at last grasping strategic works or passages, in the context of sources, analogues, historical circumstances, and the inferior subliterature whose lower pleasures it leaves behind. Lewis's selectivity showed in the works he had chosen to remember. Being fairly political then, I thought of William Morris as the author of *News from Nowhere*; but Lewis preferred *The Well at the World's End* (and persuaded me to read it). He made a good deal of room for reading simply by missing out newspapers—at the cost of being amazingly ignorant of current affairs. That shocked me; I had been taught that reading the papers was a duty, next after the Bible. I had yet to discover the revulsion from politics that Lewis had formed as a consequence of early memories of politically religious hatred in Ireland.

Lewis's choice of reading differed from that of mainstream literary critics of his time like F. R. Leavis or Wallace Robson. Lewis took a longer view; he knew the official canon was prone to change and so was happy to study authors outside it. The private canon he held in memory featured Spenser, Pope, Sir Walter Scott, Jane Austen, John Keats, Charles Dickens, and Wilkie Collins (rather than William Thackeray). George Meredith's *Egoist* he reread every year. Robert Louis Stevenson, John Ruskin, and Kipling (extracanonical then) were important to him personally. Influential models included Dr. Johnson and, in another way, George MacDonald. On the whole, a romantic emphasis. He went to Walter de la Mare and Robert Graves, even to Roy Campbell, for alternatives to modernism. He kept up with the modernists (and could quote from them) but rejected their intense introspection. Early T. S. Eliot he particularly disliked; and he read Henry James's letters for the first time in his middle fifties. He had even less interest in the movement writers Philip Larkin and Kingsley Amis. When Amis introduced himself, on the Belfast ferry, he received what he took (perhaps wrongly) as a putdown: "Amice? Amice? No, I don't believe I know the name." That would cause chagrin, for Amis admired Lewis's lecturing. (Lewis lectured fairly slowly, and Amis, who despised students, exaggerated this; he lectured at dictation speed, "so you can get it all down.")

I don't mean that Lewis closed his mind to all contemporary literature or new methods of criticism. On the contrary, he valued Virginia Woolf, W. H. Auden, and George Orwell very highly. And he even said he envied my generation our chance to work out the details of older literature. This was apropos of Kent Hieatt's work on Spenser's *Epithalamion*; Lewis read *Short Time's Endless Monument* for Columbia University Press and sent me a page proof as soon as it was published. Supervisor or ex-supervisor made no difference; Lewis always remembered to pass on new scholarship that might be relevant. He sent the Hieatt on 22 November 1960, and soon after his own review of Robert Ellrodt's *Neoplatonism in the Poetry of Spenser*, before its publication in *Études Anglaises*. We also exchanged less academic books: he made me aware of David Lindsay's *Voyage to Arcturus*, and I responded, less successfully, with Austin Wright's *Islandia*.

A corollary of Lewis's memory art was that his reading, prodigious as it was, had gaps and limits. He certainly read less widely than F. W. Bateson, the last Oxford don to keep up with all the journals.

Lewis's understanding of contemporary philosophy was inadequate, as a famous debate with Miss Anscombe painfully exposed.[3] His theology was almost exclusively biblical, rather than "systematic" or "dogmatic." And he had little interest in the visual arts—unlike his friend Nevill Coghill, for example, or John Bryson, his rival for the Magdalen Fellowship, both connoisseurs. Only belatedly, when Erwin Panofsky, Edgar Wind, and Mario Praz influenced the study of literature as well as of art, did Lewis develop an interest in iconography. Even in reading for his *OHEL* volume, Lewis followed individual predilections. He suffered criticism for his unfavorable account of the humanists—due perhaps to insufficient knowledge of the northern humanists.

Perhaps Lewis's most striking limitation was his lack of interest in literary criticism as distinct from literature. In the fifties, New Criticism and structuralism were only beginning to reach Oxford; Theory appeared no more than a harmless little cloud on the horizon. Intelligent academics could see that the new theories depended on false premises and assumed they would come to nothing. Lewis certainly knew the need to study context and could have opposed neo-Saussureanism effectively; but instead he ignored it and left Bateson to sketch a theory of contextualism. Unconcerned with phenomenology, Lewis regarded criticism simply as a report on reading. So he went on exploring his impressions, clarifying them, and determining the properties of individual works. Would theory have helped with this? Without it, he often went right to the heart of what others called critical issues. Like most Oxford dons, Lewis thought F. R. Leavis's narrow moralism more of a threat. In Lewis's view (and I agreed), to study only an approved canon was to evade literature's challenges. Literature did not merely confirm one's views but might surprise by embodying perspectives that could qualify readers' prejudices and widen their horizons.

The range of literature that Lewis held in memory was affected by the formal limitations of the Oxford English School, whose canon then ended at 1830. In the syllabus debate of the fifties, Lewis defended this arrangement against the proposal of Helen Gardner and others to extend the canon to 1900 or later. Although this would have taken in many of his favorite authors, Lewis argued against it. The proposed field would be unworkably extensive, making preparation more superficial and tending to what we now call "dumbing down." At that time I favored extending the curriculum; but I have since come to repent this. In the event, "reform" brought a radical lurch, and gave the Oxford School, like many others, a disastrously modern focus. Modern literature has proved unsuitable for undergraduate study. It is not far enough removed from our shared assumptions to challenge them. It has yet to prove itself as the memory of our history. And mostly it is not memorable. Besides, the reference books required for studying it are not yet available.

If Lewis's memory of literature was somewhat idiosyncratic, this hardly affected his supervising. For he conceived the role, not as that of manager, still less as authoritative *Doktorvater*, but rather as that of disputant, like his own Kirkpatrick. The disputations might be designed (as on the Gosse occasion) to force clearer formulation or self-defense or discovery of hidden assumptions. What, for example, did I think thinking was? "How often, Fowler, do you suppose yourself to be actually thinking?" I was about to claim, absurdly, that I spent most of my waking life thinking, when he broke in to confess that he himself thought only about once a week—twice, in a good week. The term "thinking" was to be kept for inference from ground to consequent. Another time he amiably ruminated, "You know, Fowler, you don't have enough *roughage* in your life." This must have been projection; I've never known anyone who organized his life more than Lewis himself.

Similarly out of the blue, he proposed to dispute what life's greatest pleasure was. Great art? No. Mystical ecstasy? No: something more generally accessible. Simultaneous orgasm? But that wasn't it, either. "I'll tell you," he said; "it's the pleasure, after walking for hours, of coming to a pub and relieving yourself." Probably I had been too solemn, or high-flown. But his down-to-earth example was not chosen at random. He would sometimes in the middle of a supervision go off to the next room and pee into a chamber pot, apologizing for his "weak bladder" and maintaining the flow of discourse through the open door. (Oxford was still very much a male society; senior common rooms might have chamber pots behind screens, and one of the Inklings was known to conduct tutorials from his bath.) Outside the teaching frame, Lewis was hardly less disputatious. When we had him to dinner at Church Walk, conversation turned to hot-cross buns and Jenny faulted the local variety for its paucity of raisins and spices. At once Lewis pounced; the traditional hot-cross bun had neither fruit nor spice. It was made, was it not, with the last of the unleavened bread?

Naturally, the challenges were most often literary. When Lewis praised Samuel Henry Butcher and Andrew Lang's translation of Homer, I said something in favor of T. E. Lawrence's *Odyssey*. Instantly, Lewis rubbished it, chuckling: "But the style's Wardour Street, isn't it?"—one of his favorite dismissive epithets. He thought my approval too vague and wanted to maneuver me into substantiating it. We settled, I think, for Lawrence's handling the narrative lucidly. Sometimes Lewis would take up the evidential basis of a point, giving me *en passant* a crash course in rhetoric. "Don't exaggerate claims beyond what the evidence will easily bear," he advised; "the weaker the statement, the stronger the case." Or "Make your statements only as strong as you have to." I had a propensity to overstate—an un-English tendency Lewis himself displayed, as at the English faculty meeting when he foolhardily told Helen Gardner that all *his* pupils read Calvin.

In 1955 Lewis went off to Cambridge to take up the chair of medieval and Renaissance English. Never forgetting a pupil, he passed me on to his own former tutor, F. P. Wilson, Merton Professor, compiler of the *Oxford Book of Proverbs*, and an authority on Elizabethan and Jacobean prose. Wilson was a very different supervisor: less the bold critic, more the professional scholar. He knew just what shape a dissertation should have; and his gentle suggestions, quietly put, were so clearly right as to render argument superfluous. But no single supervisor could supply Lewis's place. Soon I found unofficial mentors: Helen Gardner, the learned Ethel Seaton, Bateson of the *Cambridge Bibliography*, J. B. Leishman, and George Temple the mathematician. Besides these I could rely, of course, on my peer group; for we all mysteriously had time then for coffee in the morning and in the afternoon tea—Ian Gregor and Mark Kinkead-Weekes, the satirical rogue Claude Rawson and the laid-back Walt Litz, and sometimes George Hunter or Christopher Ricks.

During Lewis's Cambridge years I saw little of him, and by 1962 we were different people. I had finished my D.Phil., been a junior research Fellow at Queen's, taught a year in Indiana, and become a Fellow of Brasenose. Lewis too was a different person from the supervisor I remembered: he had married but lost his wife and was himself seriously ill. Visiting him in the Acland hospital and at The Kilns, I got to know him as a friend. Now our talk, more recollective and ruminative, was about anything and everything: his dreams, plum jam, The Lord of the Rings. On his side at least, it seemed without reserve. The sort of topic he proposed now was whether the pleasures of masturbation were keener than those of full intercourse. In the United States, I heard of a Lewis quite distinct from the Lewis I knew. My Lewis smoked incessantly, drank more than was altogether good for him, and appreciated bawdy, whether of the *Rodiad* or the *Eskimo Nell* genre. If he was a saint, it was not one of an austere or narrowly pious sort. Nor given to angst. He was assured, and talked of his wife, Joy, without difficulty. Retrospection now brought no unbearable sadness.

In 1963 Jack died, and with him much else. He had been laughed at for offering himself as a specimen of Old Western culture. But he proved in actuality to be one of the last of a threatened species. Before he died, he wrote, optimistically, of the tide turning back to literature. In the event, N.I.C.E. turned out to have more subsidiaries, on both sides of the Atlantic, than he ever feared.[4] Universities submitted to bureaucratic management, dons morphed into accountants, training replaced education, and Theory displaced literature. Reading simplistic codes, supplying false contexts, pursuing irrelevant indeterminacies or telltale "gaps": these have proved no substitute for the memorial grasp of literature. Now that the tide really seems to be on the turn after its fifty-year ebb, we could do a great deal worse than look back across the drift to the great reader Lewis. We need to try to recall what literature was, what it meant, and can still mean, to grasp literary works in memory.

Chapter 8

ENCOUNTERS WITH LEWIS: AN INTERIM REPORT

Paul Piehler

What a great idea, I thought. Get some of us who knew Lewis to write about the different ways in which he affected our lives. But by a fruitful serendipity, while I was starting to put some thoughts together for Hal Poe's anthology, a friend asked if I would be interested in leading a small group in a reading of Lewis's *Surprised by Joy*. I did not see much point in this at first, feeling that something more directly doctrinal and theological would lead to more useful discussion. But then it struck me that my own boyhood and conversion experiences had run oddly parallel to those of Lewis. Was there, or is there still, some significance to this, positive or negative, or was it just one of those coincidences that the life flow in which we live is wont to mock us with, those vain intimations of empty meanings?

Let us start along that trail and see how far it leads us.

Public School — and an Atheist Mentor

Always something of an outsider, I never felt myself more excluded from a group than when, at the age of thirteen, I was sent to King William's College in the Isle of Man, a boarding school with a clientele of middle-class boys from the north of England. In the tribal England of the time, it was an odd choice for a boy brought up in the south, but my father was in the Intelligence Corps during the Second World War. He was stationed in the Isle of Man, busy sorting out genuine refugees from the Nazis interned on the island. In that school I was among the very few who boasted, or rather suffered from, a south of England accent. Branded as an upper-middle-class "toff," I soon found myself stigmatized as "the aristocrat." Nor did it help that I was a year younger than normal for entrance to the school and was sent there in shorts, where long trousers were the socially essential badge of senior school maturity.

So I was inescapably in a state of cultural antagonism with most of the boys in a place with pretty rough-and-tumble standards compared with the schools in the south of England I was used to. In most respects I was as badly off as Lewis in his first and only year at "Wyvern." And like him, at the beginning I suffered most from the two practices that reinforced his successful demand to be taken away from Wyvern: the institutionalized, almost ritualistic intimidation and bullying of the juniors, and then the prevailing (though relatively innocent) homosexuality, but nonetheless disconcerting enough to a naively innocent thirteen-year-old.

Nonetheless, I never thought of trying to get myself elsewhere for an education, nor even changing to a different house in the school, although Washbourne House, as it turned out, was among the worst for bullying, as well as those two other peculiar institutions, fagging (working as personal servant for senior boys) and homosexual activities. Shortly after I left, my housemaster suffered instant dismissal after attempting to climb into bed with a boy. My rescue from the gutter life of Washbourne House differed from the experience of Lewis, but with the same result. I encountered a mentor with many of the greatest qualities of the Great Knock, Lewis's tutor Kirkpatrick, with whom he studied privately in Bookham, Surrey, during his teen years.

It happened quite by chance, without any initiative on my part, like so much that has been crucial in my life. After I had been in King William's for about a year, I was invited with a number of other boys to have tea one day with a retired doctor who had taken up residence in the Isle of Man after a career in public health in East Africa. I received a repeat invitation and was soon as welcome there as in my own home. Ironically, the very qualities that had alienated me from the other boys in the school gave me the freedom of Dr. Mel Saunderson's house. We became the greatest of friends over the remaining five years I was at King William's.

Visits to Mel's house turned into continuing dialogues on every aspect of life my circumstances had hitherto deprived me of. Not least was the opportunity to browse in his personal library, full of brilliant, disconcerting books I had never encountered in my fairly conventional previous education. And then there was the opportunity of listening to and discussing the marvelous recordings of classical music we played on his colossal radiogram. By some extraordinary stroke of luck I had found a mentor, or rather I had been found by him. It was as if I had found my way home to the true country of the mind.

Mel not only had the widest knowledge of anyone I had met but opened up for me whole ranges of intellectual exploration whose existence I could never have guessed at. The education I had been through before I met him had been sound in its own way but typically conventional, limited, and static, offering little opportunity for serious questioning or discussion. Visiting Mel offered education in action, education that offered me the essential opportunity to form my own opinions and develop my own intellectual positions. He was particularly well versed in the anthropology of Frazer's *Golden Bough*, as well as psychology of a humanistic Freudian character. From these intellectual bastions he would sally out to assail the dogmas and practices of Christianity, in a fashion, as I soon came to realize, quite prevalent among British intellectuals of the day. In any Oxford college, as I came to realize, he would have been quite a luminary.

Some of Mel's most interesting books emanated from the Rationalist Press Association, a society devoted to the exposure of the essentially unhistorical, if not mythic, character of the biblical texts. They emphasized the inconsistent and frequently gross morality to be found in some of the less edifying passages of the Old Testament, and their grotesque depictions of the nonexistent Jehovah. Prominent British philosophers found a mouthpiece in the RPA to enlighten the public by logical demonstrations of the nonexistence of any Creator or Supreme Being. They also vigorously exposed what they regarded as the incorrigible immorality of the Christian churches' policies and practices. I joined the society as a nonmember subscriber (not being considered, it seemed, as having yet reached the "age of reason" demanded of regular members) but was permitted to receive, nonetheless, a constant flow of vehemently anti-Christian polemic.

The Christian churches, it now appeared, had propagated a dogmatic, obsolete religion, fashioned in ancient times by some brilliant but obviously twisted geniuses out of a curious conglomerate of pagan myths and superstitions. Whatever its original merits might have been, Christianity had all too soon fallen into the hands of hypocritical authoritarians, who, as soon as they had the opportunity, ruthlessly inflicted savage repression and punishments on anyone who had the temerity to question their dogmas. I eagerly gulped down all Mel's heterodox ideas and books, and relieved the tedium of the King William's daily chapel services and biweekly Scripture classes by refreshing my mind with these exciting, controversial new insights. All this reading and discussions with Mel stood me in such good stead in Scripture classes that our open-minded school chaplain awarded me the Bishop Drury Scripture Prize, but obviously on the basis of my curiously extensive knowledge rather than any show of piety!

But just as important, I now realize, as any of his ideas or insights, or his esoteric knowledge, and the continuing intellectual challenge of our discussions, was the serene refinement of his house, his way of life, and most of all the continuing friendly respect and courtesy with which he treated this outsider schoolboy. Knowledge and study were no longer mere academic requirements but had come alive, essential vitamins for sustaining life and health.

I learned something too of his adventurous life, his high standing among Free Masons (whom he did not take very seriously), and his formal conversion to Islam. Curiously, he formed his own (one person!) orthodox Muslim sect, combining precepts and dogmas from the four orthodox sects to form a fifth. His conversion was rewarded by permission to journey to Mecca, the forbidden city, impelled by his omnivorous curiosity concerning the human condition.

The Years at Magdalen: Christian Tutor and Atheist Friends

Having finally quitted King William's, rather to my surprise I managed to pass an entrance exam for admission to Magdalen College, Oxford. First I was required to do a year of military service and, coincidentally, found myself gazetted as a second lieutenant in the Somerset Light Infantry, just as Lewis had been thirty years previously. Like him, I found the regiment and the officers a very pleasant and agreeable lot and was surprised to find myself blending in quite nicely, constantly delighted at the courtesy, fairness, and general reasonableness of life in a good regiment in contrast to my King William's experience.

One almost comic serendipity marked my initial basic training. To ensure neat and well-blocked ammunition pouches for parade inspections, our corporal advised us to put books in them to square them off. Accordingly, I popped into a secondhand bookshop the first time I got a chance, and asked the bookseller for appropriately sized books to fill out my ammunition pouches. In those early postwar days in Britain the army, and especially young and innocent-looking soldiers, evidently still had a kind of mystique. The bookseller obligingly searched out a couple of well-sized volumes and refused any payment.

One day I found myself at a loose end in the barracks and idly pulled out the books from the ammo pouches in case there was anything in them conceivably worth reading. One of them turned out to be a surprisingly plausible refutation of the RPA champion J. M. Robertson's claim that Jesus was a purely mythic figure. Was it possible that a real person had come to enact in real life and real time what had been so prolifically imprinted on pre-Christian imagination? After all, if the gospel accounts happened to be true, what else would one expect to find but multitudinous anticipations of the great event on which all history must hinge? This interpretation of the "mythic Jesus," reflecting Chesterton's and anticipating Lewis's views on the subject, by no means converted me back to Christian beliefs but certainly made me feel, should I say, a degree of skepticism even towards the fashionable skepticism of the time.[1]

My admission to Magdalen, with the financial support of a scholarship from Surrey County Council, was, in the first instance at least, to read Modern Greats, a course comprising politics, philosophy, and economics (PPE). Fortunately, I had plenty of time in the peacetime army to do some preliminary reading in these fields and was surprised to find myself far less enthusiastic at the prospect of these studies than

I had expected. Politics and economics I found vitiated by a kind of categorical approach which simply expanded on things I felt I already understood. The history of modern philosophy I studied did not yield one philosopher whose views I found either sympathetic or plausible.

I felt almost trapped until one day it struck me that I had achieved some relatively flattering assessments in the English literature papers for the Higher Certificate Exam, and that I might be able to persuade the college to allow me to read English instead. I got a strong feeling that if I stuck with PPE, after the three years required for the degree, I would simply know a bit more about subjects I essentially comprehended already, whereas if I studied literature I could hardly imagine where three years' study might lead me. This prospect of exploring the unknown I found far more enticing.

I ran into what seemed like one quite serious drawback. When I mentioned to a fervently Catholic uncle that I would be reading English at Magdalen College, Oxford, next year, he replied with the utmost enthusiasm, "Ah, that's just wonderful. You're really in luck. You're going to have C. S. Lewis as your tutor. You remember, that's the fellow who wrote *The Screwtape Letters*." As you can imagine this was by no means what I wanted to hear, as a recently liberated, enlightened atheist. Nonetheless, such was my determination to read English and escape the earnest boredom of PPE I decided to brave it out and ignore, or evade, the no doubt cumbersome attempts Lewis would surely make to press upon me heavy Christian interpretations of the English literature I was to study.

In the event, Lewis turned out to be an entire surprise. A plumpish, red-faced Ulsterman with a confident, jovial Ulster rasp to his voice, at first sight he could have been taken for a cheerful and prosperous ineluctable butcher rather than one of the great minds of the age. Once the tutorials started I was immediately impressed by his relaxed and friendly style, not at all the gaunt, tense dogmatist I had expected. The intensity and incisiveness one expected came out in discussion but inevitably combined with an intellectual courtesy even beyond the Oxbridge norm. Grades or exam results seemed to be the last thing in his mind; rather, we were friends discussing common interests. It was far more like being with Mel than with any other teacher I had known.

His seemingly keen interest in my efforts to form actual opinions and interpretations made me wonder if he had somehow confused me with someone who was actually quite good. (Of course this encouraged one to work exceptionally hard, to try to preserve this pleasant illusion for as long as one could.) While some students referred to him genially as "Papa Lewis," I rather saw him as an indulgent but still somewhat awesome uncle who would talk to you man-to-man but respected your privacy as much as he guarded his own. In spite of my misgivings, I discerned no hint of evangelism on his part. Though we were expected to imbibe deeply of a thousand years of Christian literature, in the tutorials his responses and comments to my papers were as strictly literary as my own contributions.

Unfortunately, I seemed to be paired too often with some of the less diligent of Lewis's students. The one drawback of tutorial teaching at Oxford was that, if anything, some of the dons were just too polite to us. Lewis seemed extraordinarily patient with some really provocatively boring, or shallowly indifferent, undergraduates and only once, in my experience and under great provocation, broke the conventions of courtesy. Jupiter thundered, but only in a tone of exasperated amusement, at which it would be hard to take offense—a hearty rudeness that would have been quite in place, I imagine, among the gatherings of his friends and fellow dons or at lunch with the Inklings. He seemed incapable of talking down to any student.

My initiatory class with Lewis was, for first-year Magdalen undergrads, a kind of pre-tutorial. In no way was it a lecture, and in no way did Lewis dominate the proceedings in the fashion depicted by Anthony Hopkins in *Shadowlands*. One or two of us would read papers each session, and this would be followed by response from Lewis and general discussion, much like a graduate seminar, in fact.

In fact, the portrayals of Lewis in the two *Shadowlands* versions, while quite understandable in their dramatic contexts, are both, perhaps inevitably, misleading. In the earlier version, Joss Ackland's Lewis is simply a nice fellow, quite unlike the extremely powerful but not necessarily affable or ingratiating personality Lewis presented.

Hopkins portrays slightly firmer shades of the iron in Lewis's character but obviously does not even try to emulate the power or charisma of his lecturing. Hopkins would simply have lacked the weight.[2] When Lewis lectured, the room seemed to shake with the strength of his personality, his enormous, somewhat rough-edged Ulster voice, and the unquestioning confidence which infused itself into every opinion, every citation. (An Ian Paisley who had found Jesus, if you will!)[3]

Of his lectures, I most enjoyed Lewis's "Prolegomena to Medieval and Renaissance Literature." He would stride in with magisterial authority, his springy gait in perfect accord with his somewhat rolypoly figure, thrusting his way through the crowd milling around the aisles of the largest lecture hall the university could provide. A massive figure on the high podium, he would boom out resonantly over the disorderly multitude below the same first instruction every lecture of the term: "Would members of the University be seated first, please!"

A hush would fall over the crowd, a silence broken only by the shuffle of seats as a hundred or so mere "visitors" — often elderly ladies, shuffled uneasily to the back of the hall, giving up their seats to us bright young undergraduates (usefully distinguished by the short black gowns then required for attending all college and university functions). Well, this was a university lecture and the students were expected to take notes! A glance at *The Discarded Image*, the scholarly work that came out of these lectures, would remind or convince anyone that the material was hardly of a character that most lecturers would choose in order to cram a hall to bursting point. Your average audience is quite content to let the Dark Ages remain that way. Macrobius or Andreas Capellanus are hardly household names today and would likely as not be quoted in Latin, the similarly obscure Layamon or Gower in equally fluent Middle English.

Nonetheless, one could not, would not miss a word, and I carried those notes around with me for years, until the book came out. I would say I got (or at least kept) my first lectureship at Columbia largely on the strength of what I took from those lectures — inspiration and subject matter alike.

Oddly enough Lewis seemed quite honestly innocent of the immense effect of these performances. One week he had been obliged to miss a session, and walking back with him to Magdalen from the Lecture Hall after the next session, I happened to ask him when we were going to get a chance to hear the omitted lecture. He seemed genuinely surprised that I was so eager to catch up on the missing talk, as if, after all, the grandeur of his performance was just part of the academic routine rather than a life-changing experience. Beneath the resonant, booming voice, it seemed, lay a genuine personal humility.

Some undergraduates, attuned to the milder, more apologetic and hesitant Oxford lecturing style, claimed to find Lewis bombastic and pompous. I believe they missed the point. True humility, in Lewis's view, should consist of a full and unapologetic acceptance of whatever role you might find yourself in, as he himself pointed out quite emphatically in his *Preface to Paradise Lost*:

> Above all, you must be rid of the hideous idea, fruit of a widespread inferiority complex, that pomp, on the proper occasions, has any connection with vanity or self-conceit.... The modern habit of doing ceremonial things unceremoniously is no proof of humility; rather it proves the offender's inability to forget himself in the rite, and his readiness to spoil for every one else the proper pleasure of ritual.[4]

Like most of the older dons at Oxford, Lewis emphasized intensive study of actual texts rather than secondary commentary. Our weekly essays for our tutors thus tended to be the result of in-depth reading in and pondering over the original literature rather than extensive citation of the modern critical positions.[5] One might occasionally quote modern commentators as a way of triggering off one's own interpretations, but it was made clear that the intimate study of the originals was the royal road to achieving the kind of literary authority that Lewis wielded so effortlessly.

In fact, we used to feel a heady Oxford superiority to friends who had ended up reading English at Cambridge and found themselves burdened with immense reading lists of secondary works. Evidently, if you were studying Shakespeare at Cambridge you would have been found dreadfully unprepared if you had not read, for example, *Those Nutcracking Elizabethans*! We could not understand how any student, however conscientious, could read so exhaustively in the critical commentaries and still have time for the deep rumination on the text on which our Oxford essays were essentially intended to be based.

Nonetheless we were lucky enough to have some contrary opinions pitched at us by our brilliant graduate tutors in Magdalen, one of whom, Robert Browning, was particularly fired up by the kind of searching, stimulating (often abrasive) new criticism hailing from the puritan, moralistic, and, we understood, largely atheistic Leavisites at Cambridge. We relished some fervent debates on this Lewis-versus-Leavis issue and gained hugely from these divergences in critical approach.[6] All Lewis's most interesting tutorial students would turn up to such discussions. A. N. Wilson reported complaints that Lewis delighted in "verbal bullying" and was unapproachable and daunting as a tutor. Not in my time. The suggestion that Lewis could be "intimidating" would have raised incredulous laughter in this group. His affectionate sobriquet was "Papa Lewis." Nor did I or anyone else ever sense or suggest that he considered tutorials "an interruption to his real work." Lewis would complain about examination chores, from which he would emerge "reeking from the slaughter," as he would put it. He also confessed some exasperation at the seemingly endless task of putting together such things as the bibliographies of the obscurer authors featured in his monumental *English Literature in the Sixteenth Century*. Nor, incidentally, in my time, could one have guessed he took the slightest pleasure in drunkenness or bawdy.

At all events, I found it easy enough to remain impervious to Christian belief, whether Lewis's or Milton's. My defenses had been considerably enhanced by the influence of a circle of quite brilliant fellow students, graduate as well as undergraduate, I was able to infiltrate. We boasted members from Australia, New Zealand, India, Canada, the States, as well as a sprinkling of token Brits. Our tone was pretty much set by the philosophers in the group, who followed the current Oxford freethinking mode. In fact, the prevailing disposition was to regard religious propositions as not even erroneous but as simply meaningless. Here we took our lead from a book that was all the rage at the time among Oxford intellectuals, A. J. Ayer's notoriously skeptical (and, as it turned out, logically precarious) work, *Language, Truth and Logic.*[7]

Oxford's student-run *Isis* magazine[8] once ran a survey on undergraduate attitudes towards religion. In the course of an eager discussion by our group, someone read out one of the anonymous comments that *Isis* reported on: "I do not accept any established religion, but I cannot rule out the possibility of a faith based on mystical experience." This led to a buzz of discussion until I cut in with "I happen to know that comment came from someone who is right now sitting in this room." Silence and skeptical, puzzled glances followed.

"Well, you ought to know by this time," I continued, "that there is only one person here who rides with the hounds and hunts with the hare like that." Further anxious glances until light broke in, and one friend broke my cover.

"You'd better confess that it was the skeptical Piehler himself, the Rationalist Press graduate, who perpetrated that sentiment."

I had to own up. "Well, a conscientious skeptic has to be distrustful about atheism just as much as any intellectual fashion" was the best I could do for a response.

I had managed to outflank the rest of the group on this point, but on reflection I was a trifle surprised by the incident myself. Was something in all this literature I was reading emitting vibrations on levels beyond the strictly academic? Or was it that the tutorials with Lewis were teaching me to keep an open mind about everything, even the academically correct skepticism of the time? Well, my youthful agnosticism survived this experience (for a while at least) "bloodied but unbowed." Nevertheless, the incident proved curiously prophetic.

Lewis's well-founded but quite boisterously confident assertiveness in all literary and religious matters may have gained him the friendship and admiration of such strong-souled Oxford figures as Coghill, Tolkien, and Dyson but notoriously offended those who preferred colleagues of quieter temperament and more limited range. Their sentiments filtered down to undergraduates from outside Magdalen, who would come up with dicta like "Isn't it rather a pity he puts so much energy into all this religious stuff when he could be contributing to real literary scholarship?"

At the time I found it difficult to disagree with this stricture. It seemed so solid, reasonable, commonsensical. A shoemaker should stick to his last, a scholar to his scholarship. And yet even then I was not quite comfortable with what seemed a rather too easy judgmentalism. Lewis in no way gave the impression of a divided, or lightly distractible, personality. It was only quite gradually that I found a considered answer to this critique. Finally, it came to me that his scholarly and religious lives were really no more separable than two sides of the same coin. How so?

Simply this, Lewis notably, some would say notoriously, put the active personal experience of literature before attempts at criticism or evaluation. Literary texts, he felt, too often get used as fodder for critical analysis by academics who show little sign of sensitivity to the sheer oomph effect (or "By Gum" response) engendered by the author.[9] For Lewis the scholar's essential role is not to ignore but to enhance that "By Gum" reaction, so that one can read an ancient text in the light of the cultural and historical circumstances more relevant to its creation. Armed with the scholar's insights one then has a better chance of following Pope's imperishable advice to read the text in the same spirit that its author writ.[10]

Not, of course, that this restoration of any ancient cultural model would necessarily command any belief, just the respect appropriate to any model or system of reality. But contemplation of, say, the medieval model of the universe may provide not only aesthetic pleasure but insight into the way in which our perceptions are conditioned by the models that dominate in our own age. Thus, all models can be seen as relative rather than absolute. In terms of *The Pilgrim's Regress*, Lewis demonstrated a type of scholarship that allows us a chance of escaping from Giant Zeitgeist's conceptual gulag.[11]

Nonetheless, we all have to make at the least a provisional choice of a model. So far as the physical universe is concerned, most educated people today no doubt settle for an uneasy amalgam of Newtonian and Einsteinian models, with at least partial acceptance of evolutionary theory, though not necessarily on strict Darwinian lines. But when it comes to metaphysical realities, a conscious decision between a theistic or a simply material model of the universe seems less avoidable, and a little more tricky. As a literary scholar and historian, Lewis at least clearly found the issue difficult to evade, if he wished to expound literature in the spirit of past Christian ages.

Significantly, he came to make his decision, in a sense, on literary grounds. His insistence that as a firm priority one must experience a work of literature to its fullest before attempting to interpret and theorize, could be seen as a natural result of his immersion in the great Nordic, Celtic, and classical myths that enthralled his childhood reveries. But how could one get closer to these experiences, actualize them? There was Arthur Rackham to inspire one's visualization, Wagner's operas to appreciate the response in musical terms, walks among the Irish hills and bog lands to appreciate the landscapes whence such legends emerged.

Nonetheless, there was always the frustrating, and yet in some way delightful, and perhaps, on a deeper level, an essential "yawning gap" between the myth, elusive as a rainbow or sunset, and its fervid admirers. The dream, it would seem, would paradoxically have to be impossible, the quest unending, if it was to inspire the profound yearning for a fulfillment that could exist only in the imagination.

So when Tolkien and Dyson started to convince Lewis that the mythic world he loved and yearned for had in cold sober fact been actualized, and indeed was still being celebrated and reenacted in every humdrum Christian congregation in commonplace parish churches and dissenting chapels, his initial response was predictably unenthusiastic. Could the yearning for the "visionary gleam" be truly assuaged and fulfilled by simple attendance at services in the college chapel or parish church? Finally, the arguments evidently seemed incontrovertible, and, however unwillingly, Lewis capitulated.

Lewis's literary and metaphysical quests had thus inevitably converged, and, in this sense I believe, the critics who condemned his writings on religion as an unprofessional distraction missed out. Personal motivations and commitments must unavoidably impel all serious investigations of the arts. The only question is whether one should be conscious of one's motivations and clarify them.

Once Lewis had committed himself to this course, it is easy to understand the second persistent criticism one heard from fellow undergraduates: "Well, you know the thing is, what people say is, Lewis writes about Christianity as if he invented it." Like the objection to his presuming to write in defense of religion, on further thought the comment turned out to be more of a compliment. If experience should precede analysis, as Lewis always insisted, then the interpretations will proceed from what will sound like living experience rather than academic discourse. All this was reinforced by Lewis's freedom from chronological prejudice, his refusal to assume that people of past ages are necessarily less smart or perceptive than ourselves.

Through the Cherwell Gates: Mystical Religion

Lewis's conversion experience was to be dramatically reenacted in my own life, but there were first some hurdles to be overcome. I sat for the exams for both the Civil and the Foreign Service, did well enough to be invited to country-house weekends by their respective interviewers, and was turned down for both. I was somewhat surprised at the time, since I felt pretty confident of success, given that I had employed the same fairly forceful assertiveness that had proven so successful in the War Office Selection Board weekend for officer status five years earlier. I am mildly but permanently grateful for the discretion of the examiners in turning me down.[12] As a bureaucrat I could see myself disrupting my department's programs with proposals for projects that would probably have been premature or impracticable.

Instead, I accepted an offer of a scholarship to study German Literature in Bonn after graduation, but characteristically I got myself diverted by an odd occurrence. One day while I was having tea in my rooms, there was a knock at the door and I found standing in the doorway a tall, gaunt foreign-looking man who introduced himself with the words "I want you to teach my students in Finland." Well, I accepted this improbable proposition. The actual position was one that I had previously hesitated to apply for, thinking myself under-qualified for any such university teaching post — at a salary, moreover, quite above my expectations. Anyway, I was soon off to Finland, not uninfluenced, I suppose, by the pictures of the marvelous-looking Finnish students he showed me.

I enjoyed life in Helsingfors immensely, as well as teaching at the College of Economics and the university. And I found time to think over some unsettled issues. One decision I came to was to take up as my research the mysteries of medieval dream visions. Yes, perhaps Lewis's favorite subject, certainly the subject of his greatest book, *The Allegory of Love*. How come, one wondered, that for so many centuries the peak form of art, literature, and even architecture seemed to have as its object the recapturing of an experience of a paradise that hopelessly exceeded anything conceivable in the waking world? Lewis himself apart, no one at that time seemed very conscious of even the question, let alone any answer.

At the same time there came into my life, as the friend of a friend, Maj-Britt Kuber, who even at the age of eighteen seemed herself a miraculous being, beyond all expectations of this world, as indeed she still does today, in her seventies. As if a Dante had actually been able to marry his Beatrice. Over the years we had four wonderful children.

But there was also time in all of this to turn to the question that had exercised the minds, if not the emotions, of my Oxford friends: this question of God's existence. He had seemed so easily dismissible by Mel and by our set at Magdalen, but how about all these people of massive intellect in all ages who seemed to find His existence beyond all question? How come Dante, Chaucer, Milton, Wordsworth had all, in their different ways, fallen for the same illusion?

One day I quite suddenly saw a way of cutting through the whole question permanently and freeing my mind for more interesting speculations and worthier endeavors. If God exists and, as the religious claim, has the slightest interest in us diminutive individuals in an unimaginably vast cosmos, then why should I have to bother with him, since his Omnipotence is obviously capable of contacting me at any time he wants? So, if God is interested in me as an individual, he can contact me. I was not going to waste time and energy looking for him anymore. In the meantime, there were plenty of other things to get on with. Admittedly, I was aware that pious monks and hermits secluded for many years in remote monasteries or desert fastnesses had reported strange experiences of realities beyond everyday consciousness. Since I had not the slightest intention of putting the existence of God to any such test, I felt perfectly confident that I would not be bothered by any such mystical experiences disturbing my absorbing professional and social life in Helsingfors.

My new god-free state, however, did not last beyond a couple of days. In the predawn hours of the second night following this seeming final solution to the God question, I found myself in a real medieval-style dream vision so intense that I was only able to sustain it for a few moments. The setting was the Magdalen College Watermeadows, which were transformed in a kind of Life-after-Life vision into a desert paradise blazing with such intolerable light and joy that I had to quit the place after three or four timeless seconds.[13]

Would the *deus absconditus* care to manifest himself, should he feel up to it? It was quite a challenge. Well, this visionary experience obviously and indisputably constituted an overwhelming response to my impudent demand. Four seconds of transcendence. Beyond that, of course, it raised questions about the nature of reality that would take a lifetime to ponder. I could hardly feel any more doubts about the existence of a reality superior to our own, and in some way containing and embracing it. Call it God if that's your favored monosyllable. But in no way did I feel committed—or uncommitted—to anything like a sectarian religious belief. I had simply experienced a paradisal place, a place that exists in more intense reality than our own. And I knew this with more confidence than I could believe in anything presenting itself as normal life.

That frivolous statement I made to the *Isis* magazine had turned into a real-life prophecy. I could believe, in fact now had no other choice than to believe, in a religion founded on mystical experience, whatever that might mean.

It seemed essential to contact Lewis. The immediate motivation was as a kind of response to *The Allegory of Love*, which had already motivated me to set out myself in quest of the medieval dream landscapes he had written about so brilliantly. Lewis surely would understand the kind of experience I had just been through.

Beyond this, it took me many years to realize how closely and mysteriously he was involved in this strange event. It was not just a matter of my vision experience initiating itself outside the windows of his tutorial rooms in the New Buildings. There was that gateway and bridge over the Cherwell I crossed to reach those transformed Magdalen meadowlands. Lewis must have entered through that gate and crossed that same bridge on 17 September 1931[14] at the start of that momentous nightlong peripatetic debate with Tolkien and Dyson on the validity of the Christian religion. As he described it in his letters to Greeves,[15] this was the momentous discussion that ended with Lewis admitting the contention that in the incarnation of Christ, myth becomes history. It was this realization, it seems, that finally enabled him to comprehend and accept the mystifying notion that Christ's sacrifice on the cross in some arcane fashion does atone for the failures of humanity, collectively and individually. This was, it seemed, the crucial incident, or "defeat" as he put it, in Lewis's long personal and intellectual struggle against conversion to Christianity.

Is Magdalen College a locale particularly conducive to such experiences? Glancing through a tutorial paper I wrote back in 1951 on Chaucer's version of *The Romance of the Rose*, I find the words:

> But as we look around our College today and see the ordered flowerbeds and lawns "right even and squar in compassing, the hye and grete trees, the deer, the conies, and the squirrels ful greet plentee," we can realize something of the beauty and power of the medieval conception of the garden within.

It would seem that some three years before my actual adventure in those paradisally transformed watermeadows, I had become open to the potentiality of the Magdalen landscape as providing a stimulus and a setting for inner experience.

Surprised and pleased by hitting on this prevenient insight, I found other anticipations of my vision experience in this essay on medieval dream visions. It had seemed to me that the dream form is significant as a step on the way to achieving a sense of remoteness. But it is noticeable that the dream is never considered sufficient in itself for this; there is always a second stage of inner remoteness, in the *Romaunt* represented by the walled garden with its gate guarded by Oiseuse; in Chaucer's *Parliament of Fowls* the dreamer has to pass through the gates of a "park, walled with green stone."

Once the dreamer enters the park, in these vision poems, he is almost overcome with the paradisal joyousness of the place. But, I wrote,

> where the nineteenth century romantics wanted to escape to the wild perimeter lands of history and geography, and today romanticism looks to outer space for sanctuary, ... the medievals sought to escape inside, into civilization ... natural enough at a time when castle and petty court are ... islands of civilization in a sea of barbarism.

I cite these early musings on medieval visions since they anticipate to an extraordinary degree my actual experience. In the vision itself I too entered through the high wrought-iron gates and found the Magdalen watermeadows transformed into that limitless park-like plain, blazing with extraordinary light, bounded only by distant mountains. This paradise was in one significant sense the very reverse of the secluded, walled-in paradises of Guillaume de Lorris, Chaucer, and so many other medieval poets and artists, and indeed the very architects responsible for Magdalen itself. What I find interesting here is that while I had not at that time read Lewis's *The Great Divorce* (having assumed the title related to some boringly sensational divorce between socially important people!) my dream experience had some interesting parallels with Lewis's (presumably quite fictional) vision.[16] Nor, for that matter, had I at that time read the Narnian paradise described in *The Last Battle*, not published until 1956.

The landscapes in each vision had some remarkable similarities—and differences. Both stretched out in unlimited vistas and offered vast spaces for exploration for those spiritually strong enough to penetrate into the interior beyond its portals, "further up and further in" to use the Narnian expression. In the evolution of landscape psychology you could call them unbounded, neo-romantic paradises. Such an ascent was, of course, something quite beyond the powers of the still very earthbound Lewis as dreamer-author in *The Great*

Divorce. My capacity to withstand "the weight of glory" in my own dream experience was even more limited, though in both instances there were other souls who were able to travel onwards joyously into the brightness and the glory.

The Missing Mentor

But there was also one significant difference. Lewis's paradisal landscape had been graced by the presence of an authority figure, George MacDonald, who had descended the celestial mountains in order to explicate to him the mysteries of the place and the spiritual principles it manifested. So much of Lewis's detail is brilliantly inventive, the bus from Hell to Paradise, the grass which resists the feet of the ghosts, but there is hardly anything more traditional than the presence of a guide and mentor in the paradisal land. Aeneas had his own father, Anchises, as mentor in Elysium, Dante had his Virgil, Chaucer a host of mentors in his dream visions, and Aslan himself was the guide and explicator of Aslan's Country in Lewis's *The Last Battle*.

So where was my missing mentor? A significant nonappearance, as in "Why did the dog not bark in the night?"[17] Possibly. Of course my contract with the obscure "nonexistent" Being had stipulated a religion based on mystical experience alone. And that is precisely what I had got. To the Hindus is attributed the saying, "God, in his infinite courtesy, manifests himself to his devotees in the form most conducive to their spiritual advancement." Maybe. But now, given the experience itself, devoid of the slightest interpretation, I instinctively started a search for the missing sage.

So this was the time when surely my personal connection with the author of *The Allegory of Love* must bear some fruit. And this is what I wrote:

[Transcript reconstructed from rough copy.]

Sep 28, 1953.
Dear Mr Lewis,
  May I thank you again for the lunch and the talk last July?

My investigation into Dream Gardens has taken on a turn which I think can never before have overtaken a research student.

Please do not suspect I am bursting into fiction. The account is truth as plain as I can make it.

I found the garden on Saturday 26th September, in as strange and potent sense as might be imagined. I have now managed to reduce the experience into a reasonably concise account, which I hope you may find of interest.

At all events you are certainly the only person who can give me much guidance on this.

Yours sincerely,
Paul Piehler

This is the account of the Magdalen Vision that I sent to Lewis in September 1953, verbatim except that for some reason I omitted the fact that the setting of the dream was an area within the college with which we were both very familiar. The importance of the setting only dawned on me later. I shall supply particulars of the setting within square brackets:

I in a dream, an early morning dream; rather vivid as these early morning dreams can be. [I was standing on one of the great lawns that front the New Buildings, the lawns, in fact that I had crossed each time on my way to Lewis's rooms up that marvelous old twisting oak wood staircase to read my weekly essay. These were the lawns that one saw from the high south facing windows of the extensive room where his tutorials were held. Not that Lewis was on my mind in the dream. I dreamed that as I faced towards the Buildings, I was confronted by three men who manifested an air of formal, and quite aggressive, hostility.]

I was standing in a diamond shaped group of figures: like thise:

x Young Man

YM's Ally   xx Fat Man

x Myself

I am pretty sure these 4 represented 4 attributes of the soul. But they are not really so interesting yet so I shall not say much about them. Sufficient to say that we were at enmity. We all had revolvers and I was pretty sure that shooting was going to break out. I was trying to pacify the Young Man who was rather puritanical and [was] furious with the Fat Man, a sensual figure. The young man's chief annoyance was now however directed at me for condoning and defending the Fat Man. At this point, rather to my surprise, the Young Man's ally, hitherto a rather shadowy figure, stepped smartly up to me and shot me through the neck. I realized I was done for. I was filled with a desire to execute some wild justice before I went down.

I shot the ally twice through the head. I took a shot at the gross man, but probably missed. At this point he anyway seemed less important. I hesitate over shooting the young man, and I feel relieved when I find myself unable — too weak — to press the trigger. As I lose consciousness I see his face elongating like some Easter Island statue. I fire three shots into the air to summon whatever authorities deal with such affairs.

There is a moment of unconsciousness, then I find myself once more standing in the same place [on the New Buildings lawn,] but facing the other direction [east towards the Cherwell Gates and the watermeadows]. The three others are standing around me in a loose group. We feel ourselves friends. It is as if a play had ended. One, I think it is the Young Man, says "You know, we must be quite close to the Great Cole Mountains here." [He has now taken the lead, which we all seem ready to accept.]

I look up. [The New Buildings, the lawns and trees retain their normal earthly beauty, as do the tall wrought-iron gates that guard the bridge over the Cherwell, just as in the waking life, but over the other side of the brook the tranquil Magdalen watermeadows, where cattle graze under the great oaks, everything is transformed.] We seem to be in some tropical region. As I look I realize that this is a land different from anything else I have ever seen before. We are quite close to a range of steep, dark-rocked mountains that rise almost sheer from the plain below. The plain itself is bathed in a warm golden light of dazzling brightness. From its shimmering sands rise luxuriant shrubs and tall trees.

All places on earth have their atmosphere, weaker or stronger, imagine a place whose atmosphere is too strong to be endurable. Instinctively and unquestioningly we walk forward into the scene [eastwards over the lawns and through the high Cherwell gateway]. But as we cross the little bridge, and walk forward into this marvelous desert I find myself undergoing a strange transformation. We are swept with nostalgia and longing, filled with a great sense of companionship for each other: the garden draws us in to its unutterable glory and peace. As we walk forward among the glades and tall trees the pressure becomes stronger and stronger, great waves roll over us of glory and love and joy, joy beyond all imagining or conception; my blood soared and pounded. The joy burned too fiercely. I was too weak to endure it.

At this moment all things were clear. "Good-bye, my friends," I call, — if my voice was not already lost to them. At the same I pushed the ground away from beneath my feet, [launched myself effortlessly into the air, surged upward and forward] and cleaved the air with great strokes of my arms. The Garden swung away below me and I made my way back to my bed as easily and confidently as if I had come in from the next room. The pale shadows of earthly life received me....

This account prompted the following reply from Lewis.

Magdalen College
Oxford
14/xi/53
Dear Piehler,
 You were not mistaken that I would enjoy your dream.

The odd thing about your account is that the words "The garden draws us" etc come as a complete surprise for you have not, till then, mentioned a garden at all. On the contrary the Plain has been described as "shimmering sands" and if a desert is not the opposite of a garden, what is? If this is intentional it renders the dream quality pretty well. Looks to me like a dream wh. is emotionally about the garden but momentarily painted over by the desert image of the Hous of Fame. I am no Daniel to interpret dreams. I even doubt if we don't feed on them best when we don't interpret them. Possibly in passing from the three figures you met (yourself fourth in the quincunx) to "attributes of the soul" one is passing from the more real to the less real? To me what a dream really reveals is the quality, the mere taste of its experience: the soul "remembering how she felt, but what she felt Remembering not."

"God tourne us every dreme to gode"![18] This is clearly a good one.

Yours,
C. S. Lewis.

My search for an instant interpreter for the dream had come to an abrupt halt. In the first place, my description of the dream had evidently missed the mark. By failing to clarify that the dream was pegged down so specifically to the Magdalen College grounds, and by making clear that what I saw on the other side of the Cherwell Bridge was a very specific landscape, a desert garden (in appearance not at all unlike those marvelous deserts around Tucson, as I learned years later), I failed to convey how solid and stable the vision was, so much so that I can replay the whole sequence through in my mind these many years later. Thus, I could hardly agree that this dream revealed merely the "quality, the mere taste of its experience," and I had, and still have, not the slightest difficulty in remembering the "what" of the dream. Lewis was right, in a sense, that "the attributes of the soul" were less substantial than the actual figures, and I am not fully convinced that every person one meets in a dream must represent a "soul fragment," as some experts have claimed.[19] Nonetheless, the three other members of our party were able to pass further and further into the lovefire without the slightest hesitation or break of pace, and I still feel that some hidden part of me remains in that blazing landscape. In fact, I find it quite difficult even now to narrate this story aloud to a sympathetic audience, since the narration plunges me back so deeply into that experience of fifty years ago that I am liable to be reduced to emotional incoherence. More than a tad humiliating but also interesting evidence that such experiences are hardly under the control of one's ego and imply no merit on the part of the recipient.

Finally, it struck me that if Lewis's dictum that dreams should be felt rather than interpreted was no obiter dictum but a well-considered position, there should be indications of this elsewhere in his writings. So I searched out one of his finest pieces, *The Weight of Glory* (Walter Hooper confidently ranks it as worthy of the great works of the patristic era). There I reread that wonderful passage where he describes himself as catching glimpses of what lies beyond the natural world and yet feeling excluded from the glory that underlies the beauties of mountain, ocean, or sunset. Significantly, I believe, he never refers either here or elsewhere to the evidence of the visionary experiences that had been for many years the subjects of his study when he was writing *The Allegory of Love*. In this, I felt my experience was entirely in the tradition of the medieval visions discussed in Lewis's great book on dream allegory, as well as his other writings on medieval literature. Was this a challenge I could meet?

Medieval Dreamers—or Visionaries?

If Lewis's letter was not going to give me the key to this dream vision, then it was clearly something that this graduate student was intended to tackle for himself, an appropriate responsibility for someone who had rejected spiritual and religious authority. So I pursued the quest of landscape mysteries with renewed zest and with greatly personal interest.

An early discovery was the fourteenth-century vision poem of *The Pearl*, arguably the most powerful religious poem in our language, perhaps in any language. (This work had been omitted from the Oxford syllabus, an error I have never been tempted to repeat in my own syllabi of medieval literature.) I felt a strange tremor of recognition when I read that the visionary poet, once he entered the paradisal place, the *locus amoenus*, had had a remarkably similar experience to my own. In quite untypical fashion for a medieval poem, the paradisal woodlands were bounded by distant mountains rather than a cozy enclosing wall. With a strange tremor of recognition I read that the further he trod into that paradisal land, the more over-powering "the strength of joy." His progress, though far beyond mine, was stopped by a stream, which, as he is informed by his brilliant, marvelous mentor, the Pearl Maiden, he may not cross. Finally, in his attempt to be reunited with her before the time of his earthly summoning to that Paradise over the stream, he attempts to leap over it and is puffed back to earth again, much as I was. Like myself, he has no regrets; it is sufficient that such a place exists. He is sure that his marvelous experience has amounted to a *veray avisioun*, a significant dream (l.1185).

One other discovery enhanced my conviction that I was on the right track in seeing the connection between my particular experience and the medieval visions. I felt an odd kinship with John Lydgate when, in the concluding lines of his *The Assembly of the Gods*[20] (early fifteenth century) he gives us some idea of the thought processes that inspire the creation of a dream allegory. When he woke up from his vision, he tells us, his body was shaking in fear from the sight he had seen, since he believed at first that it had all been true. Then after a while he began to feel it had just been "a fantasy & a thing of nought" and decided to ignore the whole matter. Then he changed his mind again and decided that since he could not really understand why he had been shown this vision, he ought to put the whole thing into writing; otherwise, he might well be accused of sloth, even though finally he could not be certain whether or not he had seen the vision with his own bodily eyes. What he seems to be saying is that if there is any chance that his vision was a valid one, he had a duty to give it to the world, whatever his doubts.

Lydgate, as a follower of Chaucer, inherited little or none of Chaucer's subtlety, or sophistication, and even his powers of exposition are pretty shaky, as the above passage would indicate. But he has a beguiling honesty about himself and his work, and there's little doubt that his *Assembly* is based on an actual dream. His conclusion, awkward as it is, seems the very reverse of a literary ploy.

Increasingly convinced by the evidence of Lydgate's *Assembly* and of the anonymous Pearl vision that what I had experienced had been a *veray avisioun*, a significant vision and not just an idle dream,[21] I now felt ready to tackle more seriously Lewis's *The Allegory of Love*, his masterly account of the great secular visions of the Middle Ages. Right away I found another clue to his attitude towards medieval vision-literature. In Lewis's view: "There is nothing 'mystical' or mysterious about medieval allegory; the poets know quite clearly what they are about and are well aware that the figures they represent to us are fictions."[22]

So the issue essentially is whether these visions are simply constructed fictions, or whether to some extent they were based on real experiences. During the Middle Ages, at least, it seems that the poets themselves and their readers considered them as essentially real. Of course, it might be asked how one could dream anything so long and complex as Dante's *Divine Comedy*. The question, in my view, is rather how much of the poem would be based on an original vision experience, and how much on imaginative extrapolation of the experience. It is also possible that the actual development of an original vision could have taken place in a state intermediate between dreaming and waking, an experience I have had myself at times.[23]

As my research continued, I found one other significant link between my vision of the desert paradise and medieval visions. Almost without exception they build up from what I designated, for want of any generally accepted term, a *"seminal image."* Such images strike the visionary's mind in a state of heightened tension and take the form of a visual image, a personification, concept, or proverbial saying. It appears first in a casual, static form, previous to entry into the vision state and then is revealed both as the stimulus for the visionary experience itself and as the foundation image or idea on which the experience is finally based.[24] I felt confident that my response to the student questionnaire in *Isis* that I could believe in a religion based on mystical experience had acted as a pretty potent and challenging seminal concept that finally got itself triggered off by my idle if not frivolous invitation to the Almighty to reveal himself to me.

Nonetheless, I was pleased to note that Lewis did not maintain his view of allegory as a consciously contrived fiction with any great consistency. Speaking of the great thirteenth-century French allegory of the "courtly love," *The Romance of the Rose*, he warns us not to be misled by modern allegory into believing that "we are retreating from the real world into the shadowy world of abstractions."[25]

This seemed an important insight, well worth pursuing further. What really were these mysterious "deep springs" that underlay and inspired the surface narrative? I found one useful clue in J. S. Lincoln's anthropological study, *The Dream in Primitive Culture*.[26] Lincoln reported that the content and imagery of dreams follow rather precisely the rituals and imagery in which our early ancestors clothed their beliefs. One function of their cults seems to be that of providing clear and consistent imagery for their dreaming, in fact spirit guides or maps to the dreamtime. But the more I read of medieval vision poetry, the more I was convinced that Lincoln's findings also applied to my own. The inherited belief-images of one's own culture, the great archetypes of our spiritual life, make possible the comprehension of the vision worlds that define and shape the lineaments of our collective consciousness.

Well, all these thoughts finally found their way into a book, *The Visionary Landscape*. It was not published until 1971, sadly too late for its originally intended role as a response to Lewis for the enormous debt I owed to him for his tutoring and his friendship. But it was the subject of a very full review by Lewis's great friend, Owen Barfield, to whom I had been introduced by Lewis while I was still an undergraduate at Magdalen. Indeed, the book was inspired as to content by Lewis, but the approach owed more to Barfield, who seemed to me to bridge in a quite convincing manner that gulf between spiritual and professional life that characterized Lewis's work in his earlier years.[27] The book thus solidified my already active friendship with Owen, a friendship that stayed vital right through to his passing in his late nineties.

I Encounter the Positivists—and Screwtape

If the experience of "The Cherwell Gates" provided me with a deep and consistent—and perhaps necessary—incentive to pursue research into medieval dream visions, it also stimulated me to explore Lewis's and Barfield's arguments against atheism. I was particularly struck by Lewis's point that skeptical materialists never seemed to be able to take in the awkward fact that their denial of the possibility of objective truth cut away the validity, or objective truth, of their denial itself.

I experienced a curious and bizarre confirmation of Lewis's point when I was a junior instructor teaching English at Dartmouth College (New Hampshire) in the year 1960–61. The provost had summoned us to a faculty debate to consider the argument that, in the light of the then dominant logical positivism, assertion of the existence of God is a meaningless proposition. If a statement is to have any meaning, it was claimed, it must in principle be objectively verifiable—a proposition supported unanimously by the philosophy department. The college chaplain doughtily asserted God's existence, but since he accepted the basic positivist position that metaphysical statements are meaningless, the trio of young philosophers were able to run rings round his arguments, until he was finally reduced to silence. The provost, chairing the debate, called for further questions or points, an appeal which elicited no response, and I realized that we were in danger of ending the debate without anyone attempting any real challenge to the positivists.

So I thought it was time to raise at least one Lewisian objection and enquired, with all the boldness I could muster: "Is not the fundamental positivist principle 'that metaphysical statements are meaningless' itself a metaphysical statement? It is obviously a principle that is itself obviously incapable of scientific verification. Is it not therefore meaningless?"

To my great surprise, there was no response from the philosophers to what I assumed would be a most elementary and easily refuted objection. "I'm no professional in this field," I continued, "but I had been given to understand that the classic weakness of logical positivism is that it short-circuits itself by this basic contradiction. The sense data which the sage scientist relies on to verify his statements is itself surely meaningless without what is normally referred to as a theory, or, in other words a metaphysical structure, to give it significance. It's only through nonverifiable, or 'metaphysical' assumptions that data ceases to be merely noise and can acquire meaning. In other words, if logical positivism was an electrical appliance, it would short-circuit itself every time you plugged it in."

There was again silence. The dean looked puzzled. "Well, if no one wishes to reply to Mr. Piehler's objections, I declare the debate over." I never heard from the philosophers. I assume they had been brought up as positivists and had never had the privilege of studying somewhere where philosophy students are exposed to rational debate. It seemed that they had simply been instructed in the orthodox positive doctrines, passed their exams, been awarded degrees, and absorbed into the system.

Unfortunately, my vision of the paradise in the Magdalen meadows had far less immediate effect on my spiritual life. A. N. Wilson, in his *C. S. Lewis: A Biography*, has some perceptive remarks on such conversion experiences:

> Since Lewis was to go on to become a faithful and devoted Christian, he writes rather as if the "conversion" were a *fait accompli*, after which nothing would be the same. But men have had such experiences and done nothing further about them ... because they could not endure the ethical and spiritual demands which were implied in the unspoken, ineffable moment of divine knowledge.[28]

I fell between these extremities, falling back, that is, into a kind of off-and-on allegiance to the Anglican churches in which I had been brought up. I had also over the years that followed participated in enough Zen, Vedanta, and Jewish spiritual practice to regard Christianity as just one among many viable modes of religious expression. In terms of my actual moral condition, however, I was somewhat in the state of an ancient Roman polytheist, giving ritual and intellectual respect to Jove as the chief god but being quite fair game for any other god whose influences came my way, whether Mars for Irritation and

Anger, Venus for Lust, or Juno, Queen of the Gods, Respectability and Career, etc., etc. . . .

Eventually, it did not work for the Romans, and by October 1976 it was no longer working for me. At that time I was living with wife and family in Montreal, enjoying my tenured status on the McGill faculty. But at home, my easy "situation ethics" type polytheism had provoked a marital crisis, and we were getting little spiritual sustenance from our local church. Where could we get some help? Maj-Britt decided to attend a diocesan retreat for women coming up, at which she found out what was happening at various churches in the diocese. The week after, armed with a list of possible churches, we decided to eliminate the most distant one first and found ourselves the next Sunday at St. Barnabas, Pierrefonds. We were initially disappointed to hear the rector was away that week, but when the assistant rector, Tom de Hoop, mounted the pulpit to announce, "Today we're going to talk about forgiveness," we knew we had come to the right place. It turned out that St. Barnabas was at the height of a charismatic renewal, and that it was hardly possible to leave after the service without acquiring a book or two about this amazing new movement. That afternoon I picked up the book we had bought with the thought I ought to read at least a paragraph or two, if only out of politeness, and found myself joyfully engulfed in Colin Urquhart's *When the Spirit Comes.*[29] It turned out to be a life-changing experience.

During the next few months we spent more and more of our time at St. Barnabas, our experiences culminating in an intensive Holy Week "seminar" on the Holy Spirit, at the conclusion of which we underwent a charismatic "laying on of hands"—perhaps a more powerful rite than I realized at the time. Our Easter Sunday dinner featured for dessert Maj-Britt's special almond torte, a great family favorite. I remember grabbing the last piece of the torte and feeling a tad greedy and selfish as I did so.

That night I was hit with what started as an extremely vivid nightmare. I was in a barely furnished upper room, with windows looking out on the street. There was a television set which seemed to be just between programs, and as I watched to see what was coming on, I heard the words "Our next program will be a horror film." Not caring for such things, I grabbed the remote control and switched channels, but the next channel was showing the same program, and the next, and the next. Now quite uneasy, I clicked the off button, but the TV and its horror program were unresponsive, so with increasing apprehension I reached over to the back of the set and pulled the plug out of the wall … once more, no response. The film continued, depicting ever more horrible scenes. Nauseated and appalled, I turned away from the TV and looked out of the window to escape the horrors. But there in the street I saw the same diabolic faces enacting the same drama that was being shown on the screen. Pulling myself together, I summoned up my newfound piety and made the sign of the cross directly at the screen. The TV blew like a bomb, shattered glass blasting round the room. The explosion hurtled me out of the dream and I found myself awake in bed lying flat upon my back.

I had not awoken into any ordinary reality. Rather I was in a strange catatonic state, shaking from the horror of what I had seen. Finally my mind started to function again. I started thinking about asking for God's help, but in spite of groping towards some devout thoughts, I remained locked firmly into this state of complete horror. Finally, with enormous effort of will, I mentally blurted out, "Jesus, help!" Immediately, a warm tremor struck powerfully through my body from head to toe. It was a sensation unlike anything I had ever felt before, and quite beyond conscious control. As the feeling ebbed away, it left me still deep in the grip of the nightmare, but now I felt the beginnings of hope and reassurance. I continued to pray these terse prayers for help and found each prayer brought this responsive wave of healing love. With each wave I felt stronger as my catatonic state began to be alleviated. Nonetheless, the shock of this demonic encounter had been so powerful that I soon realized that it was going to take quite awhile for this catatonic paralysis to be completely washed out of my body. No matter, since the therapy of these "shockwaves of love" was turning out to be an increasingly wondrous and blissful experience.

After a while I began to notice that these healing waves would vary quite markedly in intensity, the strength of the wave seeming to depend in some way on the strength and the content of the prayers. Though none of the prayers were completely without response from whatever, or wherever, was the source of this amazing spiritual therapy, yet the differentiation of response seemed to grow more and more pronounced. Prayers that were no more than repetitions or variations on earlier prayers seemed to draw progressively less powerful responses.

At this point I realized that I had a unique opportunity to test out, as it were, the power and appropriateness of our prayers, and I started to pray the Lord's Prayer. At once the shockwaves redoubled in intensity and became what I can only describe as "thunderbolts of love." Then my whole body started shaking all over, as the astonishing realization came to me that it could hardly be anyone but Jesus who was responding so directly to the prayer he had enunciated to us two thousand years ago. Impossible, absolutely impossible, and yet why not, why not? So my prayer continued on through the answering thunderbolts to its dizzying climax in "the power and glory," and at that moment I realized that the paralysis of terror had been totally washed out of my system, and my rescue was complete.

But marvelous to report, my prayers were still being powerfully and instantly responded to by these shockwaves of love, and so it struck me that I should pray in terms of the most powerful—and controversial—gospel revelations I could think of. So I invoked my mysterious Respondent in the words "By Thy Holy Crucifixion" and "By Thy Glorious Resurrection" and received the greatest, most thundering love waves of all in response to these invocations. And so I came to realize that those most central events in human history, climactic events that I had previously accepted on faith, were now being directly confirmed through this experience, beyond all shadows of doubt or skepticism. By going through Hell, pretty literally, I had found what had been missing from the vision of "The Cherwell Gates," the host of my visionary experience, the missing mentor who was Christ. Thus I encountered a closer, more intimate friend than any conception I had ever had of Christ as presented to me in text or liturgy.

I felt no need to sleep. I continued to pray and receive the responses. But now, by some mysterious shift, the responses became so sensitively attuned to my prayers that I seemed to be in direct dialogue with the source of these shockwaves of love. I remember asking questions and being deeply, blissfully satisfied with the answers. It is probably just as well that I do not remember the specific details of the dialogue. And I am pretty sure the answers were not exactly in verbal form. The one thing I do remember is that I tried asking Him about an issue that seemed very important to a lot of us Anglicans at that time (the debate over women priests), and the response came through as "Do we really want to spend our time right now on issues like that one?" And I sensed a kindly, if slightly wry, smile behind the mind-words.

One essential part of the therapy seemed to be that somehow the figures I had seen on that TV screen had become completely blotted out of my memory. Without that merciful intervention I should have, it seems, been left in the horrifying state of having caught a glimpse of one of those creatures of the "miserific vision" who, as Lewis described them, make the other discomforts of hell relatively endurable.

On reflection, I realized that I had once more stumbled into an actual experience on which Lewis had based a literary work. And, as he said, it is only people who are committed believers who are likely to suffer the direct and open Screwtape attack. Assuming the personal kind of devil that Lewis wrote about in *Screwtape*, the strategy would surely be only to appear to those who already accept the truths of the spiritual life. There was no point in them terrifying skeptics into a belief in God. Leave that to the hellfire preachers.

In the last part of the night, I reflected on what I had learned about prayer through this experience. What came to me was a story.

～⊱⊰～

The coast of a tranquil country in a peaceful part of the world had once been protected by a battery of powerful artillery. Though there seemed not to be the slightest chance of them ever being called into action, the peacetime volunteers who manned this ancient battery patiently went through their regular drills of loading, aiming, and "firing" their weapons at hypothetical targets far out at sea. But since they never used anything but dummy shells, the "firing" of the guns never produced anything more than a loud and heavy click. Their drills did, however, impress visitors and tourists, who were, according to the skeptics, the main reason that the battery had not been closed down years before.

Then one day, suddenly, out of nowhere, something quite extraordinary happened. Early one morning, as the sentries conscientiously scanned the horizon, they observed a large and menacing fleet of black warships heading straight for the bay and the little port nearby that the battery had originally been intended to defend. Sirens from the port started to whoop out a warning. The eager young volunteers tumbled out of their bunks. But what could a tourist attraction do to protect them against this fearful menace? No one seemed to know. But then the cry went up: Quickly, send for Jack! Jack was a grizzled old sergeant who went back to goodness knows when, now retired but living in a cliff-side cottage just a short way up the hill. Jack soon came panting in. "Sorry, fellas, should'a told you about the special key. Opens those old storeroom lockers three flights down. There's still some real ammo down there, s'far as I know." So they hurtle down the spiral staircase, brushing aside the cobwebs—smart young Peter has W40 ready for the aging lock, and soon they're in the ammunition store, gaping in astonishment at rack upon rack piled high with gleaming shells. "Right, lads, get that hoist going, and we'll show those pirates the way home all right."

And so a few minutes later the guns are being trained on the rapidly advancing black fleet, the skull-and-bone figureheads gleaming menacingly in the early morning sunlight. "Okay, lads, fasten those sound blockers over your ears real tight; you're going to hear a crash like nothing you've ever heard in your life before." And indeed a few seconds later the turret shakes with a roar as earsplitting as if you were hurling the thunder yourself. And as they watch in amazement, the lead pirate ship disintegrates in a blast of smoke and flame that echoes round the bay and breaks windows in the town hall.

❦

Well, that is the waking vision that came to me as the night lightened into dawn. Some Christians understandably do not care for battle imagery. Or one could say that the real use of wars and battles is to provide images for the ongoing *bellum intestinum, la guerra si del camino*, as Dante put it, the wars of our inner pilgrimage.

Do I now "believe" in Screwtape and his operatives? Well, seeing is believing, so I have to believe in them as spiritual entities. But do they affect us in the way *The Screwtape Letters* describe? I have found that it is a possible and at times rather effective model for describing what goes on in my flow of thoughts and impulses, and particularly in those moments when I feel a strong temptation to allow myself to lapse into some situation which would be highly contrary to one's best spiritual or earthly interests. In this sense, I have found the Screwtape model a highly effective means of raising one's level of awareness of the hidden motivations implied by a surprisingly high proportion of one's thoughts, when one is in certain moods. As in the case of the visionary paradises, stories that seemed at first to be just an entertaining fiction, it turned out that Lewis was, consciously or not, revealing the existence and character of extremely powerful spiritual entities, that in this age had been assumed to be discarded or at least disposable myth.

Columbia College: The Missing Tutorial

After a couple of years teaching in Finland, and a year in a private school in Palm Beach, in 1955 I was happy to find a job teaching freshman English at Columbia College in New York City, and being admitted to the Ph.D. program. The actual conditions of my admission were flatteringly generous. The facts were these. My three years of college education, comprising two hours a week of required classes for nine eight-week terms, had involved me in a grand total of about 150 "contact hours" during my time in Magdalen. (One could also attend lecture courses, but these were neither required, nor graded, nor was there any attendance taken.) So I had taken fewer required classes over three years in Magdalen than a Columbia student would take in one term of the four-year B.A. program.

I was also flattered when Columbia invited me to teach an undergraduate course on medieval comparative literature. Actually, my tutorials at Oxford had covered only English literature of this period, so the notes I took at Lewis's lectures that became the basis of *The*

Discarded Image became a marvelous survival package as I plunged quite happily into these unknown territories.

On any coherent mathematical basis or computation of class hours, Columbia might have felt themselves generous in offering me, say, three years' credit towards my B.A. As it was, however, I was provisionally awarded, right away, the equivalent status of a Columbia B.A., an M.A., and credit for half the work towards the Ph.D. I was also given the option of satisfying the next year's graduate courses by examination, without class attendance. (I actually did this in some courses and did not find any great difficulty in passing them in this fashion, since the standards were on the whole less daunting than for the Oxford B.A. exams.)

Once I started teaching I quickly realized that Columbia College students were just as intelligent as Oxford undergraduates and worked a good deal harder and, of course, for considerably longer hours. It was clear that they were being taught by a faculty who were absolutely world-class. (I was able, for example, to attend a graduate seminar cochaired by Lionel Trilling and Jacques Barzun, surely one of the great intellectual feasts of the century.)

So how on earth did it only take me three years to reach the level that required seven or so years of heavy toil on the part of a Columbia student? I was forced to the conclusion that the "Oxbridge mystique" must imply something beyond the agreeable mélange of ancient buildings, dons' sherry parties, and punting on the river, and can even show up in the guidelines of hardheaded North American university admission offices.

What's the essence of this mystique? First, there really does seem to be some magic in the Oxbridge way of teaching. In the normal system of university teaching all the dramatic weight rests on the lecturer's performance. Over the college years the student principally learns how to be a receptive member of an audience. In the Oxbridge tutorial, on the other hand, it is the student who puts on the performance and the tutor or supervisor who takes over the role of audience.

If we consider the number of courses that a student has to cope with in the course of a term, we find that five is the normal number at a place like Columbia, where an Oxbridge student is unlikely to have more than one serious class each week apart from his tutorial. If you have five courses, it is difficult to take any one of them very seriously, so no one expects the classroom to contain more than say three-quarters of the registered students on any particular day. And even once they are there, the students have no great incentive to achieve the intensity of concentration needed for giving a paper or defending its propositions.

By contrast, look at the Oxbridge demand that one complete the reading for the term before the very first tutorial session. At least the undergraduate has a fair chance of achieving some excellence in his presentation. And it also provides a reasonable guarantee that his or her colleagues are also adequately prepared. In fact, the student has the chance to prepare his tutorials in the same way his senior colleague in this community of scholars would prepare his university lectures. Even in good universities elsewhere, it always proves surprisingly difficult to cajole otherwise quite conscientious students to keep up with the reading of the texts set for class discussion. A massive and quite unnecessary dilution of the educational energies seems irrevocably built into such systems.

This suggests that the brief but remarkably intense periods of concentration demanded of the student in his preparation for and presentation of his paper in his tutorial are of far greater efficacy than the much longer periods of less intense concentration characteristic of other systems.

But the tutorial method is, I think, only one aspect of these Oxbridge mysteries we are attempting to probe. Bernard Shaw once remarked that the only difference between duchesses and cleaning ladies was in the way they were treated. At Oxbridge, we found ourselves treated like social and intellectual aristocrats, little as we might have deserved it. The best tutors seemed to have acquired the habit of talking to students more as if they were colleagues than pupils. Lewis was particularly adept at this. He constantly gave me the impression that he had somehow confused me with some other student of the same name who was really rather good. Naturally, one worked extremely hard to attempt to sustain this illusion.

As a graduate student teaching at Columbia, I was warned by my kindly chairman not to pay too much attention to my students' papers. I must concentrate ruthlessly on my own work for the Ph.D., if I ever wanted to amount to anything in my profession: standard advice, practical and totally correct. But something within me rebelled. How could I treat undergraduates like school kids when I had myself been treated like an adult by Lewis and Bennett? So one term in Columbia I decided to do some serious teaching. Any student, I announced, could rewrite his paper for extra credit — any number of times. The results were spectacular, once these brilliant students understood that their work was being taken seriously. But word got around, and I am sure that if my innovation had spread, the economic and pedagogic life of the department would have soon become impossible.

Columbia College acted with typical tact, generosity, and firmness. They rapidly founded a new Fellowship for deserving pre-Ph.D. instructors and granted one a year off without teaching responsibilities for completion of the Ph.D. dissertation. I was the first to hold it — and I had been saved from myself. In my Fellowship year I managed to complete a dissertation, "Landscape and Dialogue in Medieval Allegory," as well as draft an outline of a further book. But then halfway through the year I happened to find out that my contract as instructor at Columbia College was not going to be renewed. Understandable. Looking back on all this, I am amazed how little I learned from the incident. Essentially, I had decided that, at a pinch, Lewis as a tutor was even more important to me as a model than Lewis as the great authority on medieval visionary experience.

Berkeley: Importing Oxbridge

A couple of years later, in the mid-sixties, I had a junior teaching position on the idyllic campus of the University of California in Berkeley. Walking home through the dependably sunlit streets north of the campus, one became aware of an odd change affecting the lines of parked cars which have become such a taken-for-granted feature of the modern cityscape.

Berkeley was being invaded by the Volkswagen.

Soon one inevitably found oneself playing a game of counting the VWs on the way to campus, giving oneself bonus points for two and then even three VWs parked together. The scores grew higher and higher.

It was, of course, just at this time that the vast system of Clark Kerr's University of California Multiversity was being challenged by a revolt that, though manifesting itself through mass action on the Sproul Plaza, essentially grew out of a new "small-is-beautiful" individualistic ethos.

The trouble started over the tables. Sproul Plaza had been for some years the focal point on campus where independent student groups set up card tables advertising their club meetings and political programs. The chancellor attempted to apply some old, shaky, and tactfully neglected university rules limiting political action on campus, and wanted the tables shifted to a less conspicuous position. Students resisted, and the shock resonated around the world.

The Berkeley revolution was, in its first, world-famous, political phase, resolved quite rapidly. It was, as was said by everyone from the University President Clark Kerr down, the result of a failure in communications. Nonetheless, even after the various parties had begun to understand each other and some specific problems were settled, the campus was shaken by further protests over the next few years. The movement indeed became worldwide. For this, there were several reasons, obscurely related. First, on a superficial level, the heady, dangerous excitement of the confrontation had produced a temporary high which some students found addictive, and some wished to exploit for their own usually radical political purposes.

But more than this the Free Speech Movement, which successfully united a whole range of student protesters, had drawn the whole campus into playing out a highly intense drama, a kind of romantic morality play which was being transmogrified itself into world-class history and political science. One of the most interesting complaints made by the students is that in spite of all the work required of them for their degrees, the total process, embodied in the multifarious, endless learning fragments called courses, finally gave them no sense of any particular meaning. Well, whatever your particular stance on the revolt, it was certainly a meaningful event. And of course there was the sense of being treated not so much unfairly as inhumanly by an inhuman system, notably satirized by the students who paraded around dressed as giant IBM punch cards labeled "Do not fold, staple or mutilate."

All this added up to a sense of alienation far deeper and more widespread than the issues that touched off the initial protests. In view of this, and of the fact that the level of distraction on campus made normal teaching and research seem rather peripheral, I got together with like-minded students and faculty to see if we could tackle, in some fashion, the root causes of the problems in the university. (I had already forgotten the lessons of Columbia.)

With this constantly growing group we set up a campus-wide tutorial program to teach students in a modified version of the Oxbridge style. Essentially, what we were aiming at was a reproduction of Lewis's tutorials at Magdalen, designed in such a fashion that it would cost significantly less than either Oxbridge or North American teaching methods. At the same time, we aimed at sustaining or improving on the rate of progress achievable under the Oxbridge system. This culminated in two experimental summer colleges in residential tutorial fashion, followed by a third such college after I moved to McGill (Montreal) in 1969. We had widespread support on the Berkeley campus and felt we were making our contribution to answering the many problems in the conventional system that were being identified at that time.[30]

The Atlantis Project

Preoccupation with the Berkeley educational crisis delayed by some months the publication of my book on medieval allegory, *The Visionary Landscape*. This delay left me all too vulnerable to the strictures of some largely middle-rank faculty members who, not surprisingly, found attempts to implement such a radical change in teaching methods unacceptable from so junior a person. Fortunately, my new position at McGill offered plenty of chances for good teaching either within or outside a tutorial format. But by the eighties things turned dark once more. With savage cuts in budgets, decline in teaching standards, and the serious overworking of faculty, it seemed time to resurrect the whole project. So I wrote a new manifesto which took account of past experience of such colleges—including past mistakes (in which category I may claim some expertise). And of course I had been struck (some might say "moonstruck") by the notion that we could run the whole thing on palpably less than the conventional system. I expected to get some hard argument here, but no one at the various innovative places I consulted, New College, Sarasota, St. John's, Annapolis, or McGill itself, objected to that part of the argument.

Once I had taken early retirement in 1991 I was able to devote more time to developing these modified Oxbridge tutorials. Supported by grants and a group of interested faculty and students, I made contacts and researched tutorial methods in Oxford and Cambridge and founded what we now called "The Atlantis Project." A few published articles on the project[31] attracted a surprising degree of attention worldwide, from Singapore to New Zealand, and a listserv and a website were set up at McGill.[32] We got a surprisingly friendly reception from the McGill administration, but finally it seemed to me that there was simply not enough time or energy to carry out any changes, however beneficial.

Nonetheless, a considerable number of people experienced this version of Lewis's Oxford tutorials, and still more read about it, so that I feel convinced that one day its superior humanity, as well as its efficiency and economy, will lead to it being more generally adapted.

The Shapes of Chaos

By the late 1990s there seemed little more to be done in McGill, the Montreal winters seemed to be getting colder every year, and it felt like time for a fresh start. We discovered a pretty, little-known town on the Central Atlantic coast of Florida, where we found an affordable beachside condo, and I set up a literary and educational consultancy. So far as the Atlantis Project was concerned, I had come to certain decisions. First, that it had been unproductive to spend time and energy attempting to set up programs in places that were not ready for it administratively and psychologically, however much it may have seemed appealing theoretically to the administrators. Second, my preoccupation with Atlantis had left me far behind with my publishing plans. So I determined, before proceeding further with Atlantis, to bring out in some form or another, a follow-up for *The Visionary Landscape*.

Great works of art and literature, as Lewis remarked, tend to be energized by the great myths that lie latent within them.[33] Those of us not blessed with the *feu sacré* to create such works will nonetheless feel the impulse to pursue the manifestations of the myths in the works others have created. And so while *The Visionary Landscape* was essentially a record of a pursuit of the paradise myth latent in Lewis's own *Allegory of Love*, so my second odyssey pursues the somewhat more elusive myth of the hero's encounter with the wilderness. To plant a field of cabbages may be considered a practical act of self-preservation and economic enhancement. But to plant a rose garden or any other garden, whatever subsidiary social or economic benefits might ensue, is essentially a suprarational response to the urgings of the paradise myth, the impulse to restore Eden, whether by cultivation of the ground or of the imagination. Similarly, one may leave the security and protection of one's community for the outlands and the wilderness in quest of game or mineral rights, but what of this urge, this pursuit of the mythic quest, in order to face the challenges of the wilderness for the sake of the adventures themselves? When we look at these adventures we find they persistently shape themselves into an almost ritualistic series of encounters with monsters, seductresses, and the underworld.

The resulting text, in the form of a gradually emerging book and possible TV series and entitled *The Shapes of Chaos: Explorations of Our Inner Wilderness*, was inspired by Lewis's notion that every great work of the past has to be judged by its own standards rather than imposing upon it the limitations of our contemporary prejudices. I also found myself moving towards Owen Barfield's view that the contemplation of the historical process does produce evidence of a kind of evolution of consciousness, a view that Lewis initially branded as a kind of intellectual heresy he referred to as Historicism, but a view which he came finally, it seemed, to accept, at least as the kind of imaginative construct that underlies his last and perhaps greatest work, *Till We Have Faces*.

So *The Shapes of Chaos* has become a somewhat ambitious attempt to harmonize the Lewis and Barfield visions of our literary and spiritual history into a single unified account. I attempt to hold it together by a comprehensive theory of our intellectual evolutions from the earliest Shaman cultures up to Lewis's own visions in the twentieth century, the dynamic juxtaposition and interplay of city and wilderness providing the energizing motivations. This was inspired by Lewis's notion that the Christian professional should enter the fields where the sterility of modern materialism normally prevails and allow the evidence to speak for itself. The hope is that certain truths will emerge that would not come within the range of the materialist. In such a survey of the historical process as I am attempting, the centrality of the Incarnation seems to emerge without my being conscious of any forcing of the evidence on the part of myself as chronicler.

The new view of our wilderness literature in its historical settings has proved so fruitful of new ideas that at times one despairs of completion, but happily the gentle but persisting pressures of our TV team seem to be now compelling a no doubt long overdue closure.

Proverbially, Oxford is the home of lost causes.[34] And in certain moods I feel that the only excuse for presuming to reply to Hal Poe's invitation to contribute to this anthology is that I exemplify Oxfordian Quixotry in a particularly blatant form. My apologia is simple enough. Among those of us enjoying the privilege of a tenured position in academia, it seems right that some few of us should take the risk of attempting the really ambitious enterprises, the impossible dreams. So this stands as an interim report on my encounters with the presence, the personality, and the deep and multifarious influences Lewis had on my life and my attempts to make some kind of commensurate response. If *The Shapes of Chaos* should come to fruition and publication, it would offer vistas of a more intimate relationship between the history of humanity and our own personal spiritual evolutions. If someday the Atlantis Project, in some form or another, in whatever decade or century, should come to realization, then we should be able to offer to schoolchildren or students anywhere in the world the equivalent of a Rhodes Scholarship and the equivalent privilege of sitting in a comfortable, if aging, armchair in Lewis's study, as very Lords and Ladies of Byzantium, conversing on "What is past, or passing, or to come."[35]

Chapter 9

SMARTENED UP BY LEWIS

Christopher Mead Armitage

A s a freshman who had done well in what was then called Higher
School Certificate, I felt that, awe-inspiring and abounding
with bright students as Oxford is, I could with luck hold my own. I
decided to attend a lecture series entitled "Prolegomena to Medieval
and Renaissance Literature" by the famous C. S. Lewis.

Roundfaced and somewhat ruddy in complexion, he walked to
the podium, dressed in a dark suit and academic gown. He looked
more businesslike than the usual tweedy professor did and soon
proved that he was. Off he launched into a magical mystery tour of a
world peopled by Chalcidius, Albertus Magnus, Apuleius—ah, *him*
I recognized from *The Golden Ass*—but apparently he'd also written
something called *De Deo Socratis*. Boethius's *Consolation of Philosophy*,
which I had blithely skipped in the complete works of Chaucer, was
apparently a seminal work to which I should have paid attention. Dionysus: he always sounded like fun, but Pseudo-Dionysius and his four
books? And were there really four kinds of fairies as well as demons
and daimons? Equally disconcerting to youthful complacency was
Lewis's admonition that this kind of information was needed not only
for interpreting difficult passages but even more for ones that looked
easy. The essential message was that the life of the mind, especially
the search for the origins of ideas, mattered.

A day of judgment, if not of wrath, lay ahead for me. The completing of one's degree required an oral exam known as the "Viva"
(for *viva voce*). My examiners turned out to be J. R. R. Tolkien, Lord
David Cecil, Helen Gardner, and C. S. Lewis at his most magisterial.
Professor Tolkien easily persuaded me to acknowledge inaccuracies in

my written medieval exam. Miss Gardner, whom I had antagonized by continuing to court one of her star students after Miss Gardner had told me that she did not wish her to be "distracted by a young man," soon had me "pinned and wriggling on the wall." With my shortcomings thus exposed, Lewis apparently concluded that prolonging the inquisition would be unnecessary, so I was dismissed, duly chastened.

Intimidating as Lewis may have appeared to some in his audiences, his confident presentations were not egotistical. Clearly, to him what was important was the subject, not himself. As an undergraduate, I was unaware that he had served in the trenches of World War I or that academic politics would soon lead this quintessential Oxonian to transfer to Cambridge. Few, if any, could have predicted that before long this settled bachelor would help a self-exiled American divorcee by marrying her, later fall in love with her, but soon lose her to cancer. Yet, though Lewis did not embellish his lectures with details of his private life, his personal commitment to his public role was unmistakable: like Chaucer's Clerk of Oxford, gladly would he learn and gladly teach.

Part 3

THE PERSONAL INFLUENCE

Not all the contributors to this volume studied with Lewis. His personal influence at Oxford and Cambridge extended far beyond those who came to his rooms each week for their tutorials. Many of those who attended his well-known lectures were not his students, and others participated in the Socratic Club, of which he served as president for many years. Basil Mitchell, who succeeded Lewis as president of the club, became one of the great Christian philosophers of Oxford in the next generation. For the fiftieth anniversary of *The Abolition of Man*, Mitchell assessed the continuing significance of Lewis's apologetics. Mitchell tells no anecdotes and offers no description of Lewis's coat and trousers. Instead, he describes the legacy of Lewis for philosophy.

A famous encounter took place at the Socratic Club on 2 February 1948 between Lewis and Elizabeth Anscombe over his argument in *Miracles* (1947) that naturalism is self-refuting. Much has been written about whether Lewis won or lost the debate. He certainly felt low afterward, but Mitchell thought Lewis definitely had the stronger argument. During Mitchell's presidency of the Socratic Club, they restaged the debate in the 1960s with Anscombe presenting her critique and John Lucas standing in for Lewis. Lucas won.

Barbara Reynolds first met Lewis when she was a young scholar in Cambridge and went to hear Lewis's inaugural lecture, "De Descriptione Temporum," at the Mill Lane lecture hall. Her friend and colleague Dorothy L. Sayers had asked her to attend the lecture and send her a report, which she did. Lewis seems to have had a positive impact on a number of young people, like Reynolds, who were beginning their careers.

Sarah Tisdall did not study with Lewis, but her mother did. With Lewis, we find multigenerational relationships, for Sarah Tisdall was one of Lewis's many godchildren. Laurence Harwood was another such godchild with whom Lewis corresponded.

Finally, Lewis simply paid attention to students from his home in Ireland. David Bleakley, who went on to serve in Parliament, never studied with Lewis, but Lewis showed an interest in him when he was a student at Oxford. Some people speak of "investing" their lives in students, but *invest* implies the expectation of return. Lewis did not invest in others so much as he gave himself to others without expectation of return.

Chapter 10

AN OXFORD ENCOUNTER
WITH C. S. LEWIS

David Bleakley

W hen did you begin to think about coming to Oxford?" That was one of C. S. Lewis's first questions to me! When I replied, "In the barber's shop," he was visibly surprised. He was even more surprised when I told him the shop was Billy Graham's in East Belfast—providing a personal service with which Lewis and many generations of Strandtown people were well acquainted.

As so often happens, my way forward appeared by chance when one evening in 1945, on the way home from the Belfast Shipyard, I stopped by to have a haircut. Awaiting my turn I began to read *Picture Post*, a then famous illustrated weekly. It told the story of Ernie Fisher, a miner who had gone to Oxford with the help of an adult education bursary. "Interesting story," I thought, until a nudge from my neighbor reminded me that I was still in the barber's and that it was my turn next.

But afterward the story lingered on and then the question: "If a miner goes to Oxford, why not a shipyard engineer?"

I soon found out that the Trades Union Congress offered scholarships for open competition among trade unionists in Britain and Ireland, based on written examination, community service record, and in-depth interviews in London and Oxford. To cut the story short, I applied and was successful. The written tests proved manageable

---

This essay is reprinted with David Bleakley's permission from his book *C. S. Lewis: At Home in Ireland* (Bangor: Strandtown, 1998).

though the interviews were formidable. In fact, little time was spent on my chosen essay subject of "A Wages Policy."

This path to Oxford was new territory to Lewis, and he was interested to learn that the focus of the London interview was on what I had done with my time to date and what sort of postwar future I envisaged. He approved of this approach as a screening for university applications and thought it might be more widely used. He smiled when he heard my reply to the last question at the interview: "If you get this scholarship, what would you hope to do afterward?" The gist of my reply was: "Back to Ireland to serve the cause from Belfast," at which the Oxford don (I heard later it was Professor A. J. P. Taylor) murmured, "Mr. Bleakley, you recall that Gladstone's mission was to pacify Ireland and you know what happened to him!" Actually, my knowledge of Gladstone was slight, but I had the wit to reply, "I take the point."

A few days later I was awarded a scholarship of £250 a year with £3 a week during vacations. After seven years with wires and switches and a sharing in shipyard fellowship, I was turning to books and lectures for a while. For me it was the chance of a lifetime which I have never regretted taking and have never undervalued. My visit to Billy Graham's barber's shop had been for me one of life's defining moments.

As I subsequently discovered, C. S. Lewis, who took a holistic view of student care, was fascinated by such details and the way in which by very different routes we could arrive at the same destination. Nor did he underestimate the importance of having been employed in Harland and Wolff's shipyard. He knew the place well and from an early age had been in contact through trips to the "Yard" with his grandfather, Richard. And, of course, he and Warnie had daily eye and ear contact with H & W from their attic window in "Little Lea" and heard, with the rest of us, the 7:30 a.m. call-to-work signal of the H & W sirens. When Lewis praised the shipyard as a great "University of Life" and "a considerable preparation" for higher education, I began to appreciate his lack of regard for the English Public School system and his interest in the burgeoning adult education movement which students like myself represented.

Indeed, wartime and postwar Lewis put great energy into his lecturing programs to the armed forces and developed considerably his opportunities for popular writing and broadcasting. As I learned by experience, he had something of a soft spot for those who had come to Oxford the "hard way" and appreciated the privilege—equally he was impatient with students (for example, John Betjeman) who frittered away their time.

Ruskin College, to which I belonged, was of considerable interest to Lewis, and he was pleased to learn that many of us knew of his work. Then, as now, the American lobby was strong, and we were fortunate in having in our college Jimmy Tyrie, an American student who was well versed in things in the world of Lewis. Jimmy was for me a boon companion on many a lecturing outing to Magdalen or the Schools to hear the great man. As he put it: "Wait till I go back to the States and tell them I've actually heard C. S. Lewis with my own ears!" Together we managed to get our hero to the college from time to time, so that others could benefit from his wisdom.

Professor Lionel Elvin, our principal, a distinguished adult educationist and separated from Lewis's birthday by less than a decade, wrote to me recently reminding me of those days. He offers evidence of Lewis's willingness to "go the extra mile" in helping Ruskin College students. Frank Quinn is an example: he took Frank under his wing and prepared him for a successful application as a lecturer at Haverford College in Pennsylvania. Further evidence of Lewis's generosity comes in Lionel Elvin's comment: "Frank was of a Catholic background, but had no religion himself and said to Lewis that this would hardly commend him to a Quaker College. Lewis replied: 'You talk about English Literature—if the question of religion arises, leave that to me.'" As my principal, a much valued correspondent who shares my admiration for Lewis, observes, this typically positive action on behalf of Frank Quinn was "very much to his credit."

Equally to Lewis's credit was the special effort he made to keep in touch with his homeland and especially Ulster and the County Down; much help was given to those from home who sought his advice. To be from Strandtown was, of course, to be deemed special. *Surprised by Joy* was not yet written, but for all who knew Lewis, there was no need to have his regard for his home heath confirmed in an autobiography. His love for a whole range of things Ulster and Irish was an obvious and important side to his personality. But, and this is a point to be stressed, he saw no tension about being Oxbridge and being Irish; love of Oxford, and later Cambridge, did not lessen attachment to the homeland. Such dual loyalties were easily combined and regularly demonstrated.

As Principal Elvin told each intake, we were up at Oxford for a few years of academic life which would open up new horizons. He was enthusiastic and idealistic and pointed to an opportunity to enjoy every minute of it. It was the sort of advice which Lewis himself often passed on.

These attitudes were exactly in line with my expectations. For myself, I could hardly believe my good fortune. Grant-aided to read, write, think, and enjoy the society that is Oxford! "How, compared with industrial life, can they call this work?" I thought, as we were launched on our course of studies. Years earlier C. S. Lewis had shared a similar elation with his father.

As with Lewis in the 1920s, the late 1940s was an exciting time to be in Oxford. In the immediate postwar years it was filled with students of my own age whose desire for higher education had been both interrupted and stimulated by the war. Future "names" were generously sprinkled around the Colleges: Margaret Thatcher (née Roberts), Tony Benn, Robert Runcie, Kenneth Tynan, and Ludovic Kennedy, to name but a few. Ruskin too had its prospective panel of "futures": MPs and cabinet ministers galore, trade union leaders, industrial relations professors, high-ranking African leaders, including a future prime minister of Sierra Leone. For Lewis and his teaching colleagues the challenge was formidable.

Anxious as we were to get down to the books and catch up on the lost years of the war, there was a still "rich-beyond-the-college" Oxford to explore. Everyone—poet, politician, or preacher—was catered to. Ruskinites majored in many of the best debating encounters at the Oxford Union and our own College Hall. Selections included political personalities as diverse as C. E. M. Joad, Harold Laski, Professor

Bernal, Clement Attlee, and Christian apologists like C. S. Lewis, Donald Soper, and the Master of Balliol, A. D. Lindsay.

During my first term at Ruskin College I had the opportunity to make contact with many whose fame I had known of only through their books. On one occasion I even had to contact George Bernard Shaw on behalf of our student body. Being a fellow Irishman carried no weight whatsoever! All I received was one of his famous "no can do" postcards with his spidery writing and radically colored ink.

But as I found out to my lasting benefit, not all Irishmen were as elusive as Shaw. The special chance encounter, which meant much to me then and more so in later years, was with one of Ulster's most famous literary sons. Ordering a coffee one morning in the popular "Cadena" student cafe in Oxford's Cornmarket, I was interrupted by someone putting a hand on my shoulder and saying, "What part of Belfast gave you that accent?" Looking up I saw a farmerlike man in sports coat and "cords," who asked the question in what was clearly an Ulster accent. I told him where I came from and immediately he said, "That's not far from where I live." He was very interested to learn of my shipyard-to-university translation and before he left suggested that I might drop in to see him sometime in the college where he worked. "Magdalen," he said, "though these odd English pronounce it 'Maud-lin.'" He continued, "Just call in at the gate-lodge and ask for C. S. Lewis." The name rang a bell from home but not very loudly.

Later that night at dinner, Lionel Elvin, himself an English literature scholar, put me right: "David, my dear fellow, that's one of Oxford's most interesting men; do go and see him." I did and was always indebted for the wise advice.

We met at Magdalen from time to time (sometimes with Kenneth Tynan, one of his favorite but often teased students). C. S. was easy to talk to, and I was privileged to experience the skill of a great communicator, who got at the spiritual heart of things in language simple but memorable. Good Ulsterman as he was, a spade was a spade and not an agricultural implement.

But better than Magdalen were the times we shared the journey back to our near-to-each-other Headington home bases. They were occasions for a cornucopia of phrases, questions, and insights sufficient for a lifetime's reflection. Lewis was known to his friends as an active and lively man who loved to walk and talk, expanding on his ideas as he went along. His seemingly "out of the blue" remarks could be startling and revealing; I share a few, illustrative of his many moods.

Sometimes he could be puckish with the questions he asked. Walking together up Headington Hill one evening, this great lover of both Oxford and the County Down turned to me, feigning a need for advice: "David, could you define Heaven for me?" I tried—he soon interrupted my theological meanderings. "My friend, you're far too complicated; an honest Ulsterman should know better. Heaven is Oxford lifted and placed in the middle of the County Down."

Not bad, not bad indeed. I am sorry that I was not then better prepared to appreciate more fully this true son of my native county, but ever since I have become aware of how much C. S. Lewis "country" we have to explore in Ireland. Lewis left an enduring and much appreciated mark on all who knew him, and I was no exception. Years later I felt a fellow feeling when Simon Barrington-Ward, Bishop of Coventry, shared with me the joy he felt on discovering that he, Simon, had been given a spiritually jovial mention in one of his hero's books.

On other occasions our exchanges had to do with things back home. CSL never tired of hearing about the "goings on" in Strandtown and district. I, for my part, was fascinated by the opportunity to see my home scene through the eyes of one who, until I came to Oxford, I regarded as very much part of Ulster's ruling class—a "scion of the Big House," as many of his colleagues and contemporaries regarded him. But neither got it right: Lewis really did enjoy a "rubbing of shoulders" with his "fellow villagers" of Strandtown and was happy to contribute to a common agenda and discuss it openly.

Fortunately, I was well supplied with home news, and Lewis was glad to be made aware of the local gossip. My source of information was ample, for each week I received in the post from my godmother an envelope of cuttings from the Belfast *Telegraph* and other regional papers more than enough to keep us in touch. Mrs. Bradshaw, who was the sender, became quite a favorite with Lewis. "Have you got any more clippings from your godmother?" he would ask and was disappointed when they were not available. Warnie was anxious to have them as well.

At first I was surprised by his interest, but later I understood and appreciated the importance he placed on the everyday episodes which shape much of what we do and who we are. When I asked the reason why, he said that he just liked to know what was going on at grassroots in his own green fields of Ulster, without having to await the more lei-surely written letters from Gundreda, Kelsie, or other members of the Ewart circle. I never associated C. S. Lewis with being an avid reader of newspapers generally, but certainly he liked being kept up-to-date with Mrs. Bradshaw's weekly clippings.

Arthur Greeves, of course, remained his long-term source of what was happening at home — but this correspondence was never discussed.

From these episodes I felt that Lewis really did believe that a "bit of trivia" was good for the soul — back again to G. K. Chesterton's "divinely ordinary" things. Equally, he believed that the source should be home-based, because it represented a significant microcosm of "real people in real-life situations."

Other memories gathered from our peripatetic discussions have to do with tips about how to go about the world of learning. These were no formal seminars — even better, they were the application of a magnificent common-sense to matters of scholarship and on the gleaning of everyday knowledge.

On reading suggestions his range was wide, though sometimes I had to give up trying to keep pace with the flood of advice! (Years later I was comforted when Simon Barrington-Ward had the same experi-ence when sharing in "Lewis-led" High Table exchanges at Magdalen College, Cambridge!) But on popular nineteenth-century literature CSL was most helpful, most enthusiastic, and delighted to know that organizations like the Workers' Educational Association were doing much to develop literary studies. He approved of my regard for Trollope (much involved in Irish affairs), the Brontes, George Eliot, Thackery, and Jane Austen; and was delighted to know that they had a considerable following in Belfast adult education circles. I was disap-pointed that he could not be drawn on Helen Waddell, whose "star" was high and with whom he had much in common. Helen was a great favorite back home, where she was held in high esteem at Queen's University by noted medieval scholar Professor G. O. Sayles.

A surprise for me on one of our literary exchanges was to learn that he and I shared a favorite novel in Jane Austen's *Pride and Prejudice*. "How often have you read it?" he asked. I replied, "Many times." "Splendid," he said and proceeded to advise me not to be afraid to read a good book "time and time again." He assured me that he "dipped into" his favorites regularly and particularly *Pride and Prejudice*. About Jane Austen's classic, I often wondered how far he (perhaps unconsciously) saw parallels between the characters and action of the plot and his own complex social life: Rosings for Glenmachan, Mr. Bennett for Papy, Elizabeth for Joy, and so on.

But whichever of the many topics were under discussion, CSL was ever anxious to warn against looking for a complicated explanation when none was required. He was especially impatient with those who discarded the plain common-sense for the complex. Amusingly on one occasion he took to task those who read deep meaning into his smoking habits and his attachment to a collection of favorite pipes: "They wonder why I like to smoke a pipe and think it has something to do with getting me into a contemplative frame of mind. Do they never consider that I might just like the taste and smell of tobacco?"

I was no smoker, so our most shared consumption was not tobacco but tea. We consumed gallons of the brew together and agreed that "no cup was big enough" to satisfy our thirst for Ulster's favorite beverage. He appreciated (without endorsing!) my quotation of a popular temperance slogan: "Ulster would be a better place if the men passed more pubs and fewer resolutions!"

But sometimes CSL could be very serious during an exchange. On one rare occasion, when by chance we got on to family matters, he asked me casually about my mother and father. I had much to say about my father, a bricklayer, who had brought our family up in a radical tradition and who, like many of his generation, had sacrificed much for the sake of others. He had been proud to see me go to Oxford and promised to keep the home going until my return. Looking pensive for a moment, Lewis said I was lucky to have such a firm relationship and that I ought to value it. I have since wondered whether he had his own father in mind.

Then he broached a question which I have never forgotten and to which he never returned: "What about your mother, has she helped too?" I hesitated and then explained: "My mother is dead; she died shortly after my birth; a matter of weeks."

My companion and mentor was silent for a long moment and then asked a question which I have often pondered: "Which, my friend, is the greater loss to bear—to be separated from your mother when only a few weeks have gone or when nearly a decade has passed?"

Fifty years later I'm still trying to work that one out. Never again did we discuss our parents with each other, and I knew that we would not. We had been given a fortuitous and once-for-all opportunity to delve into a filial matter of common concern. Hopefully, we were each strengthened by the occasion. I relate it because, of all the many times we shared thoughts, this was by far the closest and most human exchange.

On academic subjects we had not much in the way of overlap. Medieval literary studies and languages were beyond me, though I had some advantage, especially by practical experience, where industrial relations and economics were concerned. So inevitably many of our "walking home" discussions had to do with the Attlee Labour Government's efforts to copper-bottom the Welfare State or, as mischievous Oxford critics sometimes dubbed it, "The Farewell State." I found CSL in many ways a traditionalist, but he was no reactionary. His acquaintance with Shaw, Wells, and Chesterton had given him a generous social vision; he even occasionally hinted that there might be a Fabian skeleton or two in the Irish family cupboard.

However, he tended to keep party politics at a distance, and I was no exception. My own stance as a Christian Socialist and pacifist in the R. H. Tawney–Keir Hardie tradition was of no avail. I suspected that he preferred total abstention to perfect moderation where the art of politics was concerned. However, I could hardly fault his final advice: "Take it to the Lord in prayer, but pray carefully lest your prayers are answered."

Fortunately, I never had to canvass C. S. Lewis for his vote, but Arthur Greeves I did canvass. To the best of my knowledge I never "made it" into his "Letters to Lewis," so I shall never know his voting pattern. However, as I canvassed I always hoped (and flattered myself) that perhaps I may, at least, have persuaded him to abstain!

The truth of the matter is that Lewis was too diverse a man to accept the traditional confines of any one political party, though I often regretted that he was not closer to Oxford's leading Christian Socialist of the time, A. D. Lindsay, Master of Balliol. Lindsay did so much to raise the sights of a postwar generation. He enthused us with his conviction that we had "to combine goodness and cleverness" so as "to harness the scientific mind in the service of the merciful heart." I always felt that these Christian philosophers had much in common on what is still a crucial issue as we prepare for a new millennium, hopefully drawing on visionaries like these two from Oxford.

Lewis was very much a "conscience of the community" man and was evenhanded in his advice to the contending political establishments. So much that when in 1951 he was offered a well-earned CBE by Winston Churchill, he refused the distinction. The refusal caused quite a stir, and many from opposing party political wings pleaded with him to accept the honor. But Lewis was firm. He let it be known that though on a purely personal level the honor would be "highly agreeable," he feared that acceptance would play into the hands of "knaves" who accused him of "covert anti-leftist propaganda" in his religious writings and of "fools" who believed the accusations. Many of us, who were neither knaves nor fools, tried to persuade him to reconsider, but he remained firm in his refusal. We respected his motives.

Nevertheless, Lewis never "shortchanged" on his community obligations; his extramural services were considerable. During the First World War he had felt it his obligation to "join up," and during the Second War he became a member of the local Home Guard in Oxford. He also opened his home for the reception of evacuees and showed an immense capacity to adapt to the pressures of wartime civilian life. Not being a car driver was an added inconvenience which often turned him into something of a "beast of burden" in the transport of domestic supplies for Mrs. Moore. At times his overladen bicycle looked like one of those encountered in an African outback.

Lewis's vast correspondence was another "extra" willingly given and in its own way provided a social service of advice to thousands far and wide. Indeed many an MP or town Councilor would have regarded the throughput as considerable — all this on top of committees and public lecturing occasions galore. Little wonder that he felt little need to join up with a political party in order to "do his bit" for society. However, he was very tolerant to those who felt otherwise and had friends across the political spectrum. His students knew this and benefited from his breadth of vision. I too was a beneficiary.

Years later, I was reminded once again of his generosity of spirit. It happened like this. During one of Lewis's visits to his beloved County Down with Joy, his wife, and when I had become a member of Parliament in East Belfast (covering "Little Lea," "Bernagh," and "Ty-Isa" as well), I took my friend on a fleeting car trip to the nearby Parliament Building which he had yet to see. After a quick tour of our legislative center we stood on the steps of Parliament, overlooking the splendor of the County Down and his evocative Castlereagh Hills. We looked hard and long at all our surroundings, and we shared reflections on the "then" of Oxford and the "now" of our native Ulster and the County Down.

It was a magic moment, during which CSL seemed to relent where I was concerned and showed acceptance and enthusiasm for my political commitment. I felt that all was forgiven as he, with a jovial wave of his hands in a double benediction to both Parliament Buildings behind us and the County Down vista before us, proclaimed: "David, my friend, you've really made it. Look behind and before you: all this and Heaven too."

"What a satisfactory conclusion," I thought, as I drove my favorite mentor back to "The Old Inn at Crawfordsburn."

Chapter 11

C. S. LEWIS ON THE ABOLITION OF MAN

Basil Mitchell

L ewis's *The Abolition of Man* is scarcely more than a pamphlet. It was published in 1943 and represents the three Riddell Lectures he delivered in 1943 at the University of Durham. The whole consists of forty pages, together with an appendix of eight pages. Its subtitle is "Reflections on Education with special reference to the teaching of English in the upper forms of schools."

The pamphlet reflects Lewis's capacity for drawing far-reaching conclusions from what appears initially to be rather trivial subject matter. He has just been reading an elementary textbook on the teaching of English intended for the upper forms of schools. The authors quote "the well-known story of Coleridge at the waterfall." He overheard two tourists, one of whom called the waterfall "sublime." The other "pretty." Coleridge endorsed the first judgment and rejected the other with disgust. On this episode the authors comment,

> When the man said *That is sublime*, he appears to be making a remark about the waterfall.... Actually ... he was not making a remark about the waterfall, but a remark about his own feelings. What he was saying was really *I have feelings associated in my mind with the word "Sublime,"* or shortly *I have sublime feelings.*[1]

This chapter was originally delivered as a lecture in Durham to commemorate the fiftieth anniversary of Lewis's original lectures on "The Abolition of Man."

Lewis points out that in point of fact, if the judgment is to be interpreted as one about the observer's feelings, they could not be *sublime* feelings but rather something like *humble* feelings, and then goes on to make his main point: "The schoolboy who reads this passage ... will believe two propositions: firstly, that all sentences containing a predicate of value are statements about the emotional state of the speaker, and, secondly, that all such statements are unimportant. [And this means that he will not learn to make discriminating judgments about English literature, but will instead be deprived of the means for doing so, all judgments of value having in advance been rendered] trivial."[2]

As against this subjectivist view Lewis maintains that there is a basic morality, common to all human beings, which has been called variously Natural Law or Traditional Morality or the First Principles of Practical Reason or the First Platitudes. He calls it the *Tao* for brevity's sake; the Chinese expression for a moral order which reflects the order of the universe. And he claims that the same fundamental principles of morality can be discerned in all the great religions and philosophical traditions of the world—Platonic, Aristotelian, Stoic, Christian, and oriental alike. The appendix to *The Abolition of Man* is intended to document this claim with extensive quotations from these sources.

This, then, is the argument of *The Abolition of Man*. In reviewing it now some sixty years later one could concentrate on either of the two main elements in it: Lewis's critique of the subjectivist view, together with his estimate of the consequences of its being generally adopted; and his account of the *Tao*, the nature and content of the First Principles of Morality. I propose this evening to dwell on the first of these. About the second I would only say that, in my judgment, a closer survey than Lewis's would reveal considerable differences between the various ethical traditions he specifies deriving, as I think, from differences between the underlying conceptions of the universe and man's place in it. To take the most obvious example there was in the ancient world nothing comparable to the Christian principle of the sanctity of human life which follows from the conviction that each and every individual is created by God and redeemed by Jesus Christ. Nor will you find any sense in Homer that humility is a virtue.

Lewis is right nevertheless in stressing what they *do* have in common—the conviction, namely, that morality is not something that we construct but something, as it were, built into the order of the universe. He rejects unequivocally the assumption conveyed in the title of the late Mr. J. L. Mackie's book *Ethics: Inventing Right and Wrong.*

How, then, does Lewis move from his identification of subjectivism as the prevailing moral tendency of our time to his conclusion that it presages the abolition of man? His argument is that once we have abandoned the conception of an objective moral order with its unavoidable constraints upon our choices, it is open to us to make what choices we like: "Let us decide for ourselves what man is to be and make him into that: not on any ground of imagined value, but because we want him to be such. Having mastered our environment, let us now master ourselves and choose our own destiny."[3]

It might appear at first sight that man has now conquered nature, including human nature, and is for the first time wholly free. But this is to forget, says Lewis, that "man" is an abstraction. The freedom which men will now enjoy will be the freedom of some men to decide what humanity shall in future be, and that means to decide what *other men* shall be. The people who have been thus conditioned by methods of psychological persuasion, selective breeding, and so on (which their conditioners will use because nothing in their makeup prevents their using them) will lack the capacity to make moral choices at all. Nor are the conditioners themselves in any way better placed:

> Every motive they try to act on becomes at once a *petitio*. It is not that they are bad men. They are not men at all. Stepping outside the *Tao*, they have stepped into the void. Nor are their subjects necessarily unhappy men. They are not men at all: they are artefacts. Man's final conquest has proved to be the abolition of Man.[4]

There is a science fiction element in all this which emerges more explicitly and more dramatically in some of his novels. But it must be admitted that we are closer now than we were in 1943 to achieving the power that Lewis anticipates. The advancement of genetic engineering has reached the stage at which it begins to look possible that we could by scientific means alter human nature fundamentally, so that it will be a moral problem of unexampled severity whether we ought to exercise these powers. Could we breed human beings who no longer had the possibility of making moral choices; or could it even be the case, as Lewis seems to think, that the very fact that people had been subject to genetic manipulation of any kind would suffice to deprive them of the capacity for moral choice?

These are deep philosophical questions which I cannot go into now, but Lewis seems justified in arguing:

1. That genetic engineering unless carefully controlled would be likely to have irreversible consequences for human nature.
2. That the control which is needed must be guided by some clear conception of what is properly human.
3. That to reduce morality to the expression of individual or group preferences is to deprive ourselves of any such clear conception.

There is, I think, nevertheless a certain lack of clarity in Lewis's argument at this point. He sees the abolition of man chiefly as the consequence of the manipulation of some men by others in such a way that these others cease to be properly men at all. Yet the manipulators—or the "conditioners" as he calls them—have, in his view, equally ceased to be men through the very fact that they no longer exercise moral choices. The abolition of man could, then, come about simply by a process of cultural change which did not involve any sort of scientific intervention. As he puts it, "Their [i.e., the conditioners'] extreme rationalism, by 'seeing through' all 'rational' motives, leaves men creatures of wholly irrational behaviour."[5] "It is the magician's bargain: give up our soul, get power in return."[6]

In the rest of this paper I should like to compare this aspect of Lewis's argument with two other discussions which are strikingly similar: one is to be found in another lecture of Lewis, his inaugural lecture at Cambridge, entitled *De Descriptione Temporum* (1954). The other is Alasdair Macintyre's treatment of "emotivism" in his much acclaimed book *After Virtue*.

The inaugural lecture was given in 1954 on the occasion of his assumption of the newly founded chair at Cambridge of Medieval and Renaissance English Literature. The title of the chair prompts Lewis to reflect upon the way we divide periods of history, e.g., the Middle Ages, the Renaissance. In particular he asks himself and his audience at what point in European history there has occurred the *greatest* division between one period and another. He concludes as follows:

> I have come to regard as the greatest of all divisions in the history of the West that which divides the present from, say, the age of Jane Austen and Scott. The dating of such things must of course be rather hazy and indefinite. No one could point to a year or a decade in which the change indisputably began, and it has probably not yet reached its peak. But somewhere between us and the Waverley novels, somewhere between us and *Persuasion*, the chasm runs.[7]

The period which is just ending Lewis calls that of "Old Western Man," and in trying to characterize the difference between it and our present age, he mentions four signal changes:

1. One is political. We used to pray "to live 'a peaceable life in all godliness and honesty' and 'pass their time in rest and quietness.' But now the organisation of mass excitement seems to be almost the normal organ of political power."[8]

2. In the arts we have work which is "shatteringly and bewilderingly new," so that even experts are in intractable dispute as to what it means.[9]

3. There has been a great religious change: "the unchristening." "In [Jane Austen's] days some kind and degree of religious belief and practice were the norm; now, though I would gladly believe that both kind and degree have improved, they are the exception."[10]

4. Finally, "Between Jane Austen and us, but not between her and Shakespeare, Chaucer, Alfred, Virgil, Homer, or the Pharaohs, comes the birth of the machines."[11] Hence for us, as not for them, what is new is best. This belief owes something, of course, to Darwin,

> but I submit that what has imposed this climate of opinion so firmly on the human mind is a new archetypal image. It

is the image of old machines being superseded by new and better ones.... Our assumption that everything is provisional and soon to be superseded, that the attainment of goods we have never yet had, rather than the defence and conservation of those we have already, is the cardinal business of life, would ... shock and bewilder [our ancestors] if they could visit our [world].[12]

The lecture has a splendid ending in which Lewis presents himself as a specimen of "Old Western Man":

I myself belong far more to that Old Western order than to yours. I am going to claim that this, which in one way is a disqualification for my task, is yet in another a qualification. The disqualification is obvious. You don't want to be lectured on Neanderthal Man by a Neanderthaler, still less on dinosaurs by a dinosaur. And yet, is that the whole story? If a live dinosaur dragged its slow length into the laboratory, would we not all look back as we fled? What a chance to know at last how it really moved and looked and smelled and what noises it made!... One thing I know: I would give a great deal to hear any ancient Athenian, even a stupid one, talking about Greek tragedy. He would know in his bones so much that we seek in vain.... Ladies and gentlemen, I stand before you somewhat as that Athenian might stand. I read as a native texts that you must read as foreigners.[13]

So he concludes:

That way, where I fail as a critic, I may yet be useful as a specimen. I would even dare to go further. Speaking not only for myself but for all other Old Western men whom you may meet, I would say, use your specimens while you can. There are not going to be many more dinosaurs.[14]

In this inaugural lecture, as in the Riddel Lectures eleven years earlier, Lewis describes a profound change in human culture. One is bound to ask how, if at all, these changes are related. Are we to take the transition from Old Western Man to our present age as identical with, or a stage in, the "abolition of Man" which he predicted in his earlier lecture? Or is that an altogether more fundamental development to which, even in our post-Christian age, we are not yet committed?

A hostile critic of Lewis might claim that, in both pieces, he shows himself to be deeply conservative. What they have in common is adherence to a world that is now past or in the process of passing, a static world which has no room for genuine originality. He does not, to be sure, attempt to relate the two discussions, but they display the same tendency to hark back to a time when a traditional stable order of society could readily be identified with the order of the universe. Although he does not spell it out, any state of affairs that departs from that is in his view tantamount to the abolition of man.

I think myself that there is some substance in this criticism. Lewis *is* temperamentally out of sympathy with modernity in most of its manifestations, and this is apparent in the approach of both lectures. But he does in *The Abolition of Man* anticipate the objection:

> Does this mean, then, that no progress in our perceptions of value can ever take place? That we are bound down for ever to an unchanging code given once for all? And is it, in any event, possible to talk of obeying what I call the *Tao*? If we lump together, as I have done, the traditional moralities of East and West, the Christian, the Pagan, and the Jew, shall we not find many contradictions and some absurdities? I admit all this. Some criticism, some removal of contradictions, even some real development, is required. But there are two different kinds of criticism.[15]

And he goes on to distinguish between development from within which accepts the spirit of morality—much as a poet may change the language while being sensitive to what the spirit of the language demands—and criticism from without which judges morality by standards quite alien to it. He concedes that it may be a delicate matter to decide in particular instances where the line is to be drawn, but the distinction is nevertheless crucial.

It remains possible, then, that Lewis would be prepared to admit (though, I suspect, reluctant to admit) that some modern developments are, to some extent, in the spirit of the language—the renewed emphasis on our obligation to the natural world might be a case in point—but he would insist that a decisive and destructive break occurs whenever morality is no longer thought of as, to use John Mackie's phrase, "required by the universe," but rather as the expression merely of individual or group preferences.

And so to Alasdair Macintyre. His book *After Virtue* develops essentially the same theme as Lewis's *The Abolition of Man* some forty years later. He cites Lewis only once—in a discussion of Jane Austen whom he agrees with Lewis in regarding as an essentially Christian writer.[16] Indeed (like Lewis) he speaks of her "as the last great effective imaginative voice of the tradition of thought about, and practice of, the virtues which I have tried to identify."[17]

Macintyre's book begins with a sustained critique of what he calls "emotivism":

> Emotivism is the doctrine that all evaluative judgments and more specifically all moral judgments are *nothing but* expressions of preference, expressions of attitude or feeling, insofar as they are moral or evaluative in character.... Factual judgments are true or false; and in the realm of fact there are rational criteria by means of which we may secure agreement as to what is true and what is false. But moral judgments, being expressions of attitude or feeling, are neither true nor false; and agreement in moral judgment is not to be secured by any rational method, for there are none.[18]

Macintyre's thesis is, in its critique of emotivism, identical with Lewis's, although worked out with greater philosophical sophistication. And it is interesting to note that, without explicit reference to Lewis, he comes to precisely the same conclusion:

> For one way of framing my contention that morality is not what it once was is that to a large degree people now think and talk and act *as if* emotivism were true, whatever their avowed theoretical stand point may be. Emotivism has become embedded in our culture. But of course in saying

this I am not merely contending that morality is not what it once was, but also and more importantly that what once was morality has to some large degree disappeared—and that this marks a degeneration, a grave cultural loss.[19]

Lewis argues that the sort of emotivism expressed by the author of the introduction to the study of English literature which prompted his Riddell Lectures will have the effect of making students feel that all judgments in the field seem trivial and unimportant, and that is undoubtedly one likely consequence. But Macintyre points out that it is not the only one. For one striking characteristic of contemporary debate on moral, political, and aesthetic issues is the prevalence of *protest*, protest which carries an enormous emotional charge precisely because there is no rational means of settling the disputes:

> It is easy to understand why *protest* becomes a distinctive moral feature of the modern age and why *indignation* is a predominant modern emotion. "To protest" and its Latin predecessors and French cognates are originally as often or more often positive as negative: to protest was once to bear witness to something and only as a consequence of that allegiance to bear witness *against* something else. But protest is now almost ... a negative phenomenon.... The self-assertive shrillness of protest arises because the facts of incommensurability ensure that protesters can never win an *argument*; the indignant self-righteousness or protest arises because the facts of incommensurability ensure equally that the protesters can never *lose* an argument either. Hence the utterance of protest is characteristically addressed to those who share the protester's premises; ... protesters rarely have anyone else to talk to but themselves.[20]

Lewis, I am sure, would not have disagreed. Indeed, he could well have written the passage himself.

I conclude, then, that in *The Abolition of Man* Lewis was not simply giving expression to nostalgia for a vanished age but was, like Macintyre, a writer whose background is in many ways different, identifying a fundamental error in certain pervasive modern or should we say "postmodern" attitudes.

You will have noticed, however, one difference between them. Macintyre talks of "a grave cultural loss" while Lewis speaks of "the abolition of Man." Is Lewis simply making his point by a rhetorical device, a pardonable exaggeration, or is Macintyre somewhat understating his case? The answer depends on whether the change is envisaged as a purely cultural one, which could in that case be reversed; or as a possible outcome of genetic manipulation which might bring about an irreversible impairment. Lewis's argument proceeds in two stages. In the first place you have human beings who, though capable of moral discrimination, choose to embrace instead a policy of unfettered choice. They remain human beings who have chosen to abandon morality but are still capable of it. This freedom they then exercise to manipulate human genes in such a way as to leave them, either intentionally or unintentionally, without the capacity for moral judgment at all, and since this capacity is essential to being human, this will amount to the abolition of man.

In the first case what has gone is the Old Western Man of Lewis's inaugural lecture, and he might be in course of time restored; in the second the loss is irretrievable.

Chapter 12

WHAT LEWIS
HAS MEANT FOR ME

Peter Milward

Ignatius Loyola, Thomas Aquinas, William Shakespeare, John Henry Newman, Gerard Manley Hopkins, Gilbert Keith Chesterton — not to mention the Bible itself — all have exercised a profound influence on my mind through their lives and writings. In one important respect, however, their varied influence on me differs from that of C. S. Lewis, giving him an advantage over them. He is the one great man whom I have actually, physically, personally met during the four years of my undergraduate life and studies at Oxford, and to whom I was deeply indebted all that time, and have been ever since.

Till the time of my going up to Oxford, for the Michaelmas Term of 1950 in October, I had been one of Lewis's many unseen and unseeing admirers — from the time of my reading of his *Screwtape Letters* and then *The Problem of Pain*. Till then, however, I had been an admirer of the other men whose names I have just mentioned, with the one exception of Hopkins, whose poetry I did not really get to know and appreciate till well after my graduation from the School of English. I suspect that Lewis himself never got to know or appreciate Hopkins, whose poetry was so unlike his own. Lewis still remained a great name for me, like those other great names, but he was not yet a living personality of flesh and blood. Like Joy Davidman, or rather Debra Winger in the film *Shadowlands*, I admired him from afar and formed my own image of what he looked like from his books: an austere, ascetic man, tall, gaunt, and forbidding. So I was in for inevitable disillusionment when I first set eyes on him at Oxford.

The occasion was during the Michaelmas Term, when Lewis had been invited as one of the master's guests for a Friday "guest night" at my college, Campion Hall. I was then a green undergraduate in the School of Classical Mods (or Moderations), engaged in the intensive study of the Latin and Greek classics for my first year and a half, and so I could only look on the great man from afar. He was seated at the master's table, at the master's right hand, and he went on with the other VIPs from that table to the Senior Common Room for what we imagined was to be a highly intellectual conversation among such Oxford dons as feature in Ronald Knox's *Let Dons Delight*. But we were mere students, relegated to the lower tables and the Junior Common Room, aloof from all contact with the senior members and their guests. Still, what I then saw of Lewis from that distance of class division came as a shock to me. With Debra Winger I could exclaim, "You don't look like C. S. Lewis!" (When I subsequently saw the film, I had the impression she was merely echoing me!)

After that, I saw much more of C. S. Lewis at closer, more democratic quarters. (After all, England is the boasted home of democracy, as well as class division, according to the motto of Alice's Cheshire Cat, "A cat may look at a king!") What I saw of him was more democratic than my imagination had been, for there had been something aristocratic, or even ecclesiastical, in that austere, ascetic creature of my imagination, something remote from common humanity. What I now saw was a red-faced, egg-headed, portly, jolly, middle-aged man, who was (like Old King Cole) fond of his pipe and his glass of beer. One might even say of him that he almost rolled along both into and out of the dining room, though he was not half so fat as that other great man whose prophetic mantle he might be said (I have always thought) to have inherited, namely G. K. Chesterton. He might even have been the model for the typical eighteenth-century Englishman, John Bull, though he was not English at all but Northern Irish. (I have only come across one other such man at all comparable to John Bull, from pictures, and he was Sir Winston Churchill.)

At that time Lewis was teaching in the School of English, and so I would not have met him in the normal course of events, owing to the "great divide" between English and the Classics. I knew, however, that Lewis also presided over a student club named the Socratic Club, which he himself had helped to found for the free discussion of matters related to "the philosophy of Christ" (as Erasmus called it), and so I made a point of joining the society and attending as many of its meetings as I could. It was indeed a most interesting group, composed of students and a few senior members from different colleges, and we met once a week during term-time (of eight weeks) with two speakers representing opposite viewpoints for the promotion of a lively discussion. (After all, if everyone said yes to each other, there would be no discussion!) Usually one of the speakers would be more or less Christian (it was not so easy to find Englishmen who were purely Christian), while the other would be more or less opposed to Christianity (for which it was easier to find a speaker). Apart from the two speakers, in an inconspicuous place sat C. S. Lewis, who would sooner or later join in the discussion once it was declared open to contributions from "the floor." (In fact, those contributions often literally came from those sitting, like myself, on the floor.) Whatever he said was pithily expressed and very much to the point, like an arrow on target. I too invariably made a point of joining in, with my previous scholastic formation of three years at Heythrop College, and I was subsequently appointed college representative for Campion Hall.

The connection became even closer when I moved from Classical Mods, in the spring of 1952, not, as would normally have been the case, to Classical Greats (classical history and philosophy) but to English, for I had meanwhile learned of my appointment to Japan, where they wanted me to take an English rather than a Classical degree. It was, of course, no easy task to "change horses in midstream," considering that I had had no previous preparation in the study of English literature and had to begin almost from scratch. But in my eyes the great advantage of this switch was the greater proximity it brought me to C. S. Lewis—who was not yet "Professor," which he only became on his transference to Cambridge in 1954, but plain "Mr." Lewis. I even hoped he might become my tutor, but I was informed by our senior tutor at Campion Hall, who was in charge of our tutorials, that Lewis was averse to receiving pupils from other colleges. So I had to content myself with attending as many of his lectures as I could, namely his two series of eight-week lectures on what he termed "prolegomena" to medieval literature (later published in the expanded form of *The Discarded Image*) and Renaissance literature (later published in abbreviated form as the introduction to *English Literature in the Sixteenth Century, Excluding Drama*).

Those classes were so memorable. For one thing, they were so well attended, far better than any others in the School of English—and that inevitably made the lecturer an object of envy among his colleagues. For who does not know, least of all Lewis himself, what a considerable part envy plays in the halls of academe? Students flocked to hear him not just because he was so famous but also because they could hear everything he said and take notes of it, he spoke so slowly and clearly, making his points both intelligible and interesting. He was not then the only great man in the School of English. There was also his little, wizened friend, Professor Tolkien, whose lectures were specially recommended to me by my tutor, Professor Wrenn. But alas! Tolkien spoke in such a small voice, one had to sit close up to his lectern to hear what he was saying, and as I came in from another important lecture, I found myself sitting at the back of the not-so-large classroom without being able to catch a single word. So I had to give up on him and content myself with Lewis.

All that time, however, I remained at a distance from Lewis without being his pupil in the tutorial sense of the word. Toward the end of my four years at Oxford I took the opportunity after one of his classes, or rather I took my courage into my hands, to ask him if I might come and speak with him privately about some matter connected with his books. So he kindly invited me to come and see him at his rooms in the New Building of Magdalen College (that is, "new" in the eighteenth century, when it really was new), overlooking the Deer Park. I especially wanted to ask him about his ideas on angels, who appear in his space trilogy under the name of "eldila," since I had a special interest from my days at Heythrop in the angelology of Thomas Aquinas. But before I could say anything, he set the ball rolling with an odd question of his own, "Why is it that so many Irish males remain bachelors?" That altogether stumped me. It was only later that I realized he must have been thinking of himself and his brother, both bachelors from Northern Ireland, whereas a certain lady named Joy had already entered his life and was about to change his bachelor status for that of marriage — of which I had heard not a rumor. As for my main question, all I remember is his getting up from his chair, going to his bookcase, and taking down a large tome of Michael Psellus, a Byzantine Platonist of the eleventh century.

Subsequently, at the viva exam after my English Finals, when it was a question of whether I would be awarded a first- or second-class degree, Lewis was on the examining board, and it was he who opened the questioning by asking me if I had read any of the minor poets of the eighteenth century, and what I thought of them. Again he had me stumped, and that set me off on a bad footing for the rest of the viva. So I went down that July, from Oxford to Japan, with only a second to my credit, while Lewis himself went off to Cambridge to take up the newly created chair of Mediaeval and Renaissance Literature, as a full professor at last. As for myself, once I had been through my studies of the Japanese language and Catholic theology, and once I had been ordained priest in Tokyo, I became first lecturer, then associate professor, and finally full professor at the Jesuit university of Sophia in Tokyo (named after Our Lady, Seat of Wisdom).

That was, however, by no means the end of my connection with Lewis, despite the divergence of our respective paths from that summer of 1954. Even while I was studying Japanese, I undertook by way of relaxation the task of writing an article on the space trilogy of Lewis for the university journal named *Sophia* (of course, in Japanese). This gave me the opportunity of writing to him both to express my gratitude for his teaching and to ask him detailed questions about his trilogy, which I had had in mind during that last (and first) interview with him at Magdalen. He at once replied to my questions in responding detail, to my full satisfaction, and so there began a long and (to me at least) satisfying correspondence continuing almost till the time of his death. (His last letter to me was unfortunately undated, but from its contents I could see he was close to death's door, and it might even have been one of the last letters he wrote.) I always sent him Japanese Christmas cards, to which he invariably replied with a letter expressing his appreciation of the religious quality of those cards in contrast to the more secular cards mostly available in England (which he held in abhorrence). Later on, for my ordination to the priesthood in 1960, he sent me a letter of good advice for my sermons, preaching what he himself had always practiced in his lectures at Oxford, and emphasizing the importance of making the points and the joints even painfully clear to the listeners.

From the time I joined the faculty of literature at Sophia University in 1962 this correspondence increased in both quantity and quality, arising out of a thesis on Lewis's space trilogy this time being undertaken by one of my Japanese students. Again Lewis replied in satisfying detail, and from then onwards we carried on an exchange of views on the subject of "allegory." Needless to say, Lewis had long since demonstrated his mastery of the subject in his great *Allegory of Love*, and it might be thought it was for me not to teach him but to learn from him. Still, the democratic tradition of Western culture and education is not only that "a cat may look at a king," but also that a disciple may argue with and even confute the arguments of his master, as Aristotle did with Plato, and as Peter Abelard did with William of Champeaux. As Aristotle himself is reported to have said, "Socrates is my friend, and Plato is my friend, but my best friend is Truth." So on this subject of "allegory" I found Lewis limiting his discussion to one, abstract meaning of the term, while I preferred a more concrete application of it, as Aquinas applies it to the Bible, and Dante to his own *Divine Comedy*, and Spenser to his own *Faerie Queene*, while I wished to carry it further even to the plays of Shakespeare.

Nor was that the only point of discrepancy I found emerging between Lewis and myself, old master with young pupil. I had no quarrel with his imaginative writings from *Screwtape* onwards. (Incidentally, it was only after my arrival in Japan that I first became acquainted with his Chronicles of Narnia, which, as he told me, happily erased the devil's name from the popular association concerning him.) Nor had I any quarrel with his other writings on Christian apologetics, which were so ecumenical as to lead not a few of his readers, including his friend Tolkien, to wonder when he would follow his precursor G. K. Chesterton into the Church of Rome. But it was with his more academic writings, in which I had been more closely involved with him as pupil with master, that I found bones to pick or rather, that gave me certain misgivings. Then on the subjects not only of "allegory" but also of "animal pain," "the Bible as literature," the "demarcation of periods," the "emergence of genius," "historicism," and even "mere Christianity" (in alphabetical order), I ventured to present my criticism of Lewis's ideas in a book entitled *A Challenge to C. S. Lewis*, which was published by the Associated University Presses in 1995. Strangely enough, and much to my disappointment, my challenge was never (to the best of my knowledge) taken up by any Lewis scholar but merely met with a cold silence, as if I was breaking a taboo. Only Walter Hooper, in his review for *The Tablet* of London, aptly explained my misgivings with reference to what Tolkien used to call "the Ulsterian motive" in Lewis's writings, that is to say, the continuing influence (much as he might endeavor to downplay it) of his Protestant, Northern Ireland upbringing. For at each stage of my alphabetical challenge I had mentioned something Protestant at the back of my uneasiness with Lewis's academic writings.

A special form of discrepancy had earlier (in 1975) made a somewhat paradoxical appearance in a book I published for the "Renaissance Monographs" in Tokyo under the borrowed subtitle of "Prolegomena to Mediaeval and Renaissance Literature." This was *An Anthology of Mediaeval Thinkers*, in which, while acknowledging my debt to Lewis for his lectures on medieval and Renaissance literature, I expressed my misgivings concerning his approach to his chosen period. For in both his lectures and the books incorporating them (as mentioned above) he had laid emphasis on the classical, pagan backgrounds of the two periods, according to the typical Oxford approach to "classical" and "modern" with hardly a nod to "medieval." It seemed to me he had done less than justice to the Catholic Christian tradition running through the Middle Ages and entering into the Renaissance. For my part, however, and for my thinkers I chose such great names as Augustine, Bernard, Thomas Aquinas, Bonaventure, and Thomas à Kempis, who were largely overlooked by Lewis. Perhaps he did this because he thought there was more continuity between their Christian thought and that of people today, whereas the older pagan cosmology was unfamiliar to them and in more need of introduction. Still, it might well be urged against this reason that their Christian thought was becoming hardly less familiar to modern readers than the preceding pagan thought and no less in need of introduction. Only, in the context of lectures to be given to Oxford and Cambridge students Lewis might have feared a hostile reaction from among his colleagues, objecting to his use of lectures as a platform for proselytizing activities. In contrast to such academic prejudice, so widespread among English universities (not to mention many of the more prestigious universities in America too), I could afford to be more open in Japan about the Christian background to English literature not only at a Christian university like Sophia but even at the national University of Tokyo, where I was also invited to give occasional lectures on this very subject.

The "Renaissance Monographs" were a series of academic publications brought out at yearly intervals by the Renaissance Institute, which I founded in the early 1970s for the express purpose of emphasizing the basic continuity in thought and culture between the medieval and Renaissance periods which was also a basic continuity of influence between Lewis and myself. So much of the secular thought of the Enlightenment, followed by the Romantic Age, had tended to divide the Middle Ages from the Renaissance even in terms of a division between darkness and light (or rather dawn). I found such a division being made everywhere in Japan in the presentation of European history, owing to the bad influence of two scholars, the Swiss Jakob Burckhardt and the Dutch Johan Huizinga, with their one-sided emphasis on the dark aspects of the Middle Ages. In contrast to them, I was happy to find Lewis strongly on the side of "the angels," owing to the delight he shared with his friend Tolkien in the literature and language of that much maligned period. Only, with his "Ulsterian motive," I found Lewis less in sympathy with the Catholic background of the period, not least with its marked devotion to the Blessed Virgin, whose name he could hardly bring himself to mention in his courses of "prolegomena" or in his study of the medieval *Allegory of Love*. Thus, when he came to give his celebrated inaugural lecture as professor of medieval and Renaissance literature at Cambridge in 1954, "De Descriptione Temporum," or the demarcation of periods, he placed "the great divide" between medieval and modern not in the Reformation of the sixteenth century, still less in the Renaissance, but rather in the industrial revolution towards the beginning of the nineteenth century. For him the dissolution of the monasteries perpetrated by Henry VIII and Thomas Cromwell was regrettable but not an unbridgeable break with England's past, and so it came in for little discussion in his lecture. Not even the rise of science or the Puritan revolution in the seventeenth century constituted any such break, but only from the time when science led to technology and industry and so entered into the whole modern way of thinking.

On one point above all I found myself in my Japanese context most in harmony with what I had learned from Lewis. With his "prolegomena" to the Middle Ages and the Renaissance, as well as his other course of lectures on Milton's *Paradise Lost* (which alas, he did not give during my few years in the School of English at Oxford), he seemed to regard it as the duty of a lecturer not so much to impart the results of scholarly research on special subjects as to introduce his audience to more general periods, leaving it up to them to follow up his suggestions in their private reading. This has also been my own approach to the teaching of English literature in Japan. My main courses for them are all in the nature of introductions, whether to "English Literature" as a whole, or to "English Thinkers" from the sixteenth to the twentieth centuries, or to "Christian Themes in English Literature," or to "Shakespeare's Plays" (a subject, incidentally, which Lewis invariably avoided as being for some reason less congenial to himself), though I might take smaller seminars for the reading of selected nature poems in English or memorable speeches in Shakespeare's plays. After all, it seems to me that the study of English literature has to be left to the students themselves, according to the saying, "You can bring a horse to the water, but you can't make him drink." The reading of English has to be left to each reader, only it needs to be guided by a teacher who may be expected to know it all. The reader has to be encouraged to develop his response to his reading in the form of subjective essays in which he may express his personal reactions to the great authors of the past. After all, the study of literature is not a science, depending on strictly scientific methods of criticism, according to a modern way of thinking that is all too widespread and no less repugnant to Lewis than to myself. As Newman pointed out long ago in his *Idea of a University*,

> Science has to do with things, literature with thoughts; science is universal, literature is personal; science uses words merely as symbols, but literature uses language in its full compass, as including phraseology, idiom, style, composition, rhythm, eloquence, and whatever other properties are included in it.

Thus, even while criticizing my former teacher, I have done so according to that long tradition of Western culture of which he was himself such an outstanding pillar. If I have found fault with him, it is largely because of certain limitations I have seen arising out of his "Ulsterior motive," with implicit support from his friend, that other great medieval scholar, J. R. R. Tolkien. Basically, we are all on the side of Old Western Man, in opposition to the rising tide of mechanized, industrialized modernity, and, I might add, vulgarity. So it might be said, somewhat whimsically, that while our heads are divided, we are, like some monster of the antediluvian age, one at heart. To me he is no idol perched on a high pedestal to receive the uncritical adoration of his worshipers, but, as Hamlet recognized and admired in his ghostly father, "he was a man, take him for all in all," and I fear "I shall not look upon his like again."

Finally, where perhaps our aims in life come closest together, there is our common Christian ideal to bear witness to the Word "in season and out of season," according to the command of the Word incarnate to his disciples to "go and preach the Gospel to all nations." Needless to say, as lecturers in the modern academic world, we both have had to "temper the wind to the shorn lamb," where by "lamb" I may include colleagues no less than students. In this refined world we cannot be open about what we hold as of first importance, any more than Shakespeare (according to my interpretation of his plays) was able to express what he held most dear, as he lamented, through the mouth of Hamlet, "But break, my heart, for I must hold my tongue!" We both have had to draw a fine distinction between what we may say in the ever-critical academic world and what we are freer to say in the marketplace. So Lewis deliberately restricted himself and drew in his horns (like a timid snail) in his academic writings, if revealing something of his "Ulsterior motive," and I too have had to avoid any appearance of proselytizing in my lectures and various books on Shakespeare, though, as I have said, I have enjoyed more freedom than Lewis did at Oxford and Cambridge, with all their academic prejudice, in the more tolerant ambient of Japanese academe. Like Lewis, if I may say so without boasting, I have achieved no small success in the wider book market, with such titles as *Things Wise and Otherwise* (an English textbook for Japanese students) and *The English and the Japanese* (in Japanese translation), which have both enjoyed sales of over two hundred thousand copies. Even books of mine on openly biblical subjects, such as *Jesus and His Disciples* and *What the Bible Tells Us* (both in Japanese), have sold up to a hundred thousand copies. Not that I wish to compare myself with Lewis, who has enjoyed far greater sales with a worldwide reputation, but I am merely showing how I have on a smaller, Japanese scale emulated his example from a humble distance.

Then, too, whereas Lewis was more of an individual in his academic world, I have been appointed by my religious superiors to teach English literature at Sophia University and so to enter into the academic world of Japan. Thus, I have to adapt my teaching to the requirements of this world while interpreting those requirements as including a reasonable explanation of the Christian background of that literature. In fact, I have found it impossible to make a rigid distinction between any Western literature and its deeply Christian inspiration, even or especially when I approach the plays of Shakespeare, which seem at first sight to be so secular. On the other hand, as a Jesuit priest and missionary in Japan, I have had the added obligation to bring the message of Christ's Gospel to the hearts of the Japanese, if outside the classroom in voluntary groups or in my writings. Then I regard it as a sowing of the seed, which I do as best I can (or what Larry the Lamb calls "my little best"), leaving the fruitful outcome in other hands, and above all in the mighty hands of God.

Chapter 13

C. S. LEWIS AND DOROTHY L. SAYERS

Barbara Reynolds

Dorothy L. Sayers and C. S. Lewis were two of the most influential British writers of the first half of the twentieth century. Their writings continue to command attention, to arouse controversy, and to challenge response. In my talk today, I will try to set before you the qualities they had in common and the extent to which they influenced and reacted upon each other. I had the privilege of knowing them both: Dorothy L. Sayers for eleven years and C. S. Lewis during his years as professor at Cambridge. They were not intimate friends; in fact, I would say that they began by being somewhat wary of each other. They respected each other's works. It is said that C. S. Lewis reread *The Man Born to Be King* every year during Lent. Dorothy Sayers greatly admired *The Allegory of Love*, of which she gave me a copy once as a Christmas present. She also admired *The Screwtape Letters* and enjoyed the two space novels and *That Hideous Strength*. But personal relations were distant. What they had in common was an enormous admiration for Charles Williams.

I have sometimes seen it stated that Sayers was a member of the group known as the Inklings. Of course, this was not so. For one thing, Sayers did not live in Oxford; for another, the Inklings was an all-male group. But professor Clyde S. Kilby, in that brilliant vision which he had of the seven authors who belonged together, was right to include Sayers alongside two of the Inklings; not just as the token woman but

Remarks made at the C. S. Lewis Summer Institute, Cambridge, 1998.

as someone who might, perhaps, be called "an honorary Inkling." She and Lewis and Charles Williams had a number of ideas and convictions in common. For instance, there is an example from the program of the 1998 C. S. Lewis Summer Institute that has this quotation from *God in the Dock* by Lewis: "We must attack the enemy's line of communication. What we want is not more little books about Christianity, but more little books by Christians on other subjects—with their Christianity *latent*."[1] That was published in 1945.

In a letter to the Bishop of Coventry from Dorothy Sayers dated the twenty-sixth of June, 1944, she writes,

> The anti-Christians have got away very successfully with an anti-religious propaganda which never openly says anything that one can pin down as a lie, but which merely *assumes*, more or less tacitly, that Christianity is aloof from daily life, uninterested in art, opposed to science and so on and so on. I believe that the time has come quietly to twist this weapon from the hand of the enemy. I mean that your Christian editor, if he really cares more for Christianity than for his paper, will be most helpful in the long run if he will sacrifice his professional eagerness for sensation and assume that an interest in jobs, science, art and what-not, is all in the day's work of the Church. For example: let us suppose that your Educational Department invites a distinguished Christian biologist to lecture on Tadpoles under your Lordship's auspices. If your Press Report comes splurging out with an excitable headline:
>
> #### BISHOP TAKES CHAIR AT SCIENTIFIC MEETING
>
> the implication is that he is a bold, and probably heterodox bishop who would fly in the Church's face by doing any such thing. Especially if this is followed up by extracts from the lecture directed to show that "Tadpoles Prove Christianity." But if the Editor will just quietly concentrate on the more absorbing aspects of the Tadpole's life, and the lecturer will quietly assume, without rubbing it in, that the Tadpole belongs to a Christian cosmogony, and that un-Christian explanations of

the Tadpole are merely irrational—then, after some months or years of this kind of thing, it will gradually filter into the public mind, and become taken for granted, that if you want to get the most up-to-date scientific stuff on Tadpoles you will find it inside and not outside the Church's sphere of influence.[2]

And it goes on at quite considerable length. And she says, like C. S. Lewis, that what is needed is books on various subjects that assume a Christian belief.

Dorothy Sayers first approached Lewis at the beginning of World War II, when she was editing a series of books known as Bridgeheads, a creation of her own designed to provide thought-provoking and morale-lifting works for a bewildered wartime public. Her fellow editors were Helen Simpson and Muriel St. Clare Byrne, and the first volume to be published in the series was her own *The Mind of the Maker*. Early on in the project she wrote to Lewis to ask him to contribute a volume on the subject of marriage, somewhat surprising at that stage in his life to be asked to write on that subject, but she had been struck by one of the *Screwtape Letters*, which deals with it. Lewis turned the invitation down and suggested she should write the book herself. She did not, but the suggestion is said to have borne fruit, and Lewis's handling of the theme of marriage in *That Hideous Strength* owes something to it.

Both writers broadcast and lectured during the war, trying to reach the general public and members of the forces on matters of faith and morality. They were both much in demand. Their lectures were published in small volumes and sold in their thousands. Both spent a lot of time and energy answering letters from strangers, advising them on their reading, straightening out their ideas. This is well known about Lewis, that he was very generous in this respect, but so was Sayers, more than is generally realized as I have now seen from editing her letters.

In March 1943, a recording of part of *The Man Born to Be King* was broadcast. The play was entitled *A Certain Nobleman*, and it is the one which deals with the miracle at Cana. A member of the public wrote angrily,

Dear Madam: I heard part of your radio play last night, but eventually switched off in disgust that such drivel should be given over the air and that a person of your standing should write it. I can quite understand people of little education accepting and taking in such things as these, but you must have made research and inquiries into the actual so-called miracle. And in view of your findings, I cannot understand why you should then write a play based on a pack of lies.

He went on for several more paragraphs, and signed himself "Yours faithfully."

Dorothy Sayers did not usually reply to such insulting letters, but for some reason this one caught her fancy and she wrote,

Dear Sir:

I'm sorry that you should have sustained such a shock. Is this really the first time you have realized that quite a large number of educated persons profess the Catholic faith?... But let me beg you not to agitate yourself too much. For a person of excitable disposition, it is extremely wearing to live in a constant state of virtuous indignation. Forget that materialism is out of fashion, that the physicists are all going metaphysicist, and that psychologists have sapped the very foundations of rationalism. Console yourself with despising us—nothing is more soothing than to contemplate the folly and depravity of one's inferior.[3]

And she went on, then signed the letter "Yours faithfully, Dorothy L. Sayers." He wrote back in the same line again, signing himself "That excitable person, and so and so and so and so."

The relationship developed, most surprisingly. At first it began "Dear Madam, Dear Sir, Yours faithfully," and once the correspondent, though beginning yet another angry letter "Dear Madam," finished by saying, as though through clenched teeth, "Yours faithfully." Then they softened a little and were writing "Dear Miss Sayers, Dear Mr. So and So," and signed their letters "Yours sincerely." Eventually, Dorothy said, "I sent him a long list of books to read." It must have taken her days to compile it. And finally, the gentleman even called—twice—to see her in her home in Witham, Essex.

In the course of this correspondence, the offending plays that comprised *The Man Born to Be King* were published and Dorothy Sayers sent an advance copy to C. S. Lewis. The letter accompanying this gift is probably one of the first she wrote to him. At any rate, it is the earliest one, extant. And you will be amused to know that she wrote it in *Screwtape* style. She invented a devil named Sluckdrib who, she imagined, had been hovering round her and who wrote in disgust to Screwtape to deplore the lack of planning which he said "seems to permeate the whole policy of the Low Command, and threatens to disintegrate our entire war-time strategy."[4] Sluckdrib's patient (that is, Dorothy herself) had been coming along nicely—and I quote—"So far as *my* department is concerned," writes Sluckdrib to Screwtape,

I can assure your Sublimity that no fault can be found. The effect of writing these plays upon the character of my patient is wholly satisfactory. I have already had the honor to report intellectual and spiritual pride, vainglory, self-opinionated dogmatism, irreverence, blasphemous frivolity, frequentation of the company of theatricals, captiousness, impatience with correction, polemical fury, shortness of temper, neglect of domestic affairs, lack of charity, egotism, nostalgia for secular occupations, and a growing tendency to consider the Bible as Literature.[5]

And so it develops. Then he demands to know what's the good of all that? He was succeeding with this patient, Dorothy Sayers, but now

A sound atheist of the old-fashioned materialist kind (that is the man who wrote to her, you see) wrote to my patient a highly offensive letter about miracles, accusing her of ignorance and dishonesty in the vulgarest language. I persuaded her to answer it still more rudely and offensively. That should have inflamed the situation. Instead, the man seemed pleased to be taken note of. His subsequent letters (though still discourteous and infidel) became more moderate in tone, and his latest effusion contained an apology and expressed readiness to read some Christian literature, if my patient would send him a list.[6]

And so on. It is too long to reproduce here, but it is a lovely, lovely letter. She breaks off there and writes to Lewis in her own persona and says,

> Thus from my Attendant. I confess it had not previously occurred to me that the corruption of all of the vices by righteousness must cause as much theological wrangling *there* as the corruption of the virtues by original sin does *here*. Meanwhile, I am left with the Atheist on my hands. I do not want him. I have no use for him. I have no missionary zeal at all. God is behaving with His usual outrageous lack of scruple. The man keeps on bothering about Miracles, he thinks Hall Caine's *Life of Christ* is the last word in Biblical criticism....[7]

And so on.

> It will go on for years. I cannot bear it. Two of [them] are yours—I only hope they will rouse him to fury. Then I shall hand him on to you. You like souls. I don't. God is simply taking advantage of the fact that I can't stand intellectual chaos, and it isn't fair. Anyhow, there aren't any up-to-date books about Miracles.[8]

That letter was written in 1943. Now C. S. Lewis's book on miracles was not published until 1947. He had preached a sermon on the subject in November 1942, and I think, and Walter Hooper agrees, that this observation of Sayers's, about there being no modern, up-to-date book on miracles, probably put it into Lewis's head to write a book about it himself, because she ends her letter:

> People have stopped arguing about [miracles]. Why? Has Physics sold the pass? or is it merely that everybody is thinking in terms of Sociology and international Ethics? Please tell me what to do with this relic of the Darwinian age who

is wasting my time, sapping my energies, and destroying my soul. Yours indignantly, Dorothy L. Sayers.[9]

Sayers's first important involvement with Lewis contained the article she contributed to the volume of essays which Lewis edited for Charles Williams. It was planned originally as a festschrift to be presented to him on his departure from Oxford at the end of the war. But as you know, he died suddenly in May 1945, and the book turned into a memorial volume. Lewis knew that Sayers had been writing to Williams about Dante all through 1944, and he invited her to contribute. She agreed at once and offered an essay on Dante compiled from her letters to Williams, which he had hoped to edit and publish. This was the first article she ever wrote on Dante. Lewis gave it pride of place in the book as the opening article, said it was a stunning essay which would, by itself, make the volume memorable.

An amusing misunderstanding arose between Lewis and the secretary of the Oxford University Press, Sir Humphrey Milford. It was assumed that the memorial volume to Charles Williams would be published by the OUP, and C. S. Lewis thought that the head of the press was dragging his feet. On the thirtieth of June 1945, he wrote to Dorothy,

> I have written to Sir Humphrey Milford about the Charles Williams volume, and he replies expressing his willingness to publish: but apparently he imagines we propose to let him do so at our expense. I have replied explaining that we had no such idea—we are seeking no remuneration, and will make over royalties to Mrs. Williams ... I wait to see if this will shame him into making an offer.[10]

Dorothy exploded with indignation.

> Dear Mr. Lewis, Good God Almighty! And Charles served that firm faithfully for nearly all his life! Does that comic little man [this is Sir Humphrey Milford] expect ME to pay for the privilege of being published by him? Pay? PAY?—Or, if it comes to that, YOU? Most publishers would be pretty glad to have our names on their list at any price.[11]

She goes on about this and suggests other publishers, and so on. And she talks about her progress with her own essay. And C. S. Lewis replied, "That's the spirit!" and so on.

C. S. Lewis had misunderstood Sir Humphrey Milford, who replied on the fourth of July, "Good gracious no!... 'Terms and prices' only meant a question of royalty and publication price. Of course I realize that you intended a book published at our expense...."[12] So Lewis adds, "Best quality Sackcloth & Ashes in sealed packets delivered in plain vans at moderate charges."[13] And Dorothy wrote back,

> Dear Mr. Lewis ...
> My menu for tonight shall be:
> HUMBLE PIE
> IPSISSIMA VERBA
> with sharp sauce
> FRUITS
> meet for Repentance
> I take it all back, including "comic little man."[14]

C. S. Lewis greatly enjoyed Sayers's letters. It is said that he destroyed most of those he received, but he did not destroy hers. In December 1945 he wrote to her, "Although you have so little time to write letters you are one of the great English letter writers. (Awful vision for you— 'It is often forgotten that Miss Sayers was known in her own day as an Author. We, who have been familiar from childhood with the Letters can hardly realize ...')"[15] To that playful flattery, Dorothy wrote another long letter, mainly to discuss her essay for the Williams volume, and she had said that Dante's style was lucid. C. S. Lewis said, "*lucid*. Great Gods!!! Yes, I know it is in *places*: but *lucid* just like that! Whose style wd. you call obscure, I'd like to know?"[16] She replied, "*lucid*—I think I do mean 'lucid'—just like that! I don't really think the style is obscure—indeed what stumps the translator at every turn is its heartbreaking simplicity."[17] She was delighted to find when she read T. S. Eliot's essay on Dante that he too had said that Dante was lucid. He said that the thought may be obscure, but the word is lucid, or rather, translucent.

Going on a little further with Lewis's pleasure in Dorothy's letters, in June 1947 she wrote to thank him for his book on miracles, which had then come out, and also she thanks him for the handsome compliment he has paid to *The Mind of the Maker*. C. S. Lewis has said, in his book *Miracles*, how a miracle can be no inconsistency, but the highest consistency will declare to those who have read Miss Dorothy Sayers's indispensable book *The Mind of the Maker*. So you see, by now they were paying handsome compliments to each other.

This letter is written in wartime, in 1947, when there isn't much food, and Dorothy Sayers just finishes her letter saying, "I have no news, except ... I have purchased two hens." Now if you were telling someone that you had bought two hens, you'd leave it at that, wouldn't you? But here goes Dorothy:

> In their habits they display, respectively, Sense and Sensibilty, and I have therefore named them Elinor and Marianne. Elinor is a round, comfortable, motherly-looking little body who lays one steady, regular, undistinguished egg per day, and allows nothing to disturb her equanimity (except indeed the coal-cart, to which most take exception). Marianne is leggier, timid, liable to hysterics. Sometimes she lays a shell-less egg, sometimes a double yolk, sometimes no egg at all. On the days when she lays no egg, she nevertheless goes and sits in the nest for the usual time and seems to imagine that nothing more is required. As my gardener says: "She just *thinks* she's laid an egg." Too much imagination in fact Sensibility. But when she does lay an egg it is larger than Elinor's. But you cannot wish to listen to this cackle....[18]

C. S. Lewis replied, "I loved hearing about Elinor and Marianne. You are a real letter writer. I am not."[19]

Perhaps you would like to hear about her admiration for *That Hideous Strength*. She says on 3 December 1945,

> What with Dante and the Litchfield play [that was her play for Litchfield Cathedral, *The Just Vengeance*], and my domestic affairs, I have never written to you about *That*

Hideous Strength. What with all this atomic stuff, we seem to be coming alarmingly close to that prospect so much desired by—which of them was it?—when there won't be a green thing left on the earth's surface. Dante put the violent against Nature and Art in *The Abominable Sand....* How right that man was! I don't so much mind if we blow up the entire planet with a bomb ... but I do dread all the promised prosperity and progress. I don't want to end up sitting in an artificial desert, eating the synthetic by-products of nuclear fission. The book [that is, *That Hideous Strength*] is tremendously full of good things—perhaps almost too full—the time-scheme at the beginning seems almost violently condensed—and I'm afraid I don't like Ransom quite so well since he took to being golden-haired and interesting on a sofa like *The Heir of Redclyffe*—but the arrival of the gods is grand and (in a different manner) the atmosphere of the N.I.C.E. is superb. Wither is a masterpiece; even with some experience of official documents and political speeches, one would not have believed it possible to convey so little meaning in so many words. And the death of Filostrato is first class—his desperate agitation, at feeling that it was all so unscientific, and "his last thought was that he had underestimated the terror." Mr. Bultitude of course, is adorable—Oh! and that marvelous confusion of tongues at the dinner. And the painful realism of that college meeting. I enjoyed it all enormously. I still admit to an unregenerate affection for the "old furry people," and was bitterly disappointed when I found I had missed the reprint of *Out of the Silent Planet* till it was too late to secure a copy. *Please* warn me in time of the arrival of a new edition. I want very much to complete the trilogy.[20]

So you see, they were getting on well.

Some of the most interesting letters they exchanged are ones which arose when Lewis invited Sayers to contribute to a series of short booklets which, as he said, should be for young people in top forms at school. He invited her to contribute one on the subject of sin. Sayers questioned whether this was the right thing for her to do, and Lewis reproached her for putting what he called her "artistic conscience" ahead, or in the way, of her duties. She let fly on this, I must say, in a long letter about artistic conscience and objecting to the use of "artistic" as a qualifying adjective to conscience. "How [the devil] does love, to be sure, putting asunder what God has joined! Conscience is conscience...."[21] And Lewis himself had said it is very difficult to decide whether one should or should not undertake a commission to write this or that.

> I've always realised, that you were bothered about this business of art and edification. But I think you're making it too complicated.... If you admit at all that gifts and talents have any sanctity in themselves ... you have to deal honestly with them and respect their proper truth. I don't believe God is such a twister as you make out. I don't believe he implants a love of good workmanship *merely* as a trap for one to walk into. Of course, one can make an idol of good workmanship as of anything else. I don't know what will happen at the moment of death, but I don't somehow fancy showing up a lot of stuff to the Carpenter's Son and saying
> "Well, I admit that the wood was green and the joints untrue and the glue bad, but it was all church furniture."[22]

Lewis had expressed doubts about himself, and she said,

> I've worried over this quite a bit, and I'll tell you what I make of it. No, of course you mustn't go by what people say ... most of them don't know what they're talking about anyhow.... They clamour for detective stories ... they clamour for religious addresses ... they clamour for personal gossip and newspaper interviews.... You must not do even the right deed for the wrong reason. You must not accept money, you must not accept applause, you must not accept a "following," you must not accept even the assurance that you are doing good as an excuse for writing anything but the thing you want to say. [That was her benchmark.]

I don't mean, of course, that you are to retire into the ivory tower and write only for yourself. You must speak to and for your audience—otherwise, you are sinning against the City. But you must not tell people what they want to hear, or even what they need to hear, unless it is the thing you passionately want to tell them.[23]

She developed this idea at great length. Then she said,

You know all this. Of course you know it. But the awful moment comes when the water-pots are empty, or the original loaf and sprats haven't been supplied; and you've either got to make *ersatz* miracles like Mr Sludge the Medium, or to say firmly: "I'm sorry; it isn't there." And I have come to the conclusion that at all costs one has got to be honest about it. One must do what one is called to do, but one isn't *really* the pole of the universe, and the thing won't *really* fall to pieces because one drops out for a moment till the next call comes.[24]

It's a wonderful letter, but I mustn't go on reading it. At too great a length she says, "If I have been impertinent, please forgive me." Lewis replied, among other things,

I don't think the difference between us comes where you think. Of course, one mustn't do *dishonest* work. But you seem to take as the criterion of honest work the sensible *desire* to write, the "itch." That seems to me precious like making "being in love" the only reason for going on with a marriage.[25]

They talked a lot about that. She wrote to him again on the subject. He said that sometimes he felt so depressed and when he had argued in favor of belief he never felt less faith in it himself than when he had written that out. And she said, "I understand all that. That happens to me." These letters, I think, are among the most intimate they exchanged. They both had doubts about what they did sometimes, and they tried to help each other this way. All I can say is, please get volume 3 of the letters.

I will now tell you about C. S. Lewis's reaction to her translation of *Inferno*. She sent him an advance copy of the first of the volumes, and on the eleventh of November 1949, Lewis, having read nineteen of the cantos by then, wrote, "This tells us one thing about your version: You have got (what you most desired) the quality of an exciting story."[26] On the fifteenth of November he wrote again: "I've finished it now. There's no doubt taking it for all in all, it is a stunning work. The real test is this, that however I set out with the idea of attending to your translation, before I've read a page I've forgotten all about you and am thinking only of Dante, and two pages later I've forgotten about Dante and am thinking only about Hell."[27]

That pleased her very much, and she said, on the eighteenth of November 1949,

Dear Dr. Lewis,

I've had a lot of nice letters about the *Inferno*, but I think yours is the very nicest, because you understood so well what the thing's all about, what the translation aims at, and why it is bound to be one thing or the other and can't very well be two incompatible things at once. I've rather ceased worrying about the border-line between liveliness and flippancy, because I learned over *The Man Born to Be King* that everybody draws it in a slightly different place. [And she agrees with him.] ...

I think the *Inferno* is really frightening. It has the quality of Hell—the infinite dreary malice and the infinite vicious monotony. Milton never frightens me—I don't think, somehow, he had ever encountered real wickedness, or felt inside himself the terrifying possibility of actual consent to the absolute will to evil. He knew all about the temptation to sin, but that's not quite the same thing....[28]

The correspondence between Lewis and Sayers is so rich that I could easily swamp you with too much material, and the temptation to do so is very strong. I'm beginning to fear I may have done so already. So I will conclude with one more item: the panegyric which C. S. Lewis wrote for the memorial service held for Dorothy

Sayers in January 1958 at St. Margaret's, Westminster. I was present; I heard this address. Lewis himself was too ill at the time to attend the service, and his speech was read for him, if I remember correctly, by the Bishop of Chichester, George Bell. Now last night you had a reenactment of C. S. Lewis's inaugural lecture here in Cambridge. I can't emulate Joss Ackland, but I will read you this address, which I think is a beautifully thought-out assessment by Lewis after the death of Dorothy, and not wholly admiring throughout.[29] There are certain reflections here and there, but I read it again in preparation for this morning and I do think he did it very well. I have a photocopy of his handwritten paper, and on the top is a little query, "Will this do? C. S. Lewis."

The variety of Dorothy Sayers' work makes it almost impossible to find anyone who can deal properly with it all. Charles Williams might have done so; I certainly can't. It is embarrassing to admit that I am no great reader of detective stories: embarrassing because, in our present state of festering intellectual class consciousness, the admission might be taken as a boast. It is nothing of the sort: I respect, though I do not much enjoy, that severe and civilized form, which demands much fundamental brain work of those who write in it and assumes as its background uncorrupted and unbrutalized methods of criminal investigation. Prigs have put it about that Dorothy in later life was ashamed of her "tekkies" and hated to hear them mentioned. A couple of years ago my wife asked her if this was true and was relieved to hear her deny it. She had stopped working in that genre because she felt she had done all she could with it. And indeed, I gather, a full process of development had taken place. I have heard it said that Lord Peter is the only imaginary detective who ever grew up—grew from the Duke's son, the fabulous amorist, the scholar swashbuckler, and connoisseur of wine, into the increasingly human character, not without quirks and flaws, who loves and marries, and is nursed by, Harriet Vane. Reviewers complain that Miss Sayers was falling in love with her hero. On which a better critic remarked to me, "It would be truer to say she was falling out of love with him; had ceased fondling a girl's dream—if she had ever done so—and began inventing a man."

There is in reality no cleavage between the detective stories and her other works. In them, as in it, she is first and foremost the craftsman, the professional. She always saw herself as one who has learned a trade, and respects it, and demands respect for it from others. We who loved her may (among ourselves) lovingly admit that this attitude was sometimes almost comically emphatic. One soon learned that "We authors, Ma'am" was the most acceptable key. Gas about "inspiration," whimperings about critics or public, all the paraphernalia of *dandyisme* and "outsidership" were, I think, simply disgusting to her. She aspired to be, and was, at once a popular entertainer and a conscientious craftsman: like (in her degree) Chaucer, Cervantes, Shakespeare, or Molière. I have an idea that, with very few exceptions, it is only such writers who matter much in the long run. "One shows one's greatness," says Pascal, "not by being at an extremity but by being simultaneously at two extremities." Much of her most valuable thought about writing was embodied in *The Mind of the Maker*: a book which is still too little read. It has faults. But books about writing by those who themselves have written viable books are too rare and too useful to be neglected.

For a Christian, of course, this pride in one's craft, which so easily withers into pride in oneself, raises a fiercely practical problem. It is delightfully characteristic of her extremely robust and forthright nature that she soon lifted this problem to the fully conscious level and made it a theme of one of her major works. The architect in *The Zeal of Thy House* is at the outset the incarnation of—and therefore doubtless the *Catharsis* from—a possible Dorothy whom the actual Dorothy Sayers was offering for mortification. His disinterested zeal for the work itself has her full sympathy. But she knows that, without grace, it is a dangerous virtue: little better than

2

the "artistic conscience" which every Bohemian bungler pleads as a justification for neglecting his parents, deserting his wife, and cheating his creditors. From the beginning, personal pride is entering into the architect's character: the play records his costly salvation.

As the detective stories do not stand quite apart, so neither do the explicitly religious works. She never sank the artist and entertainer in the evangelist. The very astringent (and admirable) preface to *The Man Born to Be King*, written when she had lately been assailed with a great deal of ignorant and spiteful obloquy, makes the point of view defiantly clear. "It was assumed," she writes," that my object in writing was 'to do good.' But that was in fact not my object at all, although it was quite properly the object of those who commissioned the plays in the first place. My object was *to tell that story* to the best of my ability, within the medium at my disposal—in short, to make as good a work of art as I could. For a work of art that is not good and true *in art* is not true and good in any other respect." Of course, while art and evangelism were distinct, they turned out to demand one another. Bad art on this theme went hand in hand with bad theology. "Let me tell you, good Christian people, an honest writer would be ashamed to treat a nursery tale as you have treated the greatest drama in history: and this in virtue, not of his faith, but of his calling." And equally, of course, her disclaimer of an intention to "do good" was ironically rewarded by the immense amount of good she evidently did.

The architectonic qualities of this dramatic sequence will hardly be questioned. Some tell me they find it vulgar. Perhaps they do not quite know what they mean; perhaps they have not fully digested the answers to this charge given in the preface. Or perhaps it is simply not "addressed to their condition." Different souls take their nourishment in different vessels. For my own part, I have re-read it in every Holy Week since it first appeared, and never re-read it without being deeply moved.

Her later years were devoted to translation. The last letter I ever wrote to her was an acknowledgement of her *Song of Roland*, and I was lucky enough to say that the end-stopped lines and utterly unadorned style of the original must have made it a far harder job than Dante. Her delight at this (surely not very profound) remark suggested that she was rather starved for rational criticism. I do not think this one of her most successful works. It is too violently colloquial for my palate; but, then, she knew more Old French than I. In her Dante the problem is not quite the same. It should always be read in conjunction with the paper on Dante which she contributed to the *Essays Presented to Charles Williams*. There you get the first impact of Dante on a mature, a scholarly, and an extremely independent mind. That impact determined the whole character of her translation. She had been startled and delighted by something in Dante for which no critic, and no earlier translator, had prepared her: his sheer narrative impetus, his frequent homeliness, his high comedy, his grotesque buffoonery. These qualities she was determined to preserve at all costs. If, in order to do so, she had to sacrifice sweetness or sublimity, then sacrificed they should be. Hence her audacities in both language and rhythm.

We must distinguish this from something rather discreditable that has been going on in recent years—I mean the attempt of some translators from Greek and Latin to make their readers believe that the *Aeneid* is written in *service* slang and that Attic Tragedy uses the language of the streets. What such versions implicitly assert is simply false; but what Dorothy was trying to represent by her audacities is quite certainly there in Dante. The question is how far you can do it justice without damage to other qualities which are also there and thus misrepresenting the *Comedy* as much in one direction as fussy, Miltonic old Cary had done in the other. In the end, I suppose, one comes to a choice of evils. No version can give the whole of Dante. So at least I said when I read her *Inferno*. But, then, when I came to the *Purgatorio*, a little miracle seemed to be happening. She had risen, just as Dante himself rose in his second part: growing richer, more liquid, more elevated. Then first I began to have great hopes of her *Paradiso*. Would she go on rising? Was it possible? Dared we hope?

Well. She died instead; went, as one may in all humility hope, to learn more of Heaven than even the *Paradiso* could tell her. For all she did and was, for delight and instruction, for her militant loyalty as a friend, for courage and honesty, for the richly feminine qualities which showed through a port and manner superficially masculine and even gleefully ogreish — let us thank the Author who invented her.[30]

Chapter 14

A GODDAUGHTER'S MEMORIES

Sarah Tisdall

There is no doubt in my mind that when my mother arrived in Oxford in 1930 she had the world at her feet: young, beautiful, and winner of the senior scholarship to St. Hugh's College, Oxford. Her name was Mary Shelley, daughter of a distant branch of the poet's family. Warmhearted, high-spirited, an accomplished violinist and draughtswoman, how is it possible that it all turned to ashes and that she left Oxford with a fourth-class degree? I think the reason partly lies in the social attitudes of the time, the terrible sense of guilt that she needlessly carried, and in the total lack of belief or confidence that she had in herself.

Oxford at that time was, by and large, contemptuous of women competing in the academic world, and my mother was very sensitive to this attitude. In addition, her family were snubbed by the small-town society of Watlington when they moved closer to Oxford from Sussex. She had a loathing for establishment attitudes and behavior to the end of her life, partly based on her experience at boarding school and partly by her experience in Oxford.

Before she came to Oxford she went to Reading University for a year, where Hugo Dyson was her tutor and where she met Cordelia Meynell, a lifelong friend and part of the famous family of intellectuals. Years later in 1991 Christine Hardie, who was also a Meynell, helped my mother with her article for *The Chesterton Review*. Around this time, Mum had a job of searching on horseback for elm trees. She was working for Ebenezer Gomb, a High Wycome timberman.

In her first year at Oxford she had to take a preliminary examination in Anglo-Saxon, always a challenge for first-year undergraduates.

C. S. Lewis became her tutor in her second and third year not only through the recommendation of Hugo Dyson but also Miss Seaton, an English don at St. Hugh's. The fact that Lewis had broken his rule never to tutor women, "whose heads," according to Vava (my mother's great friend at Oxford), "he deemed to be stuffed with cobwebs," led Vava to suppose that "C. S. Lewis was probably in love with Shelley." Vava went on to describe my mother, "Shell," as being "half nymph crowned with white violets, half racehorse" and added that "she seemed to be inviolate, unbesmirchable."

There was an incident reported independently by both Vava and my mother when Shell was mounted on horseback and met C. S. Lewis on Magdalen Bridge. My mother felt guilty because she should have been in a tutorial, but Lewis managed to give her the impression that he found her attractive. I think, reading his novels, that he especially liked people on horseback!

In his letter to her dated 18 June 1931, he gives her an outline of work.[1] It refers to Hugo Dyson, who was her tutor at Reading before she went to Oxford—so she was the "Dysonian one!" There seems to be an echo of Dionysus, but maybe I am being fanciful. In this letter he recommends reading the original texts. This is certainly a principle that I picked up from him and my mother.

Vava described their life in Oxford: "They had a triumvirate." It included Vava, my mother, and Myfanwy Evans, who later married John Piper the artist. Vava recalled to me,

> There were lovely Summer days in a punt screened by willow trees, supposedly working and afternoons in my room with our feet on the mantelpiece with Myfanwy brushing Ideum into her hair to remove the grease, Shelley and I spluttering but not objecting I just remember Shell playing the violin, her poetry, her occasional painting, the endless talk, the lovely hollow voice, the splendid disdain of all things mundane and most of all the huge luminous eyes.

There are some anecdotes from this time: the production of *The Rose and the Ring*, where Mum got so involved in the part that she hit Barbara Castle (a fellow student thespian who later became a well-known Labour Minister) really hard over the head with a warming pan.[2] How she met Lewis in the WaterMeadows on a balmy day and that this meeting was an inspiration for the watery lands of Perelandra. How hard it was to get down to writing essays. How very important her tutorials with Lewis were. How Myfanwy stole her ghost story and printed it, which was not forgiven. Years later it transpired that Mum's sister Vera had given permission. How she went to the Ruskin School to do some life drawing and play in an orchestra. How Mum sold two books of Labour raffle tickets to all the people at a conservative lecture!

Vava goes on to describe the fateful meeting between my mother and the mysterious figure who became her lover. All we know is that he was a well-known writer and the married stepfather of a friend. Vava writes, "Shelley had gone to stay with Vivian Eyles, at her stepfather's in the country. He woke Shelley up the next morning by tapping a white rose, held on a long-handled pruner, against the bedroom window, and when Shelley looked down, there he was in the garden below looking up at her, and that was that."

It is hard to appreciate in this liberal day and age how extraordinarily radical and brave my mother was to embark on an illicit affair as an undergraduate — nobody would dream of such a thing. A measure of how scandalous it was is that Vava speaks of "sordid assignations in hotels in Bloomsbury." Later the pressures of society became too much so that my mother always felt desperately guilty. At that time she was an atheist and, inspired by her wide reading, a passionate romantic and believer in free love. Why should she resist? The fact that this "cad" jilted her, however, just before her finals was partly responsible for her failing her exams. She had been confidently predicted a first. She told me that whilst she was writing the examination papers, Lewis paced up and down, agonized that she was not doing better. Vava confirms this story. There is a letter from him dated 21 July 1933 in which he says to her that she "must not run away with the idea that you are a Fourth Class mind.... I am quite clear in my own mind that you have not done yourself justice and that your real quality is far beyond the work you did in Schools."[3] He wondered if he should have been stricter, extracting essays from her and offering

215

his help should she need it. I am inclined to think that he should have been stricter with her.

After leaving Oxford she applied for a job at Dartington and asked Lewis for a reference. He wrote her such a good one that in September 1933 she got a job teaching there in preference to W. H. Auden. Dartington was a famously progressive school and estate at that time.[4] Founded by Leonard and Dorothy Elmshirst, wealthy Americans, it was based on the idea of a medieval manor [William Morris] where the whole of life was contained in one area. The school was very forward-looking at the time. Many of the ideas have become common currency in modern educational thinking. Some of the more radical ideas are perhaps not so common, such as the fact that the children did not have to attend lessons in which they were not interested. They could spend all their time on the farm if they so wished. They also had a governing council and imposed their own rules and fines. The famous intellectuals of the day sent their children there, the Huxleys and Bertrand Russell, to name but a few. My mother taught Clement and Lucien Freud. She had to endure Sigmund's granddaughter sitting at the back of her class to see if she was approved. She was! The artists of the time went there, notably Hein Heckroth, designer of the red shoes, Willy Soukop, and Cecil Collins, who were particular friends of my mother. The Ballet Russe, Ravi Shankar, and Indian dancers all visited, as did Alfred Hitchcock, the filmmaker; Tom Hopkinson, editor of *Picture Post*; Stephen Spender; and many more. There were a lot of refugees from Europe who brought ideas and variety. Altogether it was a most exciting place to be.

My father, Daniel Neylan, working in a boring job managing investments in London, read an article about Dartington, and being an idealist, he came down to look at it. My mother was detailed to show him round and they went skating! He had also won a scholarship to Oxford from the Jesuit School at Wimbledon. At Oxford he read classics at Trinity. He had rejected Christianity but was working for peace through the Federal Union. In 1934 he was appointed classical master at Dartington. My parents got married in 1935 at Hoo Mill. I also have a letter from Spain where they went on honeymoon just before the Civil War. It includes a story about seeing *Modern Times* in which Charlie Chaplin waves a red flag, at which point the whole cinema rose to its feet and shouted.

During this time my mother was enjoying teaching at Dartington and was corresponding with Lewis about literature, which they clearly both enjoyed. Lewis sent her a book list in 1937 in response to her letter. She was thrilled with the books he suggested to her. He wrote a pleased letter because she had written to say that he had brought her back to poetry.

In 1938 I was born, which was a shattering event for my mother, who was completely undomesticated.[5] She gave up teaching for the time being. When I was old enough to understand, she used to sing "the raggle taggle gypsies" to me, saying that she would like to live in a field or a caravan.

She turned to Lewis for advice. He suggested an old-fashioned nanny, which she tried, although she became jealous of the nanny's relationship with me.[6] My mother had the greatest difficulty in getting on with domestic helpers, however nice. She decided to look after me herself for moral reasons; that is, mothers should be with their children. When she tried to wean me I became very ill and was like to die. She scoured the country to find a doctor who had any knowledge of allergy, and they saved me by feeding me soya bean.

During 1938 the threat of war increased, and by 1939 there were changes at Dartington. The school decided not to have Latin anymore because so many children had been evacuated, which meant that there was no job for my father. He turned to teaching international affairs at a local further education centre. Some of the staff stockpiled tins of food, of which my parents disapproved very much. Also, many people were pacifists, and most felt that Britain would be immediately invaded.

On the third of September 1939, war was declared. At the school the art master, who was German, was interned. By that time my parents had left Dartington and were living in Headington near Oxford.

That Christmas my mother went to see Lewis. She then wrote him a long letter, thanking him for the visit and mentioning obedience, Bertrand Russell, her own experience with a psychologist, and most importantly, she mentioned that there was something that she could not avoid indefinitely.

In early 1940 my mother was not well, and I was terribly ill in hospital with whooping cough. Lewis replied to her letter about obedience.[7] She answered, saying that his letter cleared up difficulties. In April 1940 she wrote again of her problems with the marriage service. He replied with another heavyweight letter in which he asked, "Do you really want a matriarchal world? Do you really like women in authority?"[8] This illustrates Lewis's view of the position of women. There were many women, including my mother, who found this hard to accept.

It seems that my mother continued to read and think. She wanted someone to discuss things with, but she evidently came to a conclusion, because in January 1941 C. S. Lewis wrote, "Congratulations on your own decision."[9] This eventually led to Lewis's suggesting, at her request, that she see Fr. Adams SSJE, his own confessor, whom they both continued to see until Adams's death in 1953.

In 1940 my parents applied for a visa for me and my mother to go to America, under the protection of Bertrand Russell. There was some correspondence about this, and Lewis felt that my mother, father, and I should stay together, which we did.[10]

My mother told me later that Russell was very charming and good company. It is difficult to imagine the fear and uncertainty people felt in the face of war.

I was not christened until I was four years old. This marks the final conversion of my parents: first my mother and then my father. Apparently, my father had to check out everything extremely carefully intellectually before he committed himself. Lewis had agreed to be my godfather and came to my christening.[11] I vaguely remember having a nice dress and a cloudy memory of meeting someone important.

Nineteen forty-two found my mother "in a trough," and by 1943 she became really ill.[12] She had a breakdown, and I was sent to my grandparents. I did not see my mother for a year.

About this time, I can remember my mother being in floods of tears every day. I had to keep fetching handkerchiefs from the airing cupboard! She played Berlioz's "Childhood of Christ" over and over again on her wonderful gramophone and wept inconsolably. She was weeping for Dartington. She believed that she had to give up all her friends who were not Christians. She wrote to Lewis, "Why do you think that Dartington is so much worse than anywhere else?" Then again she wrote, "The teaching I enjoyed enormously and succeeded in getting them to read and write for pleasure. I started play reading at home with the idea that a good tea and social atmosphere would be a good environment in which to learn, these play readings were very successful." She also invented a game similar to "just a minute" to play with the children. She wrote,

> Dartington had never seemed to look more richly beautiful than the week we were down there packing up. There is no doubt that it is more beautiful than most places. Nor do I think the William Morris impression I got when I first went there was altogether false. The family atmosphere, the real friendliness between staff and children and the business centring round the school farm, the pet shed and the workshops, the amount of sun and fresh air and the healthiness of the children. The children are less silly and more courageous than other children.

Personally I feel that it was a great mistake for my mother to leave Dartington. The discipline of teaching held her together psychologically. She would never find another milieu that suited her so well, nor one that appreciated her so thoroughly.

By 1944 my father had a job at the War Office, and there was a congratulatory letter from C. S. Lewis.[13] My parents found a wonderful house just off Trafalgar Square, Carlton Mews, alas pulled down long ago. It had a cobbled ramp and gas lamps; friends from Dartington also lived there: the Williams Ellises; Clough, the creator of Port Merion; and his daughter Susan, a designer of pottery.

Because it was wartime I remained with my grandparents at Hoo Mill, Oxfordshire, a beautiful old mill mentioned in the Doomsday Book. My grandfather designed and made beautiful furniture using only wooden dowels and pegs, no screws or nails. The idea was stolen after the war, and one still sees vulgarized versions of his elegant work.

There I remember some visits to London, in particular my sixth birthday party where the guests were all adults. Some of the conversation referred to someone who would have come but had been killed by a bomb. On one visit the sky was all red with bombs and fire.

My parents visited Hoo Mill on weekends. I used to creep down the stairs to listen to my aunt, Vera Shelley, and my mother play Bach's "Double Violin Concerto" on violin and piano. Sometimes it would break off into a furious row between them, and I would creep back. There were always drawing and painting with my mother and aunt. I remember my mother taking me into the wood yard and telling me about Lewis and the importance of obedience, illustrating it with a story: "Suppose a bomb was falling and you were told to run and you did not. You would be killed!"

At some point during this time I went to stay with my mother in Lewis's house (or Jack as he was known to his friends). It is a vague memory for me. I must have been very young. I remember sitting in the sitting room with Jack and Warnie and my mother, having tea with the tea and cups and saucers. I think there were biscuits too, on a tray on a low table, and afterwards going out to be shown the garden and the lake or pond. I remember things being pointed out to me. Sadly, all I can see now is the edge of the lake, and a vague feeling of some kind of magic or natural presences in the bushes. I remember being put to bed very solicitously with lots of "are you all rights?" I remember the bedroom. It seemed strange to me because it had two high beds in it with oak vertical struts at either end with pieces along the top making up the bed heads and footboards. I slept in the one nearest the window which looked over the garden. There was a big wardrobe too!

In 1946 my sister was born.[14] We moved to Beaconsfield. There was the feeling of a new beginning. Liz and I were living with our two parents, a change for me.

During this time, and before, C. S. Lewis wrote me lovely letters and sent me £5 at Christmas, which was a small fortune in those days.[15] This was the magic side of his godfatherly duties. The other, as he explained, was to be dutiful. Writing back and drawing him pictures was a major effort. My mother, a most severe perfectionist, made me write and rewrite, draw and redraw. I think it was worth it, however, because I was his only godchild who got a letter from him with drawings in it!

In 1949 I was confirmed. Lewis wrote me a godfatherly message. I remember going to my first confession, which was traumatic, and owning a prayer book with a prayer in it where I called myself the greatest of sinners. Young and naive as I was, I thought it rather strange that I was so very wicked. In fact, I wondered why God had not chosen me to be the Virgin! Lewis wrote to me a lot during these years up to the time I went to the Slade in 1956.[16]

It is at Beaconsfield that I remember sitting on my mother's bed discussing the Narnia books as they came out, wishing that he would dedicate one to me. Of course, he dedicated his anthology of George MacDonald to Mum in 1946. There is a letter to her about the dedication saying how much more my mother got out of George MacDonald than anyone else.[17] I was very hurt when Susan was banished from Narnia because she liked lipstick. I felt that might be me.

I remember that in the drawer under the bed there always seemed to be a manuscript from Lewis. He used to send some of his manuscripts to her for comment. I think Mum saw him a lot during this time. I think I also saw him quite often, but unfortunately, I don't remember. I have an image of his rooms at Magdalen but not a particular occasion. I think I only remember conversations that interested me. I remember him saying how wonderfully good in quality students were after the war. I also remember him saying something about getting up early for the choir on Magdalen Tower on May Day. I also have an image in my mind of his parish church.

In 1952 my parents were introduced to the Mirfield Fathers and to Uvedale and Mel Lambert. A year later my parents had moved to Surrey, and we were installed in a beautiful place amongst a group of people who were dedicated to putting God first. Their sensitivity to art and the intellect, however, was not marked, with the notable exceptions of Jill and Donald Bell-Scott.

In 1953 Fr. Adams died. I remember him well, a darling old man. My parents and I went to his funeral and afterwards to Dyson's rooms in Oxford. I found this a most exciting experience. I was fifteen years old. It was a lovely book-lined room with a view onto the quad. There were a few people there, notably Hugo Dyson and Lewis, of course. The conversation was thrilling. Hugo and Jack discovered that I loved adventure stories, and they outdid each other in extemporizing thrilling beginnings. One that I remember was about the nose of a canoe creeping out from the reeds onto the darkening river. This was accompanied with shrieks of laughter as each tried to cap the other, making it more and more exciting. Lewis said, as we were leaving, that "funerals are so much more fun than weddings" and that it was the proximity of Heaven that made them so.

Personally, I don't think that either the film or the play about him brought out the enormous fun that Jack was. I can't imagine anyone more fun to be with. As a conversationalist he was without parallel. Lewis made the comment in a card to my mother, "Sarah at last old enough to talk to."[18] Even so, I only remember meeting him one last time.

I'm not sure when it was, but he was with Joy. We met: my father, mother, Jack, Joy, and me. We met in a field. It was near a pub in Oxfordshire. The pub had some of my grandfather's chairs in the garden and a stream running by. My mother dressed me in a horrible dress that embarrassed me: it was blue linen with pleats starting round the hips, and she said I looked lovely! I remember Joy had some difficulty with walking. We sat down for a picnic. Lewis, in brilliant form, was full of how he had traveled on a train and picked up an identical coat by mistake. In the pocket was a novel by Mary Renault. He showed us the mackintosh, demonstrating how it had happened. He was delighted by the exchange because he had had a serious work in his pocket: he hoped that whoever had it was enjoying it as much as he had enjoyed *The Bull from the Sea*.

Needless to say, my mother had serious doubts about Joy. Whatever they were, George Sayer agreed with her. I have a letter from him to that effect. I think it was extremely hard for her to accept Jack falling for Joy; however, she felt for him and read all his books about his grief and wrote to him. I found a diary of mine for 1956. It is full of cryptic entries. Tuesday August 2 says, "Saw Lewis briefly." I can remember nothing about it, but I mention it to illustrate that visits were quite frequent.

My mother shone in social situations. She was a wonderful conversationalist, a raconteur par excellence. Many of her stories were against herself. In fact, she was very funny because she was so completely impractical and unconventional. She was a sort of charming walking situation comedy.

She was also very strong intellectually, extraordinarily perceptive where other people were concerned, and an excellent artist. I think her jokes, coupled with her lack of self-confidence, led to her not being respected as she should have been. I think this was at the bottom of her rages, which terrified people.

She painted portraits of extraordinary accuracy and idyllic landscapes. In the late eighties she painted a portrait of the Bishop of Sacramento. When his son saw it after the bishop's death, he burst into tears because it was such a speaking likeness. She was tremendously supportive of anyone who had got onto the wrong side of the "elders and betters," so to speak. Indeed, Daphne Hort, great-granddaughter of Dr. F. J. A. Hort of Cambridge, who helped me with this account, owes a lot to her support and help.

Everyone loved my father. I think he was a saint, the nearest thing I have ever met to the true Christian ideal: loving, long-suffering, unselfish. A man of total integrity, a man more widely read than 99 percent of the population, with a good memory and thoughtful ideas, he was never aggressive, but he was very brave. He saved me from my mother's wrath more than once!

There is no doubt that Lewis was an all-important influence in my mother's life and that he was enormously supportive of her and brought her into the Christian faith. At that time, however, the conflict between a woman having a career and a family was not discussed or practiced as it is today. That my mother felt morally obliged to stay at home and to leave Dartington meant that she lived a life of extraordinary frustration and was obliged to do things (household chores) at which she was hopeless. I don't think Lewis tried to dispel her terrible feeling of no worth. My mother used often to say to me, "I may not have written a book but I've got you." This is a reference from a Lewis letter written when I was born that my mother quoted in an article she wrote for *The Chesterton Review*.[19] I found it quite oppressive.

It is easy to see why Lewis and my mother got on so well. The driving passion of both was literature, both reading it and discussing it. They both grew up reading the same literature. They had a mutual love for George MacDonald among many others, and they both came from severely Protestant backgrounds. Lewis was also an atheist before his conversion in the early thirties. Both got an aesthetic thrill from reading. Whenever one saw Mum she would have a book in one hand and would launch into a discussion of the contents regardless of whether one had read it or not. During the agonies of her conversion, in her draft letters, she says once or twice, "Perhaps it is not God that I desire but Mr Lewis." Finally, I think she must have told him. He says in a letter dated 1940, "You have told me rather too much" and suggested a spiritual advisor.[20] They were both generous and unworldly to a fault.

In 1963, towards the end of Jack's life, he was in hospital, and my mother visited him there several times. She was terribly upset by his illness. It is there that she drew a portrait of him.* When she visited him in the hospital he said to her, "Don't mind seeing me like this; my mind is tired." He was considerate of her to the last.

---

*Reproduced as the frontpiece—Ed.

Chapter 15

THE KILNS CELEBRATION
AND DEDICATION SERVICE

The C. S. Lewis Foundation obtained title to The Kilns, Lewis's home in Headington, in March 1988. At the time, The Kilns had fallen into a dreadful state of disrepair. Holes in the roof created holes in the floor. Windows were broken and the garden was overrun with four-foot-tall weeds. The Foundation began a faith effort to restore The Kilns as it was when Joy Lewis first came to live there. Jack and Warnie still had the blackout curtains hanging in the windows! As money became available, a team of dozens of volunteers came to The Kilns each summer to do the restoration work. Finally completed, The Kilns was dedicated as the C. S. Lewis Study Centre on 17 July 2002 during the fifth triennial C. S. Lewis Summer Institute in convocation at the Sheldonian Theatre. Laurence Harwood, Walter Hooper, and Francis Warner made remarks, and Bishop Kallistos Ware offered prayer.

Laurence Harwood

I've not stood in this room for about ten years, when I witnessed my son's graduation. That's the last occasion on which I was here, so it is a great pleasure to be here again. I have no right to be here, because when I hear all that has been achieved by you, our transatlantic friends, and those in this area for The Kilns, I feel ashamed, to be truthful, on behalf of our own country, Great Britain, that we have not done justice, as you have done, to this great man. It is therefore a particular pleasure and a privilege to be in your company today and to share in this celebration by the C. S. Lewis Foundation of the restoration of

The Kilns at Headington. The Foundation is, in my opinion, to be heartily congratulated for what has been achieved.

That name, "The Kilns," haunted my youth, as the place was often mentioned by my godfather in letters to me. Although as a boy I never actually visited the place, my mind's eye had a vivid picture of it conjured up by amusing and evocative passages in some of the letters he wrote to me. Those who heard me speak yesterday will please forgive me if this is repetition, but I think it gives you a flavor of the way he described the place, even to a young godson of his, that he loved it so much in those days.

Here's a letter he wrote to me, probably in the 1940s. He said,

> The stars have been very bright recently. This house is so funnily built that I have to go up to my bedroom by an outside stairway in the open air. As I go up, Sirius, very bright and green, looks as if he was sitting just on the top rail, and then when I reach the top I see the whole of Orion. Orion, Cassiopeia, and the Plow are the only constellations I can be sure of picking out. Do you know any more? I like Orion the best.[1]

When some years later I visited The Kilns as an adult, I must admit to great disappointment that I could see no stars outside. But yesterday, I was there again and lo and behold, thanks to Kim [Gilnett] and Don [Yanik] and Stanley [Mattson], they are there in position. So this has come true for me, this statement that he wrote to me.

Let me say a word about the grounds; he wrote a charming letter to me about something that happened in his garden:

> We are having very sharp frosts here. The pond is frozen over but not thick enough yet for skating. Our dog Bruce, who is very old and white-haired now, feels the cold very badly and has to be wrapped up in a blanket at night—he looks very funny in it.
>
> Yesterday the man who lives next door to us came into our garden when we weren't looking and cut down one of our trees. He said it had elm-disease and was spoiling *his* garden,

but as he took the wood away with him I call it stealing and we are very angry. He is an old man with a white beard who eats nothing but raw vegetables. He used to be a schoolmaster. He keeps goats who also have white beards and eat nothing but raw vegetables. If I knew magic I should like to turn him into a goat himself: it wouldn't be so very wicked because he is so like a goat already! Don't you think it would serve him right? But I suppose he would then come over and eat the bark of the trees instead of cutting them down, so we should be no better off.[2]

So when I saw The Kilns myself, I was very struck with those imaginative memories I have of it. And to some extent, notwithstanding the development round about that has sadly occurred since those letters were first written, I found that my imagination was, to a large extent, convinced.

I have had a career in the National Trust for thirty-six years, all over this country, and I know the importance of maintaining a sense of place while restoring buildings of historic interest. This has not been easy to do in the case of The Kilns, but I believe the Foundation, with the help of many, many volunteers as has been described, has done the job with great sensitivity and respect, and that Jack, were he to pay us a surprise visit, would say, "Well done." He might, perhaps, like to see a bit more pipe smoke about the house, and it might be a touch too tidy for him I suggest, here and there. But that apart, I think he would be delighted. And I am especially glad that The Kilns is being used as an international study center for further research into his life and work, an admirable purpose for the house.

I only wish that this fine example of preservation could be emulated across the water in Belfast, where I happen to know the charming Edwardian Lewis childhood home, Little Lea, has recently been under the threat of development—six houses proposed in the grounds. Happily, the Ulster Environment and Heritage Service is giving the house "listed" status, which will protect it, but there are also fears that Jack's childhood friend, Arthur Greeves's home, now known as Red Hill, formerly Bernagh, will be redeveloped. Or, perhaps, God forbid, suffer the recent fate of the poet Seamus Heaney's home, so recently demolished. So perhaps, Stanley, the Foundation can come to the rescue in Belfast.

These sad cases only serve to reemphasize the debt of gratitude that all we who honor and love the memory of Jack owe to the Foundation and all who have worked with it. And I am sure that I speak for thousands, if not millions of people throughout the world who have, in their own ways, been deeply influenced and affected by Lewis's writings.

Thank you very much.

Walter Hooper

Ladies and gentlemen, this year is the eightieth birthday of The Kilns; how appropriate that its recovery, restoration, and dedication we celebrate today continues to be one of the chief characteristics in the life of C. S. Lewis. If the walls of that house could talk, what a lot they could tell. But the story of this happy place was preceded by one of the most depressing periods in C. S. Lewis's life. When Jack Lewis returned to Oxford from the war in 1919, he began looking for a home—not only for himself but for the mother and sister of his friend Paddy Moore, who had died in France. Lewis promised Paddy that if he didn't come back, he would look after Paddy's family—a promise he took very seriously.

The twenty-one-year-old Lewis had very little money, and he was trying to stretch that little to look after the Moores. Four years later, he had taken three first-class degrees at Oxford, but there was very little prospect of a job and no prospect of a house. When he wrote up his diary on 4 July 1923, he listed the nine homes he had lived in since 1919. Number four on his list he described as Mrs. Jeffrey's flat in Windmill Road, where he says, "We were bullied and slandered and abused and so haunted by that butcher woman ... that ... I dreamed of her for months afterwards."[3] I was puzzled as to why Lewis described this landlady as a butcher until I went searching for the house and found that it was, indeed, a butcher shop with Lewis living in a room above the chopping block.

After seven more lean years, by which time Lewis had a Fellowship at Magdalen College, and Warnie was on the point of retirement, the brothers went to see a house advertised in Headington Quarry. They saw The Kilns for the first time on 6 July 1930, and it was love at first sight. The next day Warnie wrote in his diary, "We did not go inside the house, but the eight acre garden is such stuff as dreams are made of ... J[ack] and I spent an enthusiastic half hour building castles in Spain and rambling about the grounds, both agreeing that we simply must have this place if it is any way possible."[4] The Kilns was bought jointly by Jack, Warnie, and Mrs. Moore, and they spent their first night there on 11 October 1930. Lewis was still not a Christian, but immediately upon moving into The Kilns he began going to morning chapel at Magdalen College. Things were on the move.

When Lewis wrote to his old friend Arthur Greeves from The Kilns on 24 December 1930, you would have thought the entire animal population of Narnia had come on a visit:

> More than once I have seen a pair of squirrels among the fir trees, and rabbits in our own garden: and up at the top ... there is a burrow ... which ... [may] be that of a badger. Now to meet a badger on your own land ... would be almost the crown of one kind of earthly bliss!
>
> ... one thing I have noticed since the first night I slept here, is that this house has a good night atmosphere about it: in the sense that I have never been in a place where one was *less* likely to get the creeps: a place less sinister. Good life must have been lived here before us.[5]

Weeks after that letter was written, another great character had entered the story of The Kilns. Lewis and Mrs. Moore hired Fred Paxford to come there as gardener and general handyman. He too was a visitor from Narnia, because Paxford, who spent almost the rest of his life at The Kilns, was, Lewis said, the original behind Puddleglum the Marsh-wiggle, Lewis's own favorite character in the Narnia books.

Yes, if the walls of The Kilns could talk, they would speak at some length about the writing of some of the most remarkable books of this century. *The Screwtape Letters* was written there, as was *The Great*

Divorce, *Miracles*, much of *Mere Christianity*, and, I think, some of the Chronicles of Narnia. It is unthinkable that a place that has been the cradle of all this should be lost to the world. It was in this gracious house that Jack Lewis died peacefully in 1963, and it was the home Warnie returned to from his sickbed in Ireland so he too could die within its walls.

I am one of those who was heartbroken at the deaths of both Jack and Warnie, and then witnessed what I feared would be the death of The Kilns as well. The house was sold, and it was greatly butchered about, but not quite lost, however, because if clay has a DNA, maybe it will be possible to restore the old brick kilns themselves, because I have preserved one brick. Then came its rescue by the C. S. Lewis Foundation. Over the last ten years or so Dr. Stan Mattson, Kim Gilnett, and their host of noble volunteers have restored what is not only a great place in the lives of the Lewis brothers but in a great many other lives as well. If the walls of The Kilns do suddenly begin to talk, it's possible for many people here in this room to listen to what they say.

Thank you very much.

Francis Warner

It is a great honor to be asked today to say a few words as we share this service of thanksgiving and dedication of The Kilns, the home of my supervisor and friend, C. S. Lewis, from 1930 to 1963, when and where on Friday, November 22, he died a week before his sixty-fifth birthday. Apart from a week or two, my age today.

This service, then, is also my own personal thanksgiving for all he taught me and shared with me as we met regularly, for over two hours, every Wednesday morning in term in his college rooms in Cambridge. But I was only one, very young and very minor, friend. During that time I did not know The Kilns. Older and far longer friendships were enjoyed there: Hugo Dyson, Charles Williams, Tolkien, all those unfolded so succinctly and evocatively in Walter Hooper's revised edition, recently published, of Roger Lancelyn Green and Walter Hooper's *C. S. Lewis: A Biography* (HarperCollins, 2002) and also in the volumes of letters now in the process of being published.

He had a gift for friendship, perhaps an unusual one. The emotional side, in my case, was reserved entirely for letters. Face-to-face, he was not emotional at all. People reading the letters that he wrote to me, with their lengthy and meticulous annotations of my poems, or telling me of his illness, say, "What a close relationship." But it was only so on paper; personal contact was for debate—the trying out of ideas. The exploration of joint enthusiasms, even, though largely in a factual way. He was not cold; he was disciplined. Courteous. Well mannered. Eager for debate—debate in which the egos were not involved, and all energy was intent on what he called "pursuit of the fox, truth—that elusive quarry."

From him I learned every time we met. As the relationship was one between teacher and pupil, this was a gift more precious than gold. It was not quite the same among colleagues in the Oxford Magdalen Senior Common Room, who may not always have wanted debate over lunch and logic based on facts. Not that Lewis forced himself on people at all, but he did not like cant or sloppy emotion. One must not exaggerate this—he had a long and warm and happy experience of Magdalen, Oxford, and we must not forget that. He also had that at Cambridge. In the Senior Combination Room of Magdalene College, Cambridge, he found congeniality, even if the same, I'm afraid, could not be said of the Cambridge English faculty, riven as it was, as I well remember, by faction. But in his two Magdalens he could find that collegiality that he so loved. In college, at Cambridge and Oxford, and at The Kilns, he found true collegiality, places where each person respects, helps, shares, and delights in the work of each, and problems are shared. This is what The Kilns can be, now that the C. S. Lewis Foundation under, if I may say so, the inspired direction of its president, Stan Mattson, has been restored. Not a museum, but a living *locus amoenus*, a delightful place of hospitality where like-minded scholars can appreciate what it meant to Lewis and, in turn, like Castiglione and his Urbino, bring out the best in us.

For thirty-four years, my college rooms here in Oxford have looked out on Erasmus's Arch, in New Inn Hall Street, which used to be called "Seven Deadly Sins Lane." As I taught in my rooms, walking up and down and glancing out of the window, my eye would fall not only on Erasmus's Arch but on the buildings beyond, now called Frewin Hall, but in Erasmus's time, St. Mary's College. In October 1499, Erasmus arrived in Oxford with a letter of introduction to a lecturer two years his senior, John Colet, who was addressing large audiences here on the epistles of St. Paul. Erasmus stayed at St. Mary's College, the timber roof of which is now the roof of Brasenose College with a superb added plasterwork of the 1650s by John Jackson.

St. Mary's was founded by Thomas Holden and Elizabeth, his wife, primarily for canons of the Augustinian Order. Erasmus wrote a letter to John Sixtin about a dinner party which, though Sixtin was invited, he was unable to attend. Colet, later dean of St. Paul's, the affectionately respected leader of the Oxford circle, presided. On his right sat William Charnock, who was the prior of St. Mary's. On his left was an unnamed divine, who was an advocate of the old scholasticism. Next to him sat Erasmus; as Erasmus said in the letter, "so that a poet should not be wanting at the banquet." Erasmus, at this stage, still saw himself primarily as a poet.

We all know what grew out of these debates over the dinner table in this small community and others like it: the English Reformation, with all its political complexities, English humanism, and the bringing in, by such men as Colet, of the Florentine Platonism that in my own subject was to flower in the poetry of Sir Philip Sidney, Edmund Spenser, and so many more. From such meetings of minds scholasticism, humanism, Platonism, overlapped and reshaped our outlook.

The Kilns has just such a future. It is ideal. Its inspiration is a single man—a great Christian who was, and is, an inspiration to millions. Its location is Oxford—still today the center of the intellectual world, a position which it shares with its younger sister, Cambridge. Its attraction to like-minded inquirers has started in such modest beginnings as began many of the colleges around us now: like-minded scholars seeking after truth, sharing an environment, and becoming friends; collegiality, books, gardens, leisure, shared meals, above all, conversation; but more. Let me give you two anecdotes about C. S. Lewis that demonstrate his ideals; ideals that can guide the future of The Kilns. One is academic, and the other is personal.

We have all here heard and read about the Inklings, but today I want to remind you of another group: and anyone seeking a topic for research might like to explore this further. This other group was simply called the Society. It met once a term with a different host in a different college each time, and the host had to read a paper which started the discussion of the evening. The minute book of the Society is right behind me in the Bodleian Library. It's a feast of material. John Bayley gave a talk on Shakespeare's puns on the word "will." Sir Thomas Armstrong bent the rules and entertained everybody to a visit to Covent Garden to watch Margot Fonteyn and Nureyev dance. John Sparrow, Tolkien, many, many of the familiar names were members.

I had tea a few days ago with Jonathan Wordsworth, my colleague. For a while he was the secretary of this Society. When his turn came to entertain the group, in Exeter College, he chose as his topic one that Lewis rather liked, called "quaintness." Lewis was a regular and sometimes a rather brooding presence. Nevill Coghill was the ideal host: facilitator, master of ceremonies, meeting all with his boundless goodwill and Irish charm.

And the second anecdote is this: Last week I also saw my old colleague, Douglas Gray, and he told me that Frank Quinn (Is Frank Quinn present, by any chance, before I tell this anecdote? You never know in Oxford.) had been a postgraduate research student at Magdalen in the 1940s. He was one of the very first. The don assigned to him, responsible for his well-being, was C. S. Lewis, of whom he was terrified. At the end of term, Lewis summoned him to Staircase Three of Magdalen's new buildings, outside which, as Lewis described in a letter to his own father, he could see "one little stag (not much bigger than a calf and looking too slender for the weight of its own antlers) standing still and sending through the fog that queer little bark or hoot which is these beasts' 'moo.' It is a sound ... as familiar to me as the cough of cows in the field at home."[6]

When Frank Quinn had knocked, wearing of course his gown, and entered, Lewis asked how he was getting on.

"It's quite difficult, really, but I'm working hard," said Quinn, "and the work's progressing."

"I mean socially. Have you made any friends?"

"Not really. What with a wife and small child, and coming to Oxford from outside and being stretched over money, because of that I don't socialize much."

"Oh, don't worry about that. I have a fund set aside from royalties. You can borrow as much as you like to help you through, and there's no need to pay me back until you can afford to."

Two anecdotes—so typical of Lewis. We remember Wordsworth's comment in "Tintern Abbey":

> ... that best portion of a good man's life,
> his little nameless, unremembered acts
> Of kindness and of love ...

though they are remembered by his pupils and the recipients. Two anecdotes to show the outside and the inside of collegiality; and all is based on reciprocal relationships.

To end, I will quote Lewis's favorite sentences from Cicero's *De Amicitia*:

> Those people are worthy of friendship who have within their own souls the reason for their being loved.... It is characteristic of true friendship both to give and to receive advice, and on the one hand to give it with all freedom of speech but without harshness, and on the other hand to receive it patiently and without resentment.

And lastly—

> Friendship was given by nature as the handmaid of virtue, not as the comrade of vice, because virtue cannot attain her highest aims unattended, but only in unity and fellowship.[7]

So, may the warm hospitality and environment of The Kilns bring the blessing of such union and fellowship. In one hundred years' time there will be perhaps another such service of thanksgiving for the dedication that brought this Christian community into being. Small in size it may be, but in power and preciousness it will transcend all man-made memorials to Lewis. It is a living inspiration, and the remembrance of a great soul.

Appendix

THE ESTABLISHMENT MUST DIE AND ROT ...

C. S. Lewis Discusses Science Fiction with Kingsley Amis and Brian Aldiss

ALDISS: One thing that the three of us have in common is that we have all had stories published in the *Magazine of Fantasy and Science Fiction*, some of them pretty far-flung stories. I take it we would all agree that one of the attractions of SF [science fiction] is that it takes us to unknown places.

AMIS: Swift, if he were writing today, would have to take us out to the planets, wouldn't he? Now that most of our terra incognita is — er, real estate.

ALDISS: That is so; there's a lot of the eighteenth-century equivalent of SF which is placed in Australia or similar unreal estates.

LEWIS: Exactly. Peter Wilkins and all that. By the way, is anyone ever going to do a translation of Kepler's *Somnium*?

AMIS: Groff Conklin told me he had read the book; I think it must exist in translation. But may we talk about the worlds you created? You chose the science fiction medium because you wanted to go to strange places? I remember with respectful and amused admiration your account of the space drive in *Out of the Silent Planet*. When Ransom and his friend get into the spaceship, he says, "How does this ship work?" and the man says, "It operates by using some of the lesser known properties of ..." — what was it?

Reprinted with permission from *SFHorizons*, no. 1 (Spring 1964), 5–12.

LEWIS: Solar radiation. Ransom was reporting words without a meaning to him, which is what a layman gets when he asks for scientific explanation. Obviously it was vague, because I'm no scientist and not interested in the purely technical side of it.

ALDISS: It's almost a quarter of a century since you wrote that first novel of the trilogy.

LEWIS: Have I been a prophet?

ALDISS: You have to a certain extent; at least, the idea of vessels propelled by solar radiation is back in favor again. Cordwainer Smith used it poetically, Blish tried to use it technically in *The Star Dwellers*.

LEWIS: In my case it was pure mumbo-jumbo, and perhaps meant primarily to convince me.

AMIS: Obviously when one deals with isolated planets or isolated islands one does this for a certain purpose: a setting in contemporary London or a London of the future couldn't provide one with the same isolation and the heightening of consciousness it engenders.

LEWIS: The starting point of the second novel, *Perelandra*, was my mental picture of the floating islands. The whole of the rest of my labors in a sense consisted of building up a world in which floating islands could exist. And then, of course, the story about an averted fall developed. This is because, as you know, having got your people to this exciting country, something must happen.

AMIS: That frequently taxes writers very much.

ALDISS: But I am surprised that you put it this way round. I would have thought that you constructed *Perelandra* for the didactic purpose.

LEWIS: Yes, everyone thinks that. They are quite wrong.

AMIS: If I may say a word on Professor Lewis's side, there was a didactic purpose, of course, a lot of very interesting, profound things were said, but—correct me if I'm wrong—I'd have thought a simple sense of wonder, extraordinary things going on, were the motive forces behind the creation.

LEWIS: Quite, but something has got to happen. The story of this averted fall came in very conveniently. Of course it wouldn't have been that particular story if I wasn't interested in those particular ideas on other grounds. But that isn't what I started from. I've never started from a message or a moral, have you?

AMIS: No, never. You get interested in the situation.

LEWIS: The story itself should force its moral upon you. You find out what the moral is by writing the story.

AMIS: Exactly. I think that sort of thing is true of all kinds of fiction.

ALDISS: I think it is; but a lot of science fiction has been written from the other point of view: these dreary sociological dramas that appear from time to time, they started with a didactic purpose — to make a preconceived point — and they've got no further.

LEWIS: I suppose Gulliver started from a straight point of view? Or did it really start because he wanted to write about a lot of big and little men?

AMIS: Possibly both, as Fielding's parody of Richardson turned into *Joseph Andrews*. A lot of SF loses much of the impact it could have by saying, "Well, here we are on Mars, we all know where we are, and we're living in these pressure domes or whatever it is, and life is really very much like it is on Earth, except there is a certain climatic difference. ..." They accept other men's inventions rather than forge their own.

LEWIS: It's only the first journey to a new planet that is of any interest to imaginative people.

AMIS: In your reading of SF have you ever come across a writer who's done this properly?

LEWIS: Well, the one you probably disapprove of because he's so very unscientific is David Lindsay, in *Voyage to Arcturus*. It's a remarkable thing, because scientifically it's nonsense, the style is appalling, and yet this ghastly vision comes through.

ALDISS: It didn't come through to me.

AMIS: I've never got hold of it. I'm still looking for it. There are a lot of imaginative classics of this kind that one can't get hold of. Victor Gollancz told me a very interesting remark of Lindsay's about *Arcturus*; he said, "I shall never appeal to a large public at all, but I think that as long as our civilization lasts one person a year will read me." I respect that attitude.

LEWIS: Quite so. Modest and becoming. I also agree with something you said—in a preface, I believe it was—that some SF really does deal with issues far more serious than those realistic fiction deals with; real problems about human destiny and so on. Do you remember that story about the man who meets a female monster landed from another planet with all its cubs hanging round it? It's obviously starving, and he offers them thing after thing to eat; they immediately vomit it up, until one of the young fastens on him, begins sucking his blood, and immediately begins to revive. This female creature is utterly unhuman, horrible in form; there's a long moment when it looks at the man—they're in a lonely place—and then very sadly it packs up its young and goes back into its spaceship and goes away. Well now, you could not have a more serious theme than that; what is a footling story about some pair of human lovers compared with that?

AMIS: On the debit side, you often have these marvelous large themes tackled by people who haven't got the mental or moral or stylistic equipment to tackle them. A reading of more recent SF shows that writers are getting more capable of tackling them. Have you read Walter Miller's *Canticle for Leibowitz*? Have you any comments on that?

LEWIS: I thought it was pretty good. I only read it once. Mind you, a book's no good to me until I've read it two or three times—I'm going to read it again. It was a major work, certainly.

AMIS: What did you think about its religious feeling?

LEWIS: It came across very well. There were bits of the actual writing which one could quarrel with, but on the whole it was well imagined and well executed.

AMIS: Have you seen James Blish's novel *A Case of Conscience*? Would you agree that to write a religious novel that isn't concerned with details of ecclesiastical practice and the numbing minutiae of history and so on, SF would be the natural outlet for this?

LEWIS: If you have a religion, it must be cosmic; therefore, it seems to me odd that this genre was so late in arriving.

ALDISS: It's been around without attracting critical attention for a long time; the magazines themselves have been going since 1926, although in the beginning they appealed mainly to the technical side. The people who wrote a lot of it, people like Heinlein, de Camp, George O. Smith, they were engineers, and they mainly concentrated on engineering wonders. As Kingsley says, people have come along who can write, as well as think up engineering ideas.

LEWIS: We ought to have said earlier that that's quite a different species of SF, about which I say nothing at all; those who were really interested in the technical side of it—it's obviously perfectly legitimate if it's well done—

AMIS: The purely technical and the purely imaginative overlap, don't they?

ALDISS: There are certainly the two streams, and they often overlap, for instance, in Arthur Clarke's writings. It can be a rich mixture. Then there's the type of story that's not theological, but it makes a moral point. An instance—it sounds like a Scheckley story—is the one about Earth being blasted by radioactivity. The survivors of the human race have gone away to another planet for about a thousand years; and they come back to reclaim Earth and find it full of all sorts of gaudy armor-plated creatures, vegetation, etc. One of the party is saying, "We'll clear this out, make it habitable for man again"; but in the end the decision is "Well, we made a mess of the place when it was ours; but these new forms have come along, they've made a success of it, let's get out and leave it to them." Now this story was written about 1949, when most people hadn't started thinking round the subject at all.

LEWIS: Yes. Most of the earlier stories start from the opposite assumption that we, the human race, are in the right, and everything else is ogres; I may have done a little towards altering that, but the new point of view has come very much in. We've lost our confidence, so to speak.

AMIS: It's all terribly self-critical and self-contemplatory nowadays.

LEWIS: This is surely an enormous gain—a humane gain, that people should be thinking that way.

AMIS: The prejudice of supposedly educated persons towards this type of fiction is fantastic. If you pick up an SF magazine, particularly *F&SF*, the range of interests appealed to and IQs employed is pretty amazing. It's time more people caught on. We've been telling them about it for some while.

LEWIS: Quite true. The world of "serious" fiction is very narrow.

AMIS: Too narrow if you want to deal with a broad theme. For instance, Philip Wylie in *The Disappearance* wants to deal with the difference between men and women in a general way, in twentieth-century society, unencumbered by local and temporary considerations; his point, as I understand it, is that men and women, shorn of their social roles, are really very much the same; SF, which can presuppose a major change in our environment, is the natural medium for discussing a subject of that kind. Look at the job of dissecting human nastiness carried out in Golding's *Lord of the Flies*.

LEWIS: That can't be science fiction.

AMIS: I would attack you on this. It starts off with a characteristic bit of a situation, that World War III has begun, bombs dropped and all that. ...

LEWIS: Ah, well, you're now taking the German view that any romance about the future is science fiction. I'm not sure that this is a useful classification.

AMIS: Science fiction is such a hopelessly vague label.

LEWIS: And, of course, a great deal of it isn't *science* fiction. Really, it's only a negative criterion: anything which is not naturalistic, which is not about what we call the real world.

ALDISS: I think we oughtn't to try to define it, because it's a self-defining thing in a way. We know where we are. You're right, though, about *Lord of the Flies*. The atmosphere is a science fiction atmosphere.

LEWIS: It was a very terrestrial island; the best island, almost, in fiction. Its actual sensuous effect on you is terrific.

ALDISS: Indeed. But it's a laboratory case.

AMIS: This business of isolating certain human characteristics, to see how they would work out—

LEWIS: The only trouble is that Golding writes too well. In one of his other novels, *The Inheritors*, the detail of every sensuous impression, the light on the leaves and so on, was so good that you couldn't find out what was happening. I'd say it was almost too well done.

All these little details you only notice in real life if you've got a high temperature. You couldn't see the wood for the leaves.

ALDISS: You had this in *Pincher Martin*; every feeling in the rocks, when he's washed ashore, is done with a hallucinatory vividness.

AMIS: It is; that's exactly the phrase. I think thirty years ago if you wanted to discuss a general theme you would go to the historical novel; now you would go to what I might describe in a prejudiced way as science fiction. In SF you can isolate the factors you want to examine. If you wanted to deal with the theme of colonialism, for instance, as Poul Anderson has done, you don't do it by writing a novel about Ghana or Pakistan —

LEWIS: Which involves you in such a mass of detail that you don't want to go into —

AMIS: You set up worlds in space which incorporate the characteristics you need.

LEWIS: Would you describe Abbot's *Flatland* as SF? There's so little effort to bring it into any sensuous — well, you couldn't do it, and it remains an intellectual theorem. Are you looking for an ashtray? Use the carpet.

AMIS: I was looking for the Scotch, actually.

LEWIS: Oh, yes, do, I beg your pardon.... But probably the great work in SF is still to come. Futile books about the next world came before Dante, Fanny Burney came before Jane Austen, Marlowe came before Shakespeare.

AMIS: We're getting the prolegomena.

LEWIS: If only the modern highbrow critics could be induced to take it seriously ...

AMIS: Do you think they ever can?

LEWIS: No, the whole present dynasty has got to die and rot before anything can be done at all.

ALDISS: Splendid!

AMIS: What's holding them up, do you think?

LEWIS: Matthew Arnold made the horrible prophecy that literature would increasingly replace religion. It has, and it's taken on all the features of bitter persecution, great intolerance, and traffic in relics. All literature becomes a sacred text. A sacred text is always exposed to the most monstrous exegesis; hence we have the spectacle of some wretched scholar taking a pure *divertissement* written in the seventeenth century and getting the most profound ambiguities and social criticisms out of it, which of course aren't there at all.... It's the discovery of the mare's nest by the pursuit of the red herring. [Laughter] This is going to go on long after my lifetime; you may be able to see the end of it, I shan't.

AMIS: You think this is so integral a part of the Establishment that people can't overcome—

LEWIS: It's an industry, you see. What would all the people be writing D.Phil. theses on if this prop were removed?

AMIS: An instance of this mentality the other day; somebody referred to "Mr. Amis's I suspect rather affected enthusiasm for SF ..."

LEWIS: Isn't that maddening!

AMIS: You can't really like it.

LEWIS: You must be pretending to be a plain man or something.... I've met the attitude again and again. You've probably reached the stage too of having theses written on yourself. I received a letter from an American examiner asking, "Is it true that you meant this and this and this?" A writer of a thesis was attributing to me views which I have explicitly contradicted in the plainest possible English. They'd be much wiser to write about the dead, who can't answer.

ALDISS: In America, I think SF is accepted on a more responsible level.

AMIS: I'm not so sure about that, you know, Brian, because when our anthology, *Spectrum*, came out in the States, we had less friendly and less understanding treatment from reviewers than we did over here.

LEWIS: I'm surprised at that, because in general all American reviewing is more friendly and generous than in England.

AMIS: People were patting themselves on the back in the States for not understanding what we meant.

LEWIS: This extraordinary pride in being exempt from temptations that you have not yet risen to the level of eunuchs boasting of their chastity! [Laughter]

AMIS: One of my pet theories is that serious writers as yet unborn or still at school will soon regard SF as a natural way of writing.

LEWIS: By the way, has any SF writer yet succeeded in inventing a third sex? Apart from the third sex we all know.

AMIS: William Tenn invented a setup where there were seven sexes.

LEWIS: How rare happy marriages must have been then!

ALDISS: Rather worth striving for, perhaps.

LEWIS: Obviously when achieved they'd be wonderful. [Laughter]

ALDISS: I find I would much rather write SF than anything else. The deadweight is so much less there than in the field of the ordinary novel. There's a sense in which you're conquering a fresh country.

AMIS: Speaking as a supposedly realistic novelist, I've written little bits of SF, and this is such a tremendous liberation.

LEWIS: Well, you're a very ill-used man; you wrote a farce and everyone thought it a damning indictment of Redbrick. I've always had great sympathy for you. They will not understand that a joke is a joke. Everything must be serious.

AMIS: [quoting] "A fever chart of society." I'd like to say *Lucky Jim* was serious too, but not in the way they wanted it to be.

LEWIS: One thing in SF that weighs against us very heavily is the horrible shadow of the comics.

ALDISS: I don't know about that. Tidbits Romantic Library doesn't really weigh against the serious writer.

LEWIS: That's a very fair analogy. All the novelettes didn't kill the ordinary legitimate novel of courtship and love.

ALDISS: There might have been a time when SF and comics were weighed together and found wanting, but that at least we've got past.

AMIS: I see the comic books that my sons read, and you have there a terribly vulgar reworking of some of the themes that SF goes in for.

LEWIS: Quite harmless, mind you. This chatter about the moral danger of the comics is absolute nonsense. The real objection is against the appalling draftsmanship. Yet you'll find the same boy who reads them also reads Shakespeare or Spenser. Children are so terribly catholic. That's my experience with my stepchildren.

ALDISS: This is an English habit, to categorize: that if you read Shakespeare you can't read comics, that if you read SF you can't be serious.

AMIS: That's the thing that annoys me.

LEWIS: Oughtn't the word *serious* to have an embargo slapped on it? *Serious* ought to mean simply the opposite of comic, whereas now it means "good," or Literature with a capital *L*.

ALDISS: You can be serious without being earnest.

LEWIS: Leavis demands moral earnestness; I prefer morality.

AMIS: I'm with you every time on that one.

LEWIS: I mean I'd sooner live among people who don't cheat at cards than among people who are earnest about not cheating at cards. [Laughter]

AMIS: More Scotch?

LEWIS: Not for me, thank you, help yourself. [Liquid noises]

AMIS: I think all this ought to stay in, you know—all these remarks about drink.

LEWIS: There's no reason why we shouldn't have a drink. Look, you want to borrow Abbot's *Flatland*, don't you? I must go to dinner, I'm afraid. [Hands over *Flatland*.] The original manuscript of the *Iliad* could not be more precious. It's only the ungodly who borroweth and payeth not again.

AMIS: [reading] By A. Square.

LEWIS: But of course the word *square* hadn't the same sense then.

ALDISS: It's like the poem by Francis Thompson that ends, "She gave me tokens three, a look, a word of her winsome mouth, and a sweet wild raspberry"; there again the meaning has changed. It really was a wild raspberry in Thompson's day. [Laughter]

LEWIS: Or the lovely one about the Bishop who was giving the prizes at the girls' school. They did a performance of *Midsummer Night's Dream*, and the poor man stood up afterwards and made a speech and said [piping voice], "I was very interested in your delightful performance, and among other things I was very interested in seeing for the first time in my life a female Bottom." [Guffaws]

Walking Again on Addison's Walk

"And who was Addison?"
  glibly asked the chemistry professor.
A name. A man. An Oxford don.
  I never thought to ask;
Someone who liked to walk, no doubt;
  (I never really cared).
Perhaps he liked to think things through
  while strolling down the garden path.
Were they solitary strolls,
  or did he talk aloud with others?
I never strolled this path alone
  nor without some care at stake:
    concern for a brother's failed career,
    or what career to take.
Jack and Tollers walked this path one night
  with Hugo Dyson.
Would Jack have gone if he had known
  where that night's walk would lead?
These thoughts revolved inside my head,
  instead of which I simply said,
"I don't know."

Harry Lee Poe

NOTES

Foreword by Simon Barrington-Ward

1. Nevill Coghill, "The Approach to English," *Light on C. S. Lewis*, ed. Jocelyn Gibb (London: Geoffrey Bles, 1965), 57, as cited by John E. Stevens and Raphael Lyne, eds., "Centenary Readings from C. S. Lewis," *Magdalene College Occasional Papers*, no. 23 (Cambridge, 2000), 3.
2. Stevens and Lyne, "Centenary Readings," 3.
3. Ibid., 2.

Chapter 1: C. S. Lewis as Christian and Scholar

1. Leo Baker (1898–1986) was an actor with the Old Vic Company in the 1920s. He and his wife then operated a handloom weaving firm in Chipping Campden until World War II. A priest of the Anthroposophic "Christian Community," Baker taught at a Rudolf Steiner school during the war and became a national drama advisor for the Carnegie United Kingdom Trust after the war. For a biographical sketch, see Walter Hooper, ed., *The Collected Letters of C. S. Lewis* (New York: HarperSanFrancisco, 2004), 1:978. See also Baker's essay in *C. S. Lewis at the Breakfast Table*, ed. James T. Como (New York: Macmillan, 1979), 3–10.
2. See Lionel Adey, *C. S. Lewis's Great War with Owen Barfield* (Victoria, B.C.: University of Victoria, 1978).
3. Cecil Harwood (1898–1975) served as 2nd lieutenant in the Royal Warwickshire infantry during World War I. He went up to Christ Church, Oxford, in 1919. Harwood met C. S. Lewis through Owen Barfield, whom he had known since Highgate School days. Harwood became an active Anthroposophist through the influence of his wife, Daphne. For a biographical sketch of Harwood, see Hooper, *Collected Letters*, 1:998–1000.
4. Warren Lewis's books on France included *The Splendid Century: Life in the France of Louis* (1953), *Assault on Olympus: The Rise of the House of Gramont between 1604 and 1678* (1958), *Louis XVI: An Informal Portrait* (1959), *The Scandalous Regent: A Life of Philippe, Duc d'Orleans 1674–1723 and of His Family* (1961), *Levantine Adventurer: The Travels and Missions of Chevalier d'Arvieux, 1653–1697* (1962), *The Sunset of the Splendid Century* (1963), and *Memoirs of the Duc de Saint-Simon* (1964).
5. Hooper, *Collected Letters*, 1:882–83.

6. Ibid., 1:762–63. Barfield understates Lewis's remarks in which he speaks of "things in men's shapes climbing over one another and biting one another in the back: ignorant of all things except their own subjects and often even of those: caring for nothing less than for learning: cunning, desperately ambitious, false friends, nodders in corners, tippers of the wink: setters of traps and solicitors of confidence ... ," and on and on he goes.

7. Nigel Goodwin founded and serves as director of Genesis Arts Trust, an international ministry to people active in all areas of the arts.

Chapter 2: What about Mrs. Boshell?

1. Walter Hooper, ed., *The Collected Letters of C. S. Lewis* (New York: HarperSan-Francisco, 2004), 2:345–46.
2. Ibid., 2:484–85.
3. Hooper paraphrases Lewis's famous comment from the conclusion of his third Broadcast Talk. See C. S. Lewis, *Mere Christianity* (New York: Macmillan, 1952), 41.
4. "St. Anne's on the Hill" refers to the group that gathered around Ransom in *That Hideous Strength*.
5. See W. H. Lewis, ed., *Letters of C. S. Lewis* (New York: Harcourt, Brace & World, 1966).
6. Lewis made this comment in a letter to Vera Gebbert on January 17, 1960. Walter Hooper was kind enough to interrupt his own work on vol. 3 of *The Collected Letters of C. S. Lewis* to send the reference. The letter will be included in the forthcoming volume of letters.
7. Hooper, *Collected Letters*, 1:925–26.
8. Ibid., 1:932.
9. Ibid., 2:478.
10. C. S. Lewis, "Rejoinder to Dr Pittinger," in *God in the Dock*, ed. Walter Hooper (Grand Rapids: Eerdmans, 1970), 183.
11. The first C. S. Lewis Summer Institute met for two weeks in Oxford in July 1988 and was known as "Oxford 88."

Chapter 3: C. S. Lewis: Sixty Years On

1. Derek Brewer, "The Tutor: A Portrait," in *C. S. Lewis at the Breakfast Table*, ed. James T. Como (Orlando: Harcourt Brace, 1992).
2. Ann Thwaite and Ronald Hayman Thwaite, eds., *My Oxford, My Cambridge* (New York: Taplinger, 1979).
3. Ibid., 123.
4. Ibid., 199.
5. Kathryn Kerby-Fulton, " 'Standing on Lewis's Shoulders,' C. S. Lewis as Critic of Medieval Literature" (1991) in *Studies in Medievalism: Inklings and Others*, ed. Jane Chance, 3, no. 3, 257–78.